# KEYNOTES TO MODERN DANCE

by
**Dorothy E. Koch Norris, M.A.**
Professor
State University College
Buffalo, New York

**Reva P. Shiner, M.S.Ed.**
Choreographer
Educator and Consultant
Bloomington, Indiana

**Third Edition**

*Burgess Publishing Company*

Consulting Editor to Publisher

Eloise Jaeger

# FOREWORD

The early revision of *Keynotes To Modern Dance* attests to the effective and useful application of the content. Long noted for ability to simplify complex dance materials into understandable and manageable units for the teaching situation, the authors capture and record this art in printed form. This capacity to analyze continues as an outstanding characteristic of the book. The revision draws more fully upon many and varied experiences of the authors. Their ingenuity is directed toward offering succinct, practical suggestions for the benefit of the teacher of dance. By including an appendix with annotated resource references, the scope and excellence of the work has been greatly increased. The book is soundly conceived, extremely well organized and punctuated by fresh and varied illustrative materials.

The development of an artistically integrated personality is an important objective of education. Beauty of artistic expression is "its own excuse for being." Happily, however, other values related to the development of poised personalities are natural concomitants of dance. Modern dance contributes distinctly to the development of a disciplined freedom in creative expression.

Medical authorities are increasingly recognizing the value of dance as therapy for mentally and physically ill people. Such recognition serves also to underscore the efficacy of dance as an aid to the conservation of physical health and to the preservation of mental and emotional well-being.

This publication contributes to the developing sense of maturity in the arts in the United States. Modern dance is an art form naturally expressive of the democratic core of our national philosophy. This book provides a medium for helping teachers and students to an experience of artistic creativity.

GEORGE K. MAKECHNIE
Dean
Boston University Sargent College of
Allied Health Professions

# PREFACE

*This revised edition of KEYNOTES TO MODERN DANCE contains additional and inter-related materials designed to benefit prospective and beginning teachers of dance. A new chapter, Keynotes to Teaching, deals specifically with the role of the teacher and student, the planning and evolving of the lesson, and the evaluation of creative endeavor. A section on teaching guides plus an extension of the bibliography and glossary contribute further to the functional use of the contents. An added feature, resource materials for dance recordings and dance films, is contained in the Appendices.*

*All the photographs are new with an emphasis on a contemporary and an imaginative pictorialization of the modern dance art. The poetry and beauty of design in these arresting photographs should add greatly to the aesthetic enjoyment of the third edition.*

*This book endeavors to fulfill a need for a practical guide in teaching modern dance. Its purpose is to present concise and understandable materials to prospective, to inexperienced, and to experienced teachers of dance who seek a helping hand. The materials, outlined in a simplified and readily usable form, include examples of basic dance movements and related progressions that lead into the development of dance patterns — the threshold of simple dance studies and composition. The varied content, organized to meet the needs of dance teachers in junior and senior high schools, in teacher education institutions, and in colleges and universities provides a practical foundation upon which to build a course of instruction.*

*The authors hope that this book will become a keystone of challenge and service to all those inspired teachers and students of modern dance art. The contents of the book are suggested to be a pilot reference with the intention of stimulating individual creativity in the use of the materials. The potential contribution of this type of dance handbook rests with the ingenuity of the teacher in influencing the dance pendulum to swing ever forward as a vitalizing force in the art lives of people.*

*The authors acknowledge with sincere appreciation the most helpful assistance of Professor Maurice Lieberman, formerly Chairman, Department of Music, Brooklyn College, for his valuable suggestions concerning the analysis of rhythmic structure in Chapter 3. Gratitude is extended to Doctor Nelson S. Walke, Chairman Emeritus, Department of Health and Physical Education (Men), Brooklyn College, for his encouragement during the initial preparation of the book. Special recognition is due Jane Fox, formerly Associate Professor of Health, Physical Education and Recreation, Indiana University, as co-choreographer for the dance, "The House of Bernarda Alba," and for her helpful suggestions; Patti McDaniel as co-choreographer for the dance, "Song of Life"; Arlene Near Paul for her contribution of the original poetry used in the dance, "Song of Life"; and Jan Felshin for the original poetry used in the dance, "Eastport to Block Island."*

*The Dance Mobile was designed by Dan Estes expressly for this revised edition.*

*Grateful appreciation is expressed to Joan Huff, Associate Professor of Health, Physical Education and Recreation, State University College, Oswego, New York for her compilation of Selected Recordings for Dance Composition in Appendix C.*

*The authors are especially proud to present the artistic photographs by David Ahlsted for this new edition. The assistance of the staff and students of Indiana University is also gratefully acknowledged.*

*Dorothy E. Koch Norris*
*Reva P. Shiner*

# CONTENTS

APPENDICES

# LIST OF ILLUSTRATIONS

Page

FIGURE

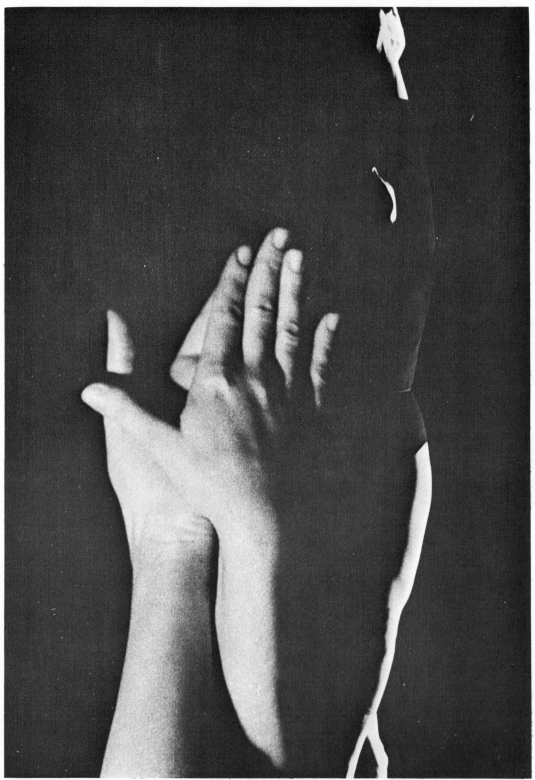

Figure One

# Chapter 1

# INTRODUCTION

Modern dance, a performing form of contemporary art, has the power to expand the horizons of each individual. To recognize that dance is an art form is not to imply that all dancers are to become professional artists. Actually, dance is for everyone with each person extracting that which serves his particular need. Some dance for the pure joy of moving. Others dance to broaden their art experiences. A few dance to become professional performers and choreographers. Whatever the reason, there is a place for everyone who wishes to dance.

As an art form, the dance of today speaks a language comparable to that of other arts. Although all arts have common elements of rhythm, line, design and the like, each art form expresses its content in its own unique way. For example, the dancer uses movement, the painter applies color, the musician employs sound, while the sculptor shapes his creation through the manipulation of mass.

Dance is a living art, and like some other arts, such as drama, it is not easily reproduced graphically. A painting as recorded on canvas is preserved for sheer beauty, for appreciation, or for study at will. A dance composition, so lifelike at the moment of performance, is not so readily documented or perpetuated. It may be reduced to a written account of its choreographic development, but mere graphic delineation eliminates the fleeting but vivid breath of life in the dance; or, it may be reproduced upon a film and yet, even here with the limitation of dimension and perspective, not all angles and surfaces of the moving body are sufficiently visible to show a perfect portrayal of the original.

In its earliest beginnings, dance existed despite its lack of aesthetic inspiration or studied meaning. Compulsively, it sprang from a prolific spontaneity of expression, vitality, and pleasure. Through the years dance forms have changed, but the appeal to dance is ever present.

The initial stages of dance experiences may be likened to the artist's use of raw materials. Through diversified motor responses the dancer gradually enlarges his experiences. He finds new ways of handling his instrument of expression — his body. He learns to organize, arrange, and modify various techniques of movement — his medium of expression. He develops the ability to create new ways of dealing with force, time, and space as elements of movement. Through utilization of rhythmic devices he discovers a variety of approaches for manipulating movement. This process of searching, exploring, and reorganizing known materials derived from past experiences opens up a wealth of novel ingredients to be explored. The more the dancer uses creative experiences, the more at ease he becomes, and the freer he feels in experimentation and invention. If the climate is conducive for creativity to flourish, the dancer discovers many ways of saying in movement that which words may not convey. Without formalization and rigidity, self-discovery and self-activity can develop. The beginner needs great freedom and liberty of movement. Let the more disciplined technique and finer muscular control be stressed later — after the seeds of spontaneity and free spirit have germinated. Initial motor experiences should serve broadly for creative opportunities. There should not be a marked separation between movement technique and composition. The creative process needs to be on-going and should permeate the simplest movement exploration. Such involvement leads the dancer more naturally from uncomplicated experiences into dance composition.

Each creation of an attitude, a reaction, a feeling, an emotion or an idea is the unique product of individual inspiration, sensitivity and imagination. Different movements mean different things to different dancers; yet, all these meanings may be perfectly valid for each composer. The choice of ideas for dance are as legion as life itself. The themes forming the content of dance composition remain constant and universal to mankind. The manner in which content is treated and expressed changes from era to era. The same theme or idea may be danced many times by many individuals. It is the fresh formulation and arrangement of movement materials and the fabrication of new ideas which crystallize the meaning of the finished product, the dance. Even then the choreographer continues to examine his composition by submitting it to the test of communication. At this stage of presentation the dance becomes most significant in that it no longer shows the problems that were so woven into the creative process itself. The effective projection of the dance idea to an audience — even to a few members of the class — validates its reason for being.

How then is it possible to motivate and challenge a dancer through these gradual but progressive steps to self-discovery as expressed finally in communicative movement? The answer lies with the teacher. There are endless possibilities for liberating the vital forces in the action lives of individuals. Whatever the approach, it should be an adventure; it should elicit fresh experiences; it should encourage the development of perception, and then discovery; it should recognize spontaneity and temper it with careful guidance. The teacher should challenge the capacity to explore and allow freedom for that exploration. Only as the dancer is given latitude to be himself will his uniqueness as an individual come to the foreground. Who can say what initially motivates a person to be creative? Perhaps this is less important than the fact that creativity has been released.

The creative process is a common denominator of all arts, and certainly the arts related to dance such as music, drama, and speech. Happily, today's contemporary dance is considered one of the arts and is spoken of as the art of dance. No longer is the awareness of art in life limited to formal appreciation courses in music and fine arts. Individuals are becoming much more aware of dance and its potential values. The professional dance concerts and television have done a great deal to enliven this perception. The arts festivals and developing centers for the performing arts that have sprung up in many sections of this country have stimulated an added interest in dance. A number of state councils on the arts have been organized and implemented. Breadth in liberal arts offerings is constantly increasing. More dance is being included in the arts curricula of higher education. There is a trend for colleges and universities to form regional dance groups. This makes possible an interchange of ideas, an exchange of dance programs; and the combining of efforts and funds to sponsor master lessons, professional concerts, dance symposia, and dance artists in residence. The focus on dance reaches all levels of education. Dance in therapy is expanding. The beginnings of subsidy for dance are being realized. Closer integration of dance with drama and speech, both amateur and professional, is in evidence. Through countless innovations the lay public is being made much more aware of the potential of dance.

The surging rapidity of present-day progress intensifies the continued need for creative teachers of dance. Each teacher, in his own way, should share the joy of dance — traditional and creative — with the tyros as well as the experienced. Untried approaches in keeping with the many cultural changes in contemporary society will undoubtedly challenge the teaching of dance. Just understanding part of the teen-age vocabulary may provide one approach for reaching this respective group. Unusual and original means for utilizing movement will be disclosed. Novel proposals for compositional development will be unveiled. These creative teachers will be the pioneers of dance. The crusaders of today carve the dance image of tomorrow. As an expressive and communicative art, dance must continue as a creative and vital force, and must maintain its rightful place in a changing social order.

The materials presented in the following chapters offer many approaches for inexperienced as well as experienced teachers. While concrete examples are included as definite points of departure from which to work, they should never be looked upon as ends in themselves. The content is deliberately organized to lead from simple to more complex materials, and from familiar and traditional to the less familiar and more creative approaches. There is danger in working straight through the book verbatim. A more imaginative approach would be to spot the special interests of the respective class and dwell longer on areas which tend to satisfy their enthusiasms. For instance, music majors may be more interested in rhythmic problems applied to movement; art majors may envision the use of line and mass in manipulating groups in choreographic projects; beginning dancers may have a great desire to develop a variety of skills; advanced dancers may wish to concentrate on choreography; boys may be disposed to perfecting skills and techniques of movement; and very young children may be intrigued by moving for the sheer joy of moving.

The structure of this book is formulated to serve as a resource guide. If utilized as a broad outline, the content is comprehensive and sequential. It is suitable for all ages providing the teacher adapts and modifies the material according to the needs, interests, and abilities of each respective group. It is imperative that the diversified experiences involve the participant in a dynamic way — looking beyond mere techniques of movement to the heart of dance. The actual manner of using the materials is left to the discretion of each teacher and reader. Nothing offered is intended to be arbitrary. The teacher, himself, must chart new areas to stimulate creative endeavor. The final challenge rests with the teacher.

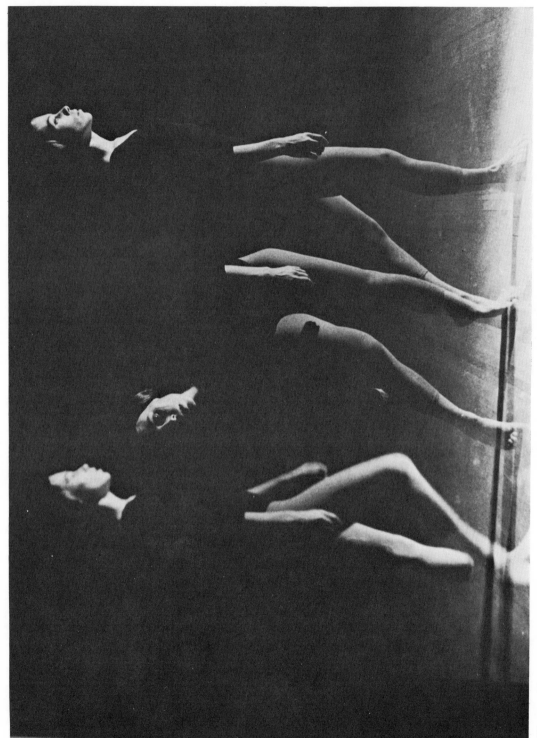

Figure Two

# Chapter 2

# KEYNOTES TO TEACHING

No two teachers will approach their classes in the same manner. Each one must find his own distinctive way of reaching his respective group. The teacher should develop gradually his own philosophy and convictions while remaining flexible to new ideas and adaptable to change. He should establish a purpose which steadies the evolvement of each lesson. The class must be structured, but not so systematized as to cause erosion of the freedom necessary for creativity. Each lesson must have a goal toward which to strive. It is not possible to achieve all benefits in any one lesson, but each lesson should focalize on selected goals.

The limits of achievement will vary with each individual. The student must be motivated and challenged continuously to work in the direction of his greatest capacity. The teacher, then, becomes the guiding power who inspires the dancer to stretch toward his fullest potential. Through a variety of diversified movement experiences, the student should gradually broaden his understanding, knowledge, and appreciation of contemporary dance as an art form. He should be led into a kinesthetic awareness of the human body as an intelligent instrument of expression. He needs sufficient time to analyze his own movements. His concepts, his thinking, his feelings, and his movement reactions are all part of the process of becoming consciously perceptive to the possibilities of self-identity and self-discovery.

If the range of perception is to be expanded and projected beyond the immediate limits, the teacher must plan thoughtfully to extend the movement explorations through varied dance experiences which do not resolve into mere exercises – a fault of some inexperienced dance teachers. One should not be misled into believing that dance is just a matter of piecing together a number of movements performed without regard to control, quality, and form. Quite the contrary. Good dance requires discipline – preferably self-imposed – and hard work. If the student has the desire to achieve, he will put forth the concentrated effort to attain his goals. In addition, the dance atmosphere should be relatively permissive, yet tempered with self-discipline. The teacher must allow just the proper balance between freedom and limitation, freedom to be creative within a given assigned problem to be solved, and sufficient limitation to keep the student from becoming frustrated because he has an embarrassment of choice. For example, after presenting a familiar 2-beat swing to the class, encourage each student to experiment in order to discover his own 2-beat swing. Allow him to use one arm or one leg at a time, varying the direction of the swing and employing the different planes of high, middle or low. This defines the problem, sets limits on the parts of the body to be used, and at the same time allows freedom of creativity in the way, in the direction, and in what plane the dancer chooses to solve the problem in his own unique way.

The power of the teacher should not be minimized. If he sets forth clearly defined goals, if he has genuine interest in and believes in the worth of his students, if he can excite the students to throw off complacency and lethargy, he can become the impelling force which taps the spontaneity of action and creative endeavor.

How does the dance teacher plan and evolve the lesson? Initially, he should decide on the over-all purpose of the lesson. This particular emphasis may be developed and carried to completion in one lesson or in a number of lessons, as in the unit plan, depending upon the need. A lesson plan is simply a way of organizing materials in a consciously planned series of procedures which ultimately lead to a successful culmination. Since there are many ways to achieve goals, there is no standardized formula to follow. Each teacher in his own way will construct, work out, and develop his plan according to his philosophy of dance as related to the needs and potential capacities of his students. Above all, his aim must be to view each dancer as a human being with the dynamic energy and wisdom to be inspired to grow in stature and to become sensitive, perceptive, and discriminatory in movement expression.

The following general outline of a plan may assist the less experienced teacher in framing a lesson. It should be noted that not all the materials will necessarily be included in any one plan. At best, it may serve as a point of departure.


## OUTLINE OF A LESSON PLAN

I.  **Over-all Goal**

II. **Objectives**

III. **Facilities and Equipment**
    A. Supplies and Aids.
        1. Piano, record player, records, percussion instruments.
        2. Films, projector, screen, tape recorder, tapes, video tapes and cameras.
        3. Photographs, scrapbooks, dance articles for bulletin board.
    B. Space to be used.

IV. **Organization**
Attempt to use space efficiently and imaginatively. Utilize a variety of formations and floor patterns. See pages 18-21, utilizing the space adequately.)

V.  **Outline of the Content**
    A. Begin with preparative movement patterns.
    B. Include vigorous movement with emphasis on exact rhythmic response.
    C. Include locomotor and non-locomotor movement experiences and combinations and variations of these. Present these creatively.
    D. Include creative problems to be solved — movement variations, movement patterns, or compositions.
    E. Plan creative approaches throughout the lesson with opportunities for individual expression, and for individual and group creative endeavor.

VI. **Procedures**
    A. The approaches employed will center around explanation, demonstration, participation, question-answer, discussion, problem solving in student leadership and followership, and in challenging student creativity.
    B. Progressions should be emphasized.
        1. Begin with familiar movements and gradually lead into less familiar ways of moving.
        2. Start with simple and progress to more complex movements.
        3. Provide sufficient repetition to insure accomplishment and satisfaction.

   4. In teaching rhythm-centered movements:
      a. Listen to the music or rhythmic accompaniment.
      b. Clap the timing, phrasing, accents.
      c. Step it out in place.
      d. Move to it through space.
   5. Practice movements on both the left and right sides of the body.

## VII. Evaluation
   A. Student accomplishments in terms of stated objectives.
      1. Skills and abilities.
      2. Knowledges and understandings.
      3. Attitudes and appreciations.
   B. Teacher's appraisal.
      1. Of the lesson.
      2. Of self.

## EXPANDING THE ABOVE OUTLINE
## AS APPLIED TO A SPECIFIC LESSON

## I. Over-all Goal
The application of sustained and percussive movement to a created pattern of designated length.

## II. Objectives
   A. To provide understanding of and experience with two different qualities of movement, namely, sustained and percussive.
   B. To review the characteristics of each movement quality.
   C. To provide varied experiences with sustained and percussive movements.
   D. To stress technical proficiency in the performance of these movements.
   E. To challenge creative endeavor through the development of a sustained-percussive movement pattern.
   F. To add enrichment and enjoyment to the dance experience.

## III. Facilities and Equipment
Drum, gong, beater.

## IV. Organization
Have class spaced informally with all facing in the same direction. Change the formation as needed.

## V. Outline of the Content
   A. Preparative movement.
   B. Discussion.
   C. Review.
   D. New material.
      1. Divide class into smaller groups.
      2. Assign problem to be solved.
      3. Limit the time to solve the problem.
      4. Have a short practice period with the accompaniment.
      5. Present demonstration performance of groups with part of the class watching.
   E. Evaluation.

VI. **Procedures**
   A. Present preparative movement emphasizing review of sustained and percussive movements including Sustained Walks, Head and Torso Rotation, Arm Reaching and Pulling (See Chapter 6, pages 131-132); Percussive Contrasted with Sustained Movement (See Chapter 6, page 135).
   B.
   1. Divide the class into groups of fives. Assign two of the five to create a non-locomotor pattern emphasizing sustained movement to four measures of 4/4 meter with a change of level for each measure; and the other three to devise a locomotor pattern stressing percussive movement to four measures of 4/4 meter with the strongest accented movement on every first beat of each measure. The latter group, although moving out of a stationary position, should relate their movement to the stationary group which is performing sustained movement. Both groups are to move in unison. The result may take on an effect of "attack and retreat" or of "aggression and submission." The exact relationship is to be determined by the concerted planning of both groups. The form should involve a specific beginning, a middle section, and a solid ending. This is a short assignment and should be finished as quickly as possible.
   2. After the groups have completed their patterns, allow a short practice period to 4/4 accompaniment. A drum serves well for the percussive movement while a gong stroke (struck with a soft beater only on every first beat of each measure and permitted to resound for the next three beats) will help prolong the sound vibrations to support the sustained movement.
   3. Select two or three groups with fine patterns which successfully show effective relationships of one group to the other. Arrange them spatially and have these groups perform in unison. Shift one or two out and replace with others until all have had an opportunity to perform. As the remainder of the class watches these choreographic experiments, ask for their suggestions in trying different arrangements. Point out especially interesting effects, and note the added efficacy made possible by noticeable group relationships.

VII. **Evaluation**
   A. Student evaluation may be simply the achievement of solving the problem successfully; and the evident and involved sharing in the experimental arrangements of the larger groups.
   B. Teacher's appraisal.
      1. Of the lesson.
         a. Was the setting conducive to student initiative and spontaneity?
         b. Was sufficient time allowed for the activity presented?
         c. Did the content build to a climax?
         d. Was the accompaniment dynamic in support of the movement?
      2. Of self.
         a. Was the problem well explained or was the group confused about what was expected of them?
         b. Were the suggestions presented in a positive and helpful manner?
         c. Was guidance a prime motivator of the lesson?

There are many types of movements which may be danced with equal skill and conviction by both sexes, yet it is a fallacy to expect that men should move like women and vice versa. Male dancers should be encouraged to seek and strive to use those qualities which best exemplify their manliness. Extra care should be given by the teacher to influence the male dancers in the class to utilize those uniquely masculine abilities which require strength and vigor. This is not to imply that all dance movement performed by men should consist of great bounding jumps and leaps. The result would be a disastrous stereotype with the man providing a limited function unnecessarily.

At all times the human body must be honored without violation of the laws governing its function and action. Correct alignment must be observed, good body mechanics respected, and strained positions avoided. Preparative movements will allow the body to become more fluent and ready for the work which is to follow.

Isolated movement techniques are uninteresting and boring. After introducing a specific movement, it should be developed through a series of variations expanding it progressively in dynamics, rhythm, and space. Starting with an initial movement and exploring (1) the possibilities related to the way energy is expended, (2) the contrast resulting from changing tempo or accent, and (3) the stimulating space possibilities which evolve from altering the direction, dimension, level, and focus is far more challenging and exciting than merely performing one given movement. By dividing the class into several groups and having them execute a movement pattern at timed intervals may be more satisfying than performing in unison.

After a skeletal movement is presented, the class should be permitted adequate time to experiment with new and different ways of using the movement. Too much leeway of choice may result in a dead end. Set a goal that is attainable. Define specific limits to be reached, and be certain that each student understands what he is attempting to accomplish. Then, leave the class to sort out, organize, and arrange the dance material in their own expressed form. Permit the group to be independent and to rely on their own thinking in solving the problems. The assignment of problem solving is one of the finest procedures for motivating individuals to persevere in self-discovery. The teacher should give verbal suggestions and pose questions for consideration. The student should feel free to ask for further assistance if he reaches an impasse. If allowed this latitude, the student tends to find a surprising number of meaningful ways to move.

Occasionally, creativity may just happen. More frequently the setting which results in discovery is planned. The student must feel comfortable, secure, and have no misapprehensions regarding the possible ridicule or down-grading of his efforts. Already the teen-ager as well as the adult has developed inhibitions with fears of expressing himself outwardly. Only with patience, understanding, and assurance will these individuals be given confidence necessary for successful accomplishment. In the earlier stages of development, embarrassment will be minimized by having all the small groups in the class show their projects at the same time. Later on, two or three may perform at the same time. Finally, one group at a time may give their presentation.

As self-confidence develops and self-identity becomes more significant, the student gradually ceases to be hesitant about the new and the unknown. As self-assurance is heightened, as body efficiency is increased, as familiarity with terminology is assured, and as creative experiences are extended in breadth and depth, the student begins to lose himself in what he is doing and arrives at partial or complete absorption in his personal adventure.

If movement techniques are approached creatively, it becomes increasingly easier for the student to build dance patterns. In turn, the simplest dance patterns, if structured in relation to dynamics, rhythm, and space with a specific beginning, a middle portion, and an ending, commence to manifest a semblance of form as the bare essentials of a dance composition materialize. Even then, beginners tend to develop compositions which may be pantomimic and literal with static and extraneous transitions. It is important to emphasize that simple movements well developed and performed will convey greater intent than complex movements poorly controlled and executed. Time and patience are of the essence in helping each student grasp the ways in which group suggestions may be combined effectively. Working as a member of a group in developing a composition is a new experience for many students.

If the teacher continues to plan comprehensively, the process of moving into and experiencing dance composition should prove to be one of natural growth. Gradually the student should begin to use the human body as an intelligent and sensitive instrument of expression, and to feel successful in projecting ideas, feelings and emotions to an audience — even a peer audience. The successful created product will be one which has weathered the processes of trial and error, re-arrangement, and refinement. This is equally true for the simplest dance and for the more complex composition. Standards set both by the teacher and the student should be kept high and, at the same time, attainable.

Each presentation of small assignments, solved problems, simple dance patterns, studies, and dance compositions should be followed with some form of evaluation. This may result in an informal discussion about that which has been viewed. At times the observations may be expanded to include reactions to that which was felt and heard as well as to that which was seen. This form of evaluation seems to elicit greater oral response from inexperienced dancers. Later, an analysis type of appraisal may replace the less formal discussion. At that time it may be necessary for the teacher to initiate the discussion by asking such questions as, "How did they use space in order to communicate the idea?" "How did they achieve unity and balance?" "Was the choice of movement right for the intended idea?" "How did they achieve group relationship?" "Did they need all the dancers included to successfully project their dance concept?" "Was contrast in evidence?" "Was the selection of accompaniment suitable?" "Did the use of a prop add or detract from the communication of the idea?" These and many more such questions could stimulate peer discussion of that which was performed.

If the teacher finds it necessary to give a grade evaluation, he may set up a point or letter grade system for each class. A certain number of points may be given each dancer for skill performance, for improvement, for cooperation with peers, for participation in verbal evaluation, for performance in projects, studies and compositions, and for written work. Or, these same classifications may be transcribed into percentage equivalents for letter grades. The teacher should decide the basis on which individuals and groups are to be graded, and ascribe values to each requirement of the course.

## PROBLEM AREAS IN DEVELOPING STUDENT CREATIVE WORK

There are certain trouble areas which students seem to encounter in the process of developing their creative work. The teacher needs to be aware of these as he guides his students toward maturity and mastery of the dance art. The following represent some of the most common problems:

1. **A mechanical presentation**
    This common fault is understandable when one considers that a rather arbitrary form has been set, a course of action has been carefully outlined, and

certain rules have been established which must be followed. Still, in spite of all this seeming regimentation, a sense of dance must happen. To overcome a heavy and static rendering of material, the movement must first be alive and dynamic; and secondly, it must flow not only from each separate movement to movement, but also from one section of the dance to another. The teacher should urge more concentration on the actual doing of the movement, less consideration of self, and more freedom and joy in the action.

2. **Weak transitions**
   The flow of the dance from one movement to another and from one section of the dance to another is termed transition. A sense of completion should occur at the end of each section, but a continuing relationship should exist between sections. Just as one sentence builds to another until a paragraph is completed, so one movement weaves into another until a unit completes itself. Ways to tie one movement to another must be experimented with and thought about. The teacher should encourage trial and error explorations for solutions.

3. **Poor phrasing**
   Transitions are closely related to phrasing. A sense of phrasing in dance can be helped by planning specifically for timed spaces between movements and sections. A pause to allow for a movement to come to completion; a breath or impulse for beginning again are ways the dancer can more satisfactorily project a sense of phrasing.

4. **Difficulty in starting to work together constructively**
   A division of responsibilities might be a positive way to start. Using as an example the resultant rhythm outlined under the next section, Evaluating Creative Work (See page 16), one person could act as a coordinator working on transitions, helping with counts, establishing tempo, and the like. Another person could be primarily responsible for devising, selecting and setting movement for the eight measures of 3/4 meter; another for the eight measures of 4/4 meter; another for the four measures of combined 12/4 meter; and another for the ending. Each dancer should be encouraged to contribute ideas to the whole project.

5. **Difficulty in cooperating together**
   At the outset the group should decide what action should be followed in the event of a disagreement. Either the majority rule will settle the conflict of opinion, or the person previously selected to be responsible for that portion of the dance shall decide the course to be followed. The decision once made must then be graciously accepted by all and progress on the project resumed.

6. **Timid experimentation**
   Some dancers are fine technically and follow all the ground rules, but still seem earth bound and unimaginative. At this point the teacher may step in and suggest one or two possibilities. For instance, change the tempo — play with it. Try one section rapidly, the next slowly; or, increase or decrease the tempo gradually. A group which has been doing non-locomotor movement may be asked to perform the same movement theme on one knee, while sitting, or while trying a variety of different levels. Each member of the group may experiment by starting in a new position, facing a new direction, or forming a new grouping. The teacher should avoid offering too many suggestions. Actually, many times all the group needs is one single little push and the momentum for their own creative ideas gathers speed.

7. **Working alone**

For beginners, more varied experiences and educational opportunities in a relatively brief time span are possible if the dancer works cooperatively with a group on a combined effort approach. However, the values derived from making one's own dance should not be ignored. Often, the best dances are the result of one person's conception. The teacher may start by structuring a very simple problem for one person to be performed by him. For example:

Purposes:
To understand how contrasting tempo affects movement.
To be given the opportunity to work alone.
Problem:
To use changing tempo as a rhythmic device to form a dance study.
Limitations:
A. Solo.
B. Devising a movement phrase using four measures of slow 4/4 meter.
C. Using the same movement phrase with slight variations and moving to four measures of quick 4/4 meter.
D. Repeating the slow movement phrase with slight variations for four measures of slow 4/4 meter.
E. Establishing a definite ending.

Later, have the above solo dancer develop his study with three dancers and exclude himself from performing. He must now consider group relationships, and face the problem of teaching and expressing his desires to other dancers in order to achieve his concept of the dance. He might be influenced by and take suggestions from his dancers, but the direction he takes and the results he attains — accepting both the responsibility for mistakes and the satisfaction of success — belong to him and to him alone.

## EVALUATING CREATIVE WORK

When one dances and is viewed communication occurs. The teacher is obliged to assess the success of this communication in terms understandable to the student and to the authorities concerned with grade marks. One coach said that he judged all gymnastic events as if every performer were an olympic star. In other words, the teacher judges against perfection as he understands it. Technical competence is likely the most obvious factor in evaluation, and perhaps the easiest to rate. But the dancer's art involves itself with the communication aspect as well as the skill area. It is in this facet that the teacher faces his greatest challenge in evaluation. In judging composition, the teacher tries to follow the dancer's intellectual struggle for communication as well as to appreciate the excellence of the technical execution.

Before judgment can be made a structured situation must exist. Therefore, it is important to set a problem with clearly defined limits at the onset of creative endeavors. A stated problem tends to give purpose and direction to movement and design. The student must be fully cognizant of the purpose of the creative assignment and of the boundaries within which he must work. For example:

Purposes:
    To understand resultant rhythm.
    To work cooperatively within established limits to develop a dance study which is well performed, original in approach, and aesthetically pleasing in its presentation.
Problem:
    The use of resultant rhythm as a rhythmic device in a dance study.
Limitations:
    1. Working with five people in a group.
    2. Establishing a definite 3/4 meter in eight measures.
    3. Establishing a definite 4/4 meter in the next eight measures.
    4. Combining the meters in the twelve-beat phrase for four measures of 12/4 meter.
    5. Devising a solid ending lasting from one to twelve beats.

Having formulated the ground rules, the first task of the student is to see that these designated guide lines are given utmost consideration. The teacher's evaluation is made more manageable by checking these same points to determine if they were adhered to, and then to judge the success of the dance.

**Teacher's Evaluation Card For Each Student:**

Student's Name _____

Skill in performance . . . . . . . . . . . . . . . . . . . . . . . . . . . . . . . . . . . . . . . . 1 2 3 4 ⑤

Resultant rhythm clearly demonstrated . . . . . . . . . . . . . . . . . . . . . . . 1 ② 3 4 5

Followed established ground rules . . . . . . . . . . . . . . . . . . . . . . . . . . . 1 2 3 ④ 5

Effective ending . . . . . . . . . . . . . . . . . . . . . . . . . . . . . . . . . . . . . . . . . 1 2 3 4 ⑤

Original in approach . . . . . . . . . . . . . . . . . . . . . . . . . . . . . . . . . . . . . 1 2 3 4 ⑤

General impression of presentation . . . . . . . . . . . . . . . . . . . . . . . . . 1 2 3 4 ⑤

Total points = 26

    With reference to the group creative problem above, all but the first item on the Teacher's Evaluative Card pertains to each group of five people. The same evaluative categories would be more or less applicable for individual creative problems. In appraising creative endeavor, particular attention should be given to the unique purposes and limitations which have been established.

## TEACHING GUIDES

    The following suggestions may give more specific assistance to less experienced teachers. At best, they represent guiding factors which may be varied, changed, or amplified according to the particular setting and relevant need.

## VARIED APPROACHES

Many different approaches contribute to the learning process. The degree of visual, auditory, and kinesthetic perception varies with students. One may respond quickly to the visual sensation of seeing a movement demonstrated, while another may be reached more directly by feeling the movement as he tries to do that which he understands as the result of a verbal analysis. The learning-response-experiences of seeing, hearing, and feeling presented as motivators aid the student in becoming more perceptive. The teacher is the catalyzer who stimulates and challenges the student to develop greater sensitivity and awareness.

## PLANNING THE LESSON

1. Find out as much as possible about the background of the class. Are they all beginners? How many have had previous experience in some form of dance? What are their goals?
2. Develop objectives for each lesson in terms of the student needs and goals.
3. Prepare each lesson carefully and build the progressions to reach a satisfying climax. As the beginning teacher grows in experience and gains self-confidence and self-assurance, his lesson plans should become more flexible; and his ability to grasp the significance of a creative response and to develop it should become more evident.
4. Be completely familiar with the music chosen as dance accompaniment. Prior to the class meeting listen to the music to analyze its structure and form. (See Appendices for lists of musical composers and dance recordings.)
5. Be familiar with a variety of percussion instruments to be used as accompaniment for dance. Be able to maintain a steady tempo. Keep in mind that each individual establishes his own tempo in his daily activities, and that adjustments may be necessary for individuals to maintain the tempo set for the group.
6. Use interesting and current audio and visual materials as motivators such as films (See Appendices for listing), photographs, bulletin board displays, articles related to contemporary dance artists and dance trends, and copies of up-to-date dance programs.
7. Whenever possible, incorporate the related arts as an integral part of the lesson: the space or visual arts of painting, sculpture, and architecture; and the time arts of music, drama, and poetry. Dance as a space-time art includes many of the principles of rhythm and form which are basic to the space arts and the time arts.

## UTILIZING THE SPACE ADEQUATELY

1. A large group in either an informal standing or lying position will have greater individual work space if they face a specified corner of the room.
2. Vary the ways in which groups are to move.
   A. Informal traveling, clockwise or counter-clockwise, in a circular pattern. This permits a "togetherness" feeling of comfort and security within the group.
   B. Moving down the floor en masse. This is a good method for early learners to try out the movement. It saves time by giving each one the opportunity to test his own ability, to clarify his problems, and to understand that which he is trying to accomplish.
   C. Moving down the floor in smaller groups arranged in couples or lines with all

Figure Three

facing in the same direction. At designated time intervals, each couple or line moves forward to the opposite end of the room. In a "cast off" procedure the left half of the line walks around the left side of the room as the right half of the line walks around the right side of the room, bringing both groups back to their starting points. This maneuver provides for continuous movement of a large group, requires individuals and groups to become alert for their next starting moment, and allows a greater area through which each dancer may move.

D. Moving diagonally across the floor by working on diagonal lines is more complex and somewhat more confusing than working on the square of a room. In general the compensating benefits of utilizing diagonal crossings are that the overall movement design becomes more exciting and less static, there is a heightening of spatial awareness, and the class movement as a whole is more nearly related to the actual dance experience with timed entrances and exits, with nearby related figures, and with passing and opposing figures.

1) If the class is small, arrange separated partners in a column at one corner facing the opposite corner. They move to the opposite corner, walk across the end of the room and back up the side to their starting point. The travel path is triangular in shape. This particular plan allows the teacher an opportunity to make brief verbal corrections to specific dancers as they move across the floor. Also, since the path is continuous, each dancer does not feel as conspicuous as if he were moving alone on the floor. The walk around allows a few minutes for recovery from exertion.

2) If the class is larger, arrange two groups with half in one corner and the other half in the opposite corner of the same side of the room. Each group may be placed with twos or threes standing side-by-side at convenient distances from each other. At a given signal one group moves en masse diagonally forward to the opposite corner. After the first group has passed the center of the floor, the other group repeats the pattern to their opposite corner.

3) As a variation of 2) above and to increase the difficulty of accurate rhythmic response, the first line of dancers in group one moves forward diagonally on a given signal. After one phrase the first line of dancers in group two moves forward diagonally. This movement is repeated alternately with the second line of dancers in group one and two respectively. This sequence continues until all have crossed the floor. Such a plan is challenging and requires a sensitive alertness to a starting signal.

## PROCEDURES FOR PRESENTING THE LESSON

1. Set an atmosphere which will allow the class to feel comfortable and secure. Let them know that their best efforts will earn respect and appreciation.
2. Recognize the uniqueness of each individual despite varied abilities.
3. Give judicious attention to correct body alignment and good body mechanics. Emphasize that a simple movement well performed with control is far more efficient and pleasing to watch than a complex movement poorly executed.
4. Use correct names for body parts.
5. Utilize both sides of the body equally in practicing movement techniques.
6. Consider the total body. In giving directions, include concise instructions for the use of arms, head, and torso as well as for the feet and legs. Beginning learners tend to

concentrate their movement in the feet and legs and give less attention to the torso, head, and arms.

7. While facing the class, present demonstrations on the side opposite to that of the class. This demonstration is a "mirror" type procedure. In other words, if the class is stepping sideward on the left foot, the teacher steps sideward on the right foot.

8. Begin each activity class with preparative techniques to warm the body, to increase the circulation, and to prepare the body for the more strenuous work to follow.

9. Limit the amount of talking and begin the class with immediate action. Charge the group to be alert at all times. When moving across the floor at spaced time intervals, challenge each individual to know exactly when to begin moving.

10. Avoid teaching dance techniques as ends in themselves. Use techniques to improve body coordination, agility, flexibility, extension, balance, and overall efficiency. Teach the techniques creatively by providing varied and exploratory experiences as preliminary to the enjoyment of composing dance patterns, dance studies, and compositions.

11. Break down new movements into their smallest components, having the class experience them slowly at first; then, in exact timing, build to their completion.

12. Be observant! Spot errors in movement and make corrections without pointing out particular individuals. Re-analyze if necessary. Avoid negative criticism. Encourage improvement and give recognition and praise for accomplishment.

13. Refrain from dancing too long with the group; otherwise, the class will resort to teacher imitation rather than self-direction.

14. Alternate vigorous activity with moments of temporary pause to revitalize physical resources. These pauses may serve for purposes of explanation, demonstration, discussion, review, and evaluation.

15. Provide enough time for students to practice difficult movement coordinations at their own tempos.

16. Place limits on the choices allowed for creating or developing a movement study. If limitations are not indicated, the beginner can become confused and even frustrated simply because he does not know where or how to begin.

17. Urge each student to make his contribution by showing the results of his creative effort even though it may be unfinished. At the same time, a responsibility to complete the assignments should be encouraged so that the fullest sense of accomplishment may be achieved.

18. Attempt to have assigned projects completed within one or two class periods. Especially is this necessary for beginners. Indicate the time limit for solving problems.

19. When time permits, follow the presentation of patterns, projects, dance studies, and dance compositions with a verbal evaluative discussion. Encourage every member of the class to make constructive comments.

20. Make each class experience enjoyable and pleasurable.

## ADDITIONAL MOTIVATORS

1. Plan small informal class programs with suggestive costumes, props, and limited staging.
2. Keep bulletin boards attractive and up-to-date.
3. Have available many fine pictures, books, and films related to dance.
4. Start a dance club in the school or college.
5. Initiate exchange dance workshops with schools or colleges in the nearby area.

Figure Four

6. Have classes or smaller groups attend dance symposiums offered by other schools and/or colleges.
7. See other groups perform: both amateur and professional.

## EVALUATING THE LESSON AND GRADING THE ACHIEVEMENT

1. Following each lesson presentation, evaluate the success of the plan. Re-check the objectives in relation to the lesson as they are reflected in the resulting accomplishments of the class.
2. Determine the basis on which grades are to be resolved. Classify the areas of the course to be used in the appraisal process. Assign point or percentage values to each area.

The role of the teacher is highly significant. It is his responsibility to provide a favorable setting conducive to learning. By careful preparation, through knowledge of subject matter, by means of positive presentation of material and objective evaluation, the teacher may accomplish his function. Yet, the teacher is only one part of the transaction. The student also plays a vital role in this process. There must be ample latitude for both individuals, teacher and student, to grow together in an educational environment which is broadly and deeply conceived A sensitive rapport between teacher and student is needed to stimulate effective progress which leads to achievement. The unity of purpose widens the potential of this dual adventure. By reason of maturity and experience, the teacher reveals the possible vistas and guides the student into liberalizing his educational perspective both in breadth and depth. He challenges the student to explore new experiences. As the student derives personal satisfaction from his new impressions, knowledge, and skills, he alters and refines his attitudes and perceptions. Thus, the twofold process is germinated and unfolds.

Figure Five

# Chapter 3

# ELEMENTS OF DANCE MOVEMENT

In order to reveal the technical significance of dance movement, it becomes important for the dancer to examine and analyze the very core-substance which comprises his art. Such an analysis requires breaking down the whole into its essential materials. This dissecting process is not to be construed as an end in itself, but rather as a means by which constituent movements may be developed into a meaningful composite whole.

With respect to movement there are three elements to be noted namely, space, dynamics, and rhythm. Whenever the human body moves, these three elements are evident.

## SPACE — AN ELEMENT OF MOVEMENT

Dance is both a space art and a time art. Dance employs the use of space and requires and utilizes a certain amount of time. These two elements, space and time, are inseparable. In the study of space there are six different aspects to be considered.

1. **Floor Pattern**

    A floor pattern develops as an individual or a group moves through a pathway in space. This pattern may take the shape of complete, partial, or combined geometric figures. For example, one effect may be achieved by progressing in a straight line toward an object, while a very different effect may result by progressing toward the same object in a zig-zag line. Or again, a dance composition may evolve into a more complex floor pattern as the dancers move interchangeably to form symmetrical or asymmetrical designs.

    For purposes of visual interest and clarification, various floor patterns may be drawn on paper or on a chalkboard with different colored chalk to represent the respective dancers in a group study or composition.

    Dance techniques employing a variety of floor patterns help the student become more consciously aware of his use of space. He discovers many different ways of handling his body as he moves away from a fixed position and explores the myriad floor designs which are possible. Although many of his movements may be prompted by a visual stimulus, the act of moving at one's own volition involves thinking and feeling. As the student continues to move with conscious awareness, he sharpens his kinesthetic perception. Having experienced many varied floor patterns in short studies, the dancer is better prepared to draw upon the use of floor designs in developing dance composition.

    Floor patterns tend to be either symmetrical or asymmetrical. In a symmetrical design the floor pattern on both sides of the spatial area correspond to each other. This plan seems simpler and less involved for the beginner to experience first. Due to its structure, it is explicit and formal.

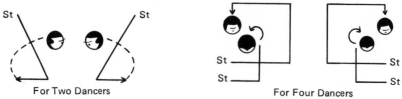

Diagram 1. Symmetrical Floor Patterns

In an asymmetrical design the floor pattern of the spatial area is not blocked equally on both sides. This allows for greater freedom, interest, and contrast as the dancer grows in experience.

Diagram 2. Asymmetrical Floor Patterns

(See pages 142-146 for Variations of Floor Pattern.)

## 2. Direction

Direction becomes evident whenever some part of the body is in action. While remaining on a pivot, the body may lean or bend in a forward, backward, or sideways direction, or may bend from one direction to another. As the body moves through surrounding space, choices of direction immediately become apparent. The movement may be forward, backward, sideways, or a combination of the foregoing arranged in phrases of short or long duration.

Due to the anatomical design of the human body, it is more natural and comfortable for a person to move in a forward direction. Also, daily life activities are characterized more by forward locomotion than any other direction. The pathway in space may occur in straight or curved lines.

The beginning dancer should first experience fundamental locomotor movements such as walks and runs in a forward, straight path. As he gains control and balance, he should be encouraged to explore many other directions such as forward-down, forward-up, sideward-left, sideward-right, diagonal-left, diagonal-right; and combinations of a variety of directions built into short sequences.

When combined, directional lines marked by sharp angles can form various shapes such as squares, zig-zags, triangles, rectangles, and other geometric figures. Following the initial experiences of moving forward, the difficulty can be increased by having the dancer maintain a forward direction of his body while moving sideward or backward. The complexity can be further enlarged by combining partial or complete turns with, and in contrast to, geometric directional patterns. Increasing the tempo while performing movements with directional changes provides an opportunity for greater sophistication.

Moving through circular floor patterns effect kinesthetic feelings which are different from those resulting from straight line patterns. Moving away from a straight line direction into a curved path tends to pull the body off balance. While traveling in a circular path, an impelling force draws the moving body toward the center of rotation. This requires additional control in maintaining balance.

Curved pathways can be explored by moving diagonally forward left, and then right while the body faces in the moving line of direction. Experimenting with semi-circles, circles, scallops, serpentines, spirals, figure-eights, and combinations of these will enhance the dancer's sensitivity to the aesthetic effects which accrue.

In the development of dance composition, it is imperative that the choreographer be aware of the psychological impact his use of space may have on his viewers. The dancer should know that his specific use of directional line can elicit certain responses from his audience. For instance, a forward-down-center path on the stage while facing forward can convey a feeling of authority, confidence, and strength. Contrariwise, a backward-up-center path while facing forward can express the feeling of retreat, resignation and weakness. The directional plan is a significant ingredient of a dance composition. (See pages 146-149 for Variations of Direction.)

3. **Focus**

Focus involves the conscious attention and movement of the eyes, the alert tensing of the body, or the inclining of the body in terms of directional line or plane. Thus, focal effects may be achieved by the specific use of arms, legs, head or torso. When focus is coupled with intense concentration, the communicative impact is powerful.

In daily life, focus is a potent means of communication. The lone person looking skyward or pointing a hand upward at some particular object will capture the interest of others who, in turn, will stare in the same focal direction.

Focus is a natural and mutual accompaniment of movement. A variety of dance experiences can center on special problems emphasizing focus. For example, as an introductory experiment have individuals walk on a straight or curved line across the long diagonal of the room while concentrating (thinking and feeling) on a focal point in the upper far corner of the room. Or, suggest that they walk slowly and informally about the room while directing the eye and head focus upward on a certain spot on the ceiling.

To bring about a person-to-person relationship, have partners sit opposite each other. One devises an 8-beat movement phrase employing concentrated eye and head focus downward. At the same time, the other partner creates movement with eye and upper body focal concentration changing from up to down.

To further the movement-focus exploration, assign a short composition in which changing focus is stressed. Such ideas as confusion, frustration, and wandering may grow out of this experience.

The effective use of focus in dance composition helps to determine the successful communication to the audience of the intended idea or mood. The result can become a vicariously moving response on the part of the audience. (See pages 149-151 for Variations of Focus.)

4. **Level**

Gradations of level may range from the highest possible jump-reach to a recumbent position. The existence of shifting level is noticeable both in locomotor and in non-locomotor movement. Many procedures may be tried to accentuate the awareness of body level. To illustrate, arms may describe circles, arcs, squares, lines, loops, triangles and combinations of these at various levels. In turn, these patterns may be further extended into space by means of locomotor movement.

32

The upright vertical position of the body gives a feeling of stability and balance. As the body moves away from this vertical line toward a diagonal or horizontal plane, the ever-constant pull of gravity tends to cause a sense of imbalance and insecurity. The process of changing from a vertical to a horizontal level tips the body through a diagonal level – the intermediate plane. Upon reaching the horizontal plane, the body again re-gains the composure of balance and security. When the body or a part of the body bends at a given point to the degree that the line is parallel with the floor, that bent portion is in a horizontal plane.

It may be less complicated for beginners to work first with one directional plane. The assignment may be to develop a movement pattern to attain the greatest height followed by the most complete depth, and then a return to the original vertical position. This involves the process of lowering the body to the floor. Whenever so-called falls are included, they should represent an outgrowth of a motivating concept which necessitates their use. Usually some form of partial or complete recovery follows the falling process. Falling to the lowest possible level requires kinesthetic control and does not evolve into complete collapse of the body with a letting go of all muscle tension.

Falls, *per se*, convey little or no meaning. If falls are not performed with correct body alignment and with utmost care, they can be injurious. Falls are used to provide contrast and to give emphasis and climax to the development of certain dance ideas. Unless a completely collapsed fall is used to end a dance composition, the fall is followed by at least some degree of recovery. A recovery is an upward impulse that tends to lift the body. (See pages 113-122 for Lead-ups and Examples of Falls and Recoveries.) (See pages 151-152 for Variations of Level.)

5. **Dimension**

Dimension connotes range or possible change in size within varying limits from the very smallest to the largest movement. Movements may continue small in range or may be amplified to the point of exaggeration. Again, they may show gradual or sudden variations within a given limit. For example, contrast the dimensional effect of tiny, pert steps with that of wide, vigorous leaps.

Dimension relates to the range of the floor pattern. The dancer must be aware of his surrounding space and needs to have many experiences in the varied use of space. Gradations of range are affected by and become apparent in terms of the ideas to be conveyed. Small or expanded movements will relate directly to the ideas to be expressed. Limited movement in a confined area may suggest a feeling of restraint or timidity. Expansive movements may invoke a feeling of liveliness or recklessness.

Dance patterns and compositional studies may be approached through space problems. The emphasis may be wholly on small movements, on a limited use of space, on an expansive use of space, or on gradations of space as determined by the idea to be expressed. With regard to dimension, the movement possibilities may be further extended by utilizing a pattern of vivid contrasts. Abrupt changes from gross exaggeration to a minute indication can be startlingly effective in dance composition and very enjoyable to do in dance class studies. Establishing a form (e.g., A B A = small, large, small; A B A B = large, small, large, small) is one possible device that may be used to illustrate differences in movement range.

The projection of a dimensional impact may be affected by the number of dancers on stage, the size of the spatial area, and the number, size, and placement of stage sets and props. (See pages 152-156 for Variations of Dimension.)

6. **Contour**

Contour refers to the body either stationary or moving, as outlined or silhouetted against the background of space. It is applicable to an individual or group. Each time an individual or group moves any part of the body, changes direction or level, the contour is altered.

Divide the class into two groups, the one participating and the other observing. The moving group standing close together walks eight steps forward while focusing downward, makes one-quarter turn and walks forward still maintaining the focus downward, slowly changes level to kneel with the focus directed upward and holds position. The observing group notes the changing contour and the empathic effect resulting. Reverse the groups and repeat the experiment. (See pages 156-157 for Variations of Contour.)

## DYNAMICS – AN ELEMENT OF MOVEMENT

Dynamics, a second element of movement, is the force of movement or the way in which energy is applied or exerted. It gives strength or power to movement. It may be exerted in varying degrees. In dance this force is controlled and tempered according to the will of the individual. At times the dynamics of movement may be visible and even audible as in the stamping of the feet; at other times the exertion of energy may be hardly noticeable. The manner of application may be a gradual surge, or again it may be a sharp charge. The way force is expended and disbursed relates to the quality of movement. The quality of movement is determined by the manner in which energy is applied, continued, and arrested. In terms of energy release, these qualities of movement are characterized under the following headings. (See pages 157-161 for Variations Built from Changing Dynamics.)

1. **Swinging Movement**

In swinging or pendular movement the impulse is noticeable, the momentum is continuous, and the follow-through is unrestrained. Swinging movement is executed by the arms or legs and the head and torso in limited fashion in various arcs, from one plane to another, or in any direction. The moving part or parts may sway from side to side or rock forward and backward. (See pages 122-130 for examples of Swinging Movement.)

2. **Sustained Movement**

In sustained movement the impetus and the completion of movement are not easily discernible. The muscle groups involved are equally balanced in force resulting in a fusion of the impulse and the follow-through — comparable to a slow motion film. (See pages 131-133 for examples of Sustained Movement.)

3. **Percussive Movement**

Percussive movement shows a marked impulse with a completely checked follow-through. It is staccato in quality and is executed against resistance. Any part of the body may be involved in the use of percussive movement. Various ways in which the body may move percussively are a sharp, forceful, hurling or lashing movement as though striking something, a sudden and dynamic shifting of the body position, or an abrupt tensing of certain parts of the body. (See pages 133-136 for examples of Percussive Movement.)

4. **Vibratory Movement**

In vibratory movement the impulses occur so rapidly that the contractions and relaxations come very close together. The sharp, powerful impulses exerted with extreme intensity against the resistance either of the body itself or of surrounding space give an effect of repetition and produce a shaking, quivering or tremulous quality of movement. Obviously this type of movement could not go on indefinitely, else the muscles would become fatigued and thus cease to function. (See pages 136-140 for examples of Vibratory Movement.)

5. **Suspended Movement**

Suspended movement, though not static in quality, is characterized by a momentary interruption of the continuity of movement. In this type of movement a lower part of the body becomes a stationary axis which supports above it one or more parts to be suspended. It is initiated with a marked impulse so that movement continues until certain parts of the body reach their peak of elevation. At this point the essential forces are so balanced that movement appears to stop completely. Actually the movement is prolonged, bringing about an equalization of forces required to maintain the suspension. After this delayed follow-through, the suspended part or parts return to the original position, or continue with a new movement. (See pages 140-142 for examples of Suspended Movement.)


## RHYTHM — AN ELEMENT OF MOVEMENT

Rhythm, a third element of movement, is a distinctive and essential quality inherent in nature and in man. This intrinsic force is the pulse of life itself and as such has existed from the beginning of mankind. History tells us that the primitive sacrificial rites of early tribal society were characterized by movements and sounds of rhythmic quality. Throughout the ages, rhythm and song have been an inextricable part of work and play.

Despite the unlimited manifestations of rhythm as translated into the sensory impressions and reactions of seeing, hearing, feeling, touching, or moving (real or apparent), rhythm remains elusive and not easily defined. However, certain characteristics are recognizable. To be rhythmic, there must be present a formed pattern in motion, sound, or design issuing from a three-fold cycle. The three parts of this cycle include: 1) a proportioned and regulated flow of energy and stress organized in duration and intensity; 2) a timed succession resulting in balance, unity, and harmony; and 3) a repetition of a regular and symmetrical grouping sufficient to form a pattern. In other words, an orderly sequence is evident whenever rhythm exists. This three-fold cycle involves preparation, impulse, and exertion of effort; accomplishment and fruition; and finally, recovery, and rest. Following the rest period, repetition occurs. During the state of relaxation, energy is re-generated. The delicate balance between tension and relaxation determines the degree to which energy is used harmoniously.

Rhythm is universal and has a universal appeal. It emerges as a controlling, active force, astoundingly varied, and inherently revealed in the world about us. Not only does life itself bespeak rhythm, but nature exemplifies rhythm in the swaying of trees, in the ebb and flow of water against a shore line, in the systematic changes of celestial bodies, in the incessant erosion of wind and water, and in the flight of birds and the movements of insects.

The characteristic action of the human organism with all its complexities is one of the simplest examples of rhythm; the physiological and psychological processes along with the functioning of thinking and memorizing respond rhythmically in their alternations of contractions and relaxations. Even the senses behave rhythmically. Pulsation is as necessary as the rhythmic beating of the heart.

Rhythm is an attribute common to all art. Art does not exist without rhythm; design is harmonized; line and color are in evidence; words, phrases, and sentences are combined into a related entity; gestures, voice sounds, and poses are correlated; and the human body moves in a symphony of balance and unity with varied intensity and duration. Rhythm may tend to deter strain, confusion, and chaos. It insures regularity, unity, and harmony.

A close parallel of this rhythmic process exists between music and dance. Thus, the analysis of rhythmic structure in music is firmly allied with the rhythmic structure of dance movement. Any motion of the human body resolves itself into an established rhythm that occurs with respect to space, stress of energy, and duration of time. Likewise, each human organism is distinctive by his own individual, natural, and particular rhythm. Even though each individual has his own unique rhythm, he uses many different rhythms every day. Rhythm is not static, it changes frequently. The rhythm of coordinated movement is quite different from the rhythm of less controlled movement. This is apparent in the highly skilled dancer in contrast with the in-experienced beginner.

As a time-space art, dance utilizes a rhythmical structure of movement similiar to that found in music which uses the beat as a time measuring unit. The grouping of these time units or pulsations in a series are distinguished by a regularly recurring strong or primary accent which tends to be stressed more than other beats. As this series of units is continued successively to form a group — measure in time — it becomes evident that the first unit or beat in each group receives greater emphasis or accent than the unit or units which follow. In music this formed measure in time is recognized by a vertical line (bar line) preceding each primary accent. Basically, the measure is divided into a uniform number of time units or beats. This division, indicated in the time signature (metrical signature), is commonly known as meter. In the following example of four measures forming a grouping, the primary accent falls on the first unit or beat after the bar line in each measure. The 3/4 fraction represents the time signature with the top number 3 indicating the number of underlying or constant beats (strong, weak, weak) contained in each measure; and the bottom number 4 signifying the type of note (quarter note) receiving one beat or count. This quarter note is the metrical unit of the measure. The metrical unit may vary depending upon the time signature indicated. (See page 36 for the Triangle of Relative Time Values.)

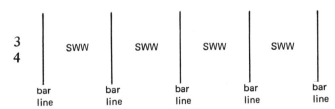

Frequently groups of two, three, or four units or beats are common to each measure. A less common rhythm may not follow the regular pattern of strong and weak beats charted above. In such an instance, the strong beats will not be equally spaced.

Fundamentally all meter tends to fall into one of two classes, duple or triple. Duple meter is characterized by an alternation of a strong and a weak beat. Triple meter is characterized by one strong beat followed by two weak beats.

Simple meters, units of two or three, have a strong accent falling on the first beat of the measure. Examples of simple meters are 2/2, 3/2, 2/4, 3/4, 2/8, 3/8. Compound meters, multiples or combinations of simple meters, have a strong accent falling on the first beat and one or more weaker accents occurring on the other beats in the measure. Examples of compound meters are 4/4, 5/4, 6/4, 7/4, 9/4, 6/8, 9/8, 12/8.

The steady fundamental beat of the measure represents the skeletal structure of meter and may be called the underlying or primary rhythm.

Examples of primary rhythm:

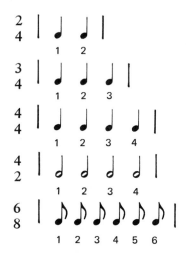

When the fundamental beat is varied but maintains a value equal to the original, the rhythm resulting may be called secondary. This may be comparable to the melody of a song. In the frequent use of chords in marches and hymns the secondary tends to coincide with the primary rhythm. Although there should be an awareness of primary and secondary rhythm in dance movement, it is unnecessary to step out every note; this procedure is rather trite and detracts from the phrasing of the rhythm, and thus, of the movement itself. Each note has a relative time value. In the following chart each note is successively divided into two equal parts. This type of division is known as binary.

### The Triangle of Relative Time Values

Examples of secondary rhythm with binary division:

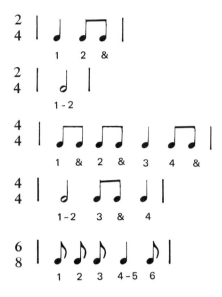

When a beat is arbitrarily divided into thirds, this is known as ternary division. The three notes (triplets) are usually written ♩♩♩ , or ♩♩♩ with each of the three given notes having equal duration and with the total value of each group of three notes being equal to one quarter or one eighth note respectively. In each instance it means that the three grouped notes of triplets must be completed in the same amount of time required to execute an equivalent quarter or eighth note, however indicated. Examples of secondary rhythm, with ternary division:

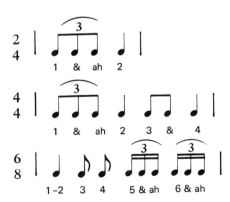

At times rest symbols are used to replace the absence of heard tones or sounds without disturbing the flow of the beats. These symbols are equivalent in length to the silent beats. The following table of rest symbols shows the equivalents for specific note values:

## Table of Rest Symbols

| | | | | |
|---|---|---|---|---|
| ▬ | whole rest | = whole note | 𝅝 | |
| ▬ | half rest | = half note | 𝅗𝅥 | |
| 𝄽 | quarter rest | = quarter note | ♩ | |
| 𝄾 | eighth rest | = eighth note | ♪ | |
| 𝄿 | sixteenth rest | = sixteenth note | 𝅘𝅥𝅯 | |

Dotted notes are utilized to lengthen parts or fractions of one or more full beats. The dot symbol in music (written • ) has value only in relation to the note which precedes it. This value is equal to one-half the value of the note it follows. For example, in the following table assume that the quarter note is equal to one count or beat:

## Table of Dotted Note Values

| Basic Note Values | | | Dotted Note Values | |
|---|---|---|---|---|
| whole note | 𝅝 | = 4 beats | 𝅝. | = 4 + (½ of 4) or 2 = 6 beats |
| half note | 𝅗𝅥 | = 2 beats | 𝅗𝅥. | = 2 + (½ of 2) or 1 = 3 beats |
| quarter note | ♩ | = 1 beat | ♩. | = 1 + (½ of 1) or ½ = 1½ beats |
| eighth note | ♪ | = ½ beat | ♪. | = ½ + (½ of ½) or ¼ = ¾ beat |
| sixteenth note | 𝅘𝅥𝅯 | = ¼ beat | 𝅘𝅥𝅯. | = ¼ + (½ of ¼) or 1/8 = 3/8 beat |

A phrase is a rhythmic or movement unit — ordered, progressive, and proportioned in form. It is comparable to a partial or a complete thought in a sentence. Usually phrases contain 4, 8, or 16 measures (occasionally 2). Phrasing may be regular consisting of an equal number of measures (8-8-8), (4-8-4). Phrasing may be regular as indicated above or irregular and at the same time contain odd numbers of measures such as 3, 5, 7, 9. The cadence representing a point of repose marks the ending of the phrase.

A phrase consists of one or more rhythmic patterns made up of variable combinations or divisions of beats. A given rhythmic pattern may be repeated within a phrase. Likewise, phrases themselves may be repeated.

In dance, phrasing is used to give a semblance of form which becomes the framework for the further development and progression of movement phrases or composition.

Tempo is the rate of speed (fast, moderate or slow) at which a given passage of music or movement progresses. Tempo may vary in great extremes from fastest to slowest, in gradations of rate, or in sudden changes of one speed to another. Variations in tempo lend variety, interest and contrast to, and affect the quality of music and movement. Slow speed tends to emphasize the control of force and balance exerted, while rapid speed tends to obscure the control of force and balance exerted. This becomes evident in performing a run at either a very slow or a very fast pace.

Intensity is the relative degree of loudness or softness, or the amount of energy exerted. In movement this strength or power may remain constant or may increase or decrease gradually or suddenly. The dancer employs a variety of changes in intensity. Extremes of intensity may be used alternately to heighten the contrasts of specific movements. Again, a prolongation of a particular intensity may be maintained to build a climactic effect.

## ADVANCED DEVELOPMENT OF RHYTHM

### SHIFTING ACCENTS OF UNDERLYING RHYTHM

Consecutive accents. For purposes of variation the accents within a group of like measures may be transferred from one beat to another. This involves the underlying beats of measures occurring in consecutive order. It may develop by accenting the first beat of the first measure, the second beat of the second measure, the third beat of the third measure, and so on to complete the rhythmic series.

Or, by accenting the last beat of the first measure, the next to the last beat of the second measure, the third to the last beat in the third measure, and so on down to the first beat in the last measure.

Variable accents. As a contrast to the above, accents within a group of like measures may be shifted from one beat to another in variable order.

### SHIFTING ACCENTS TO WEAK OR UNACCENTED PARTS OF BEATS

Syncopation is a rhythmic device of shifting the accent from the established, regular beat to a fraction of a beat and continuing past the beginning of the next beat. Or the accent may be placed on a weak or unaccented beat and extended past the following regularly accented or strong beat. During these moments of unheard tones (silences) the silent tones are felt. The resulting in-between-the-beat accents produce an exciting and delightful rhythmic effect. This is equally true both of dance movement and of music. Even inexperienced dancers respond favorably and eagerly to syncopated accompaniment. Examples of syncopated measures follow.

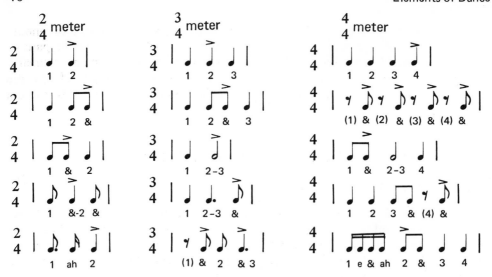

Samples of Syncopated Rhythmic Patterns

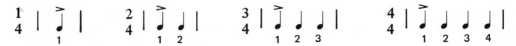

## ACCUMULATIVE AND DECUMULATIVE METER

Accumulative meter is the process of adding one or more beats to each successive measure in a given sequence. Decumulative meter is the process of subtracting one or more beats from each successive measure.

In dance the term accumulative has often been used to include both accumulative and decumulative meter. An accumulative meter may begin with one beat per first measure and continue by adding a beat for each succeeding measure for as many measures as desired.

The decumulative meter would reverse the order by starting at the highest number of beats per measure and continuing to the lowest.

Again, the starting point may begin with two, three, or more beats per first measure and continue to complete that given sequence.

$\frac{2}{4}$ | ♪ ♩ | $\frac{3}{4}$ | ♪ ♩ ♩ | $\frac{4}{4}$ | ♪ ♩ ♩ ♩ | $\frac{3}{4}$ | ♪ ♩ ♩ | $\frac{2}{4}$ | ♪ ♩ |
　1 2　　　1 2 3　　　1 2 3 4　　　1 2 3　　　1 2

Beats may be increased or decreased by twos, threes, or their multiples; but there must be an ordered progression. For example:

$\frac{1}{4}$ | ♪ | $\frac{3}{4}$ | ♪ ♩ ♩ | $\frac{5}{4}$ | ♪ ♩ ♩ ♩ ♩ | $\frac{3}{4}$ | ♪ ♩ ♩ | $\frac{1}{4}$ | ♪ |
　1　　　1 2 3　　　1 2 3 4 5　　　1 2 3　　　1

$\frac{2}{4}$ | ♪ ♩ | $\frac{4}{4}$ | ♪ ♩ ♩ ♩ | $\frac{6}{4}$ | ♪ ♩ ♩ ♩ ♩ ♩ | $\frac{4}{4}$ | ♪ ♩ ♩ ♩ | $\frac{2}{4}$ | ♪ ♩ |
　1 2　　　1 2 3 4　　　1 2 3 4 5 6　　　1 2 3 4　　　1 2

$\frac{1}{4}$ | ♪ ♪ | $\frac{3}{4}$ | ♪ ♩ ♩ ♪ ♩ ♩ | $\frac{5}{4}$ | ♪ ♩ ♩ ♩ ♩ ♪ ♩ ♩ ♩ ♩ | $\frac{3}{4}$ | ♪ ♩ ♩ ♪ ♩ ♩ | $\frac{1}{4}$ | ♪ ♪ |
　1　1　　　1 2 3　1 2 3　　　1 2 3 4 5　1 2 3 4 5　　　1 2 3　1 2 3　　　1　1

## MIXED METER

Mixed meter is one in which the metrical units may change from measure to measure. At any place within a composition the time signature may vary from that of the established one. Sometimes a different time signature extends through one measure, a number of measures, a complete phrase, or even a group of phrases. A single musical selection may include many varied meters such as 4/4, 7/4, 6/8, 1/4.

Examples of Mixed Meter

A. $\frac{4}{4}$ | ♩ ♩ ♩ ♩ | ♩ ♩ ♩ ♩ | $\frac{6}{8}$ | ♫♫ ♩ ♪ | $\frac{4}{4}$ | ♩ ♩ ♩ ♩ |
　　　1 2 3 4　1 2 3 4　　　1 2 3 4-5 6　　　1 2 3 4

B. $\frac{3}{4}$ | ♩ ♩ | $\frac{1}{4}$ | ♩ | $\frac{4}{4}$ | ♩ ♩ ♩ ♩ | ♩ ♩ ♫ | $\frac{1}{4}$ | ♫ | ♩ |
　　　1 2-3　　　1　　　1 2 3 4　1 2-3 4 &　　　1 &　1

C. $\frac{7}{4}$ | ♩ ♩ ♩ ♩ ♩ ♩ | $\frac{1}{4}$ | ♩ | $\frac{5}{4}$ | ♩ ♫ ♩ | $\frac{2}{4}$ | ♩ ♩ |
　　　1 2-3 4-5 6 7　　　1　　　1-2 3 & 4-5　　　1 2

## COUNTERPOINT

Counterpoint is the combining of two or more melodies and may be called plural melody. Thus, two or more groups may dance contrapuntally with each other moving at the same time to differing rhythmic patterns.

Examples of Counterpoint

A. Rhythmic Pattern I

Rhythmic Pattern II

B. Three Rhythmic Patterns

## POLYMETER

Polymeter, a type of counterpoint, results when two or more contrasting meters are used at the same time. Resultant rhythm in which cross accents are produced is a common form of polymeter used in dance. However, the accented beats do not coincide unless the rhythms are continued until the multiple of one with the other is reached. For example, a common accent of a two against a three will not coincide until six beats have elapsed. Note in example one that both first beats would coincide on count 7. The coincidence of beats is found by computing the mathematical least common denominator for 2 and 3 which is 6; for 3 and 4 which is 12; for 4 and 5 which is 20; or 2, 3, and 4 which is 12.

Examples of Resultant Rhythm

1. Charting 2 against 3

|                   |   |   |   |   |   |   |
|-------------------|---|---|---|---|---|---|
| Total beats:      | 1 | 2 | 3 | 4 | 5 | 6 |
| Total accents:    | > |   | > | > | > |   |
| Resultant rhythm: | 1 |   | 3 | 4 | 5 |   |

## 2. Charting 3 against 4

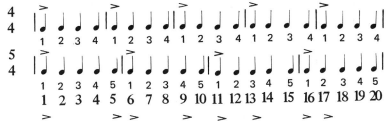

| Total beats:       | 1 2 3 4 5 6 7 8 9 10 11 12 |
|--------------------|----------------------------|
| Total accents:     | >     > >   >    > > |
| Resultant rhythm:  | 1      4 5    7    9 10 |

## 3. Charting 4 against 5

| Total beats:       | 1 2 3 4 5 6 7 8 9 10 11 12 13 14 15 16 17 18 19 20 |
|--------------------|----------------------------------------------------|
| Total accents:     | >      > >    >    >    >     > > |
| Resultant rhythm:  | 1      5 6    9    11    13    16 17 |

## 4. Charting 2 against 3 and 4

| Total beats:       | 1 2 3 4 5 6 7 8 9 10 11 12 |
|--------------------|----------------------------|
| Total accents:     | >    > > >   >    > > |
| Resultant rhythm:  | 1    3 4 5   7    9 10 11 |

## SEQUENTIAL FORM

Sequential form refers to the arrangement of one or more pharases, sometimes simple and other times complex in construction, making up the musical or dance composition. This sectional building of phrases, each of which is characterized by a cadence, gives balance, continuity or contrast to the whole.

Sequential types include one-part, two-part and three-part forms. One-part form represents a complete unit in and of itself and may be repeated. It may be described symbolically as A, and if repeated, as $A^1$. Illustrations of the one-part form may be found in such familiar songs as "Round and Round the Village" and "Atisket Atasket."

Two-part form consists of two independent but related phrase units. The second part becomes a contrast to the first. The phrases may be repeated without changing the original form and written as A $A^1$ B $B^1$. Examples of the two-part form may be found in such well-known songs as "Pop Goes the Weasel," "Oh Susannah," "Blue Tail Fly," and Brahms' "Lullaby."

Three-part form comprises three distinct phrase units. The second part gives contrast the the first. The third part is either an exact or a varied repetition of the first. This return to the original idea, recognized as a familiar theme, gives a sense of completion to the entire form. The three-part form, symbolized by the letters A B A, exemplifies balance, variety and unity. Here again, any one of the individual sections may be repeated without varying the fundamental form. Symbolically the repetitions may appear as A $A^1$ B A, A B $B^1$ A, A $A^1$ B $B^1$ A $A^1$ and others. Many folk songs are written in this form. Examples of the three-part form are found in such songs as "Captain Jinks," "Swanee River," and "Joshua Fit de Battle of Jericho."

## RONDO FORM

The rondo is characterized by the introduction of a principal statement or theme which recurs several times, with each repetition being interposed with a new but related theme. The number and length of contrasting parts may vary, their function being mainly to point up by contrast and to give balance to the principal statement. Symbolically the rondo is described as A B $A^1$ C $A^2$ D $A^3$ and so on. Examples include Bach's "Rondo in C Minor" from Third Partita, Beethoven's "Rondo Capriccio on a Lost Farthing," and Mozart's "Rondo from Pianoforte Sonata in B Flat."

## CANON FORM

The canon comprises two or more voice parts. It gives a contrapuntal effect as one voice leads off alone for one or two measures and is restated exactly by an imitating voice. After having started, the two parts occur simultaneously to the end of the composition. In terms of dance, a voice would correspond to a dancer or a group of dancers. The following example is charted in two different ways: the first is illustrated by letter symbols; the second, a rhythmic pattern, is shown by notation.

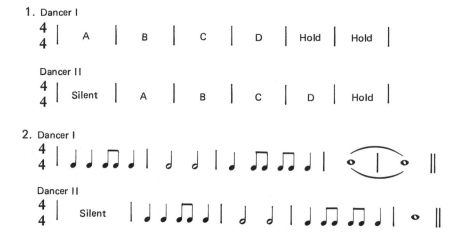

## ROUND FORM

The round is a type of imitation in which one voice leads off alone for an entire phrase, after which a second voice enters on the next phrase, and possibly a third on the following phrase. At the same time the first voice continues a new phrase while the second and third voices in respective order continue to repeat the exact melody. At no time do any of the voices resolve in a common ending but go on and on repeating the entire melody as often as desired.

Examples of a few simple rounds are "Three Blind Mice," "Row, Row, Row Your Boat," and "Little Tom Tinker."

## THEME AND VARIATIONS FORM

The theme, which constitutes the basis of the composition, is introduced first. It is a simple presentation of the statement, devoid of embellishments. The theme is reproduced in a number of variations while maintaining the essentials of the original phrase. Symbolically, it may be written A $A^1$ $A^2$ $A^3$ $A^4$ $A^5$ and so on. An example of a theme and variations is Cyril Scott's "Passacaglia."

In dance there are many ways in which a theme may be varied, namely, through the different aspects of space, through the many gradations of force, and through the diversified constituents of rhythm.

## FREE FORM

The free form is not restricted to a set structural technique; nor is there any standardized plan for arranging the order of the material. Any composition which may not be classified as one of the formal set forms may be considered as a relatively free form. The word relative is here used to imply that even a free form is not lacking in some organization which shows growth and development of content.

Although phrases making up the free form may be arranged in many different ways, the following examples show a few possibilities: A B C A D, A B C B A, A B C D A E A.

(See pages 161-168 for Variations Built from Rhythm.)

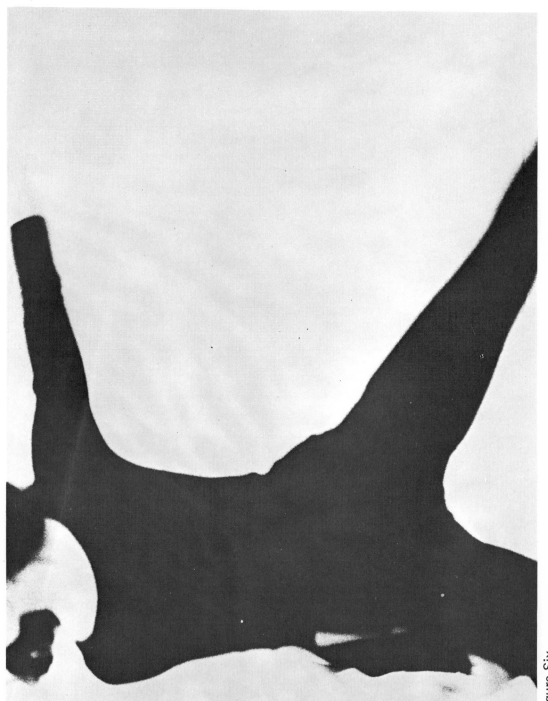

Figure Six

# Chapter 4

# CLASSIFICATION OF BASIC DANCE MOVEMENTS

In relation to a traveling or stationary floor pattern, movement may be classified in two main categories: first, locomotor movement which relates to those movements which leave a fixed position or base and cover space in any direction and plane; second, non-locomotor movement which refers to those movements performed on a pivot or in a moderately fixed position with respect to space. It is possible to combine any non-locomotor movement with that of a locomotor movement and thus project it further into space. The term non-locomotor is interchangeable with that of axial. These basic dance movements, both locomotor and non-locomotor, should serve as a starting point for the exploration of movement leading to creative expression.

## LOCOMOTOR MOVEMENTS

The fundamental locomotor movements represent the roots from which all other locomotor movement derives. The intermediate locomotor movements are outgrowths of the fundamental locomotor movements. Throughout life, from childhood onward, these locomotor movements are basic to our daily activities. In most instances they become so familiar and natural that they are performed without giving conscious attention to the process. In dance it is important that these basic steps be executed in accordance with the principles of good body alignment. Correct foot usage – push-offs and landings – should be applied in all movements of elevation. The dancer's control of the torso and the arms should be in evidence.

FUNDAMENTAL LOCOMOTOR MOVEMENTS

1. **Walk or Step**
    There is one transfer of weight, in place or in any direction, from the supporting to the non-supporting foot. While one foot is receiving the weight, the other foot is still in contact with the floor. In continuous walking steps the weight is taken on alternate feet.
    Although walking may be taken in any direction, the human body tends to move forward most frequently. Like running and leaping, walking is a process of falling and recovering. As a forward step is taken, the body momentum continues in a forward and slightly downward plane. The dancer utilizes unlimited variations of the basic walk. (See pages 62-64 for Variations of Walking.)

2. **Run**
    There is one transfer of weight, in place or in any direction, with a spring from the supporting to the non-supporting foot. As the spring is taken, there is a moment of suspension in which neither foot is in contact with the floor. In continuous running steps the weight is taken on alternate feet.
    Running is similar to walking except that the body is inclined further forward, the force of the push-off from the ball and toes of the foot is greater, the toes receive the

first weight on the start of the landing, and very little weight reaches the heels. The steps are extended and may be faster than in walking. The higher the elevation, the greater is the flexion of both the knee and the ankle. (See pages 64-65 for Variations of Running).

3. **Hop**

There is a spring, in place or in any direction, from the supporting foot followed by a landing on the same foot. There is no transfer of weight from one foot to the other involved in a hop. Continuous hops are taken on the same foot. The path of movement is directly upward. Probably the greatest difficulty in hopping is in sustaining the necessary balance. (See page 66 for Variations of Hopping.)

4. **Jump**

There is a spring, in place or in any direction, from one or both feet, followed by a landing on both feet. There is no transfer of weight in a jump. For example, should one be standing with his weight on the right foot, and then execute a jump landing on both feet, obviously his center of weight would have shifted from his right side to a balance between both feet. However, this is not considered a transfer of weight in the same sense as is that of the step. In other words, the transfer of weight must be absolute and complete with the foot or feet losing contact with the floor; or else there is merely a shifting of the weight over a stationary base.

In continuous jumps both feet leave the floor and return together. Only on the first jump may the spring be taken from one foot. Otherwise, a two-foot jump take-off ending with the weight on first one foot and then the other becomes a jump run.

The preparation for the jump begins in a plié with the knees turned out and pointed directly over the toes. This flexion of the knees and ankles is the preliminary motion for the push-off upward. At the greatest height the knees and ankles are fully extended with powerful force. On the landing the toes touch first, then the balls of the feet, and finally, the heels with extreme flexion of ankles, knees and hips to absorb the shock of the force. It is important to maintain the landing weight over the balls of the feet. (See pages 66-67 for Variations of Jumping.)

The rhythm of the four basic locomotor movements is usually thought of as being even and simply performed to 4/4 meter with all quarter notes. But actually these movements may be done to various meters, to even or uneven rhythmic patterns, or in any combination of meters and rhythmic patterns. The development of these movements into interesting rhythmic patterns will be shown in Chapter 5, Approaches to Dance Patterns.

## INTERMEDIATE LOCOMOTOR MOVEMENTS

1. **Leap**

The leap is an extension of a run. There is one transfer of weight, in place or in any direction, with a spring from the supporting to the non-supporting foot. Greater force is used in executing a leap and the result is a movement of higher and/or wider dimension than a run. Likewise, when both feet have lost contact with the floor, the moment of suspension is longer. Continuous leaps are taken on alternate feet.

Leaping for distance requires the greatest extension of both the reaching and the pushing leg. Due to the increase in knee and ankle flexion in preparation for the push-off, it is difficult to achieve a series of continuous leaps. Therefore, leaps are

Figure Seven

frequently combined with running steps. Especially is this true in leaping for height. (See pages 71-75 for Variations of Leaping.)

2. **Skip**

The skip is a combination of a hop and a step. Immediately following the hop there is one transfer of weight in place or in any direction from the supporting to the non-supporting foot. One of the characteristic qualities of the skip is the uneven rhythm. The hop begins the movement on the upbeat of the rhythmic pattern. Continuous skips are taken on alternate feet. The most common meter used is 6/8, and occasionally 2/4 or 4/4. (See pages 75-77 for Variations of Skipping.)

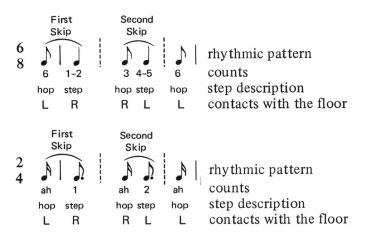

3. **Slide**

The slide is a combination of a step and a run. The step is followed by a quick drawing of the free foot up to and replacing the supporting foot as the supporting foot springs from the floor and cuts out toward the moving line of direction. The rhythmic pattern is identical with that of the skip. The rhythm, therefore, is uneven. However, the movement does not start on the upbeat, but rather on the first beat of the measure. There are two transfers of weight in a slide. Continuous slides lead off on the same foot. Meters used are 6/8, 2/4 or 4/4. (See pages 77-81 for Variations of Sliding.)

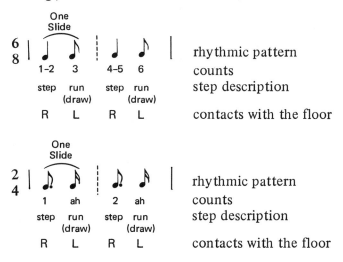

### 4. Gallop

The gallop is an exaggerated slide, and has identical notation, counts, and rhythm. It is composed of a step and a leap. Before taking the weight on the first step, the free foot is lifted in a bent knee position, giving a pawing effect to the movement. The free pawing foot steps forward. Following this the rear foot leaps in to replace the supporting foot that springs up into its original bent knee position. Meters used are 6/8, 2/4, or 4/4.

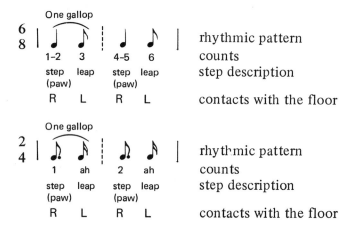

## COMBINED LOCOMOTOR MOVEMENTS

The combined locomotor movements are more highly developed forms of the fundamental and intermediate locomotor movements. They result from a combination of the various fundamentals.

### 1. Step-hop

The step-hop is perhaps the simplest of the combined fundamentals. A step is followed by a hop on the same foot. There is only one transfer of weight in a step-hop. Successive step-hops are taken on alternate feet. The rhythm is even, the meter 2/4 or 4/4.

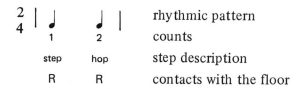

The quality of movement is buoyant and lifted. An almost perpetual bounce results from continuous step-hops. Since their rhythmic patterns and qualities of movement are the same, the step-hop and the schottische may be combined in many interesting ways. (See pages 81-84 for Variations of the Step-hop.)

### 2. Schottische

The schottische step is composed of three runs and a hop swinging the free foot forward in a low kick from the hip. There are three transfers of weight in a schottische. Successive schottische steps are taken on alternate feet. The rhythm is even, the meter 4/4.

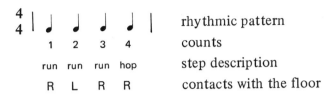

The quality of movement is gay, buoyant, and moving. (See pages 85-87 for Variations of the Schottische.)

3. **Waltz**

The waltz consists of three gliding steps. In the first two steps the feet are apart, while in the third step the feet come together in a closed position. There are three transfers of weight in a waltz. Successive waltz steps are taken on alternate feet. The rhythm is even, the meter 3/4.

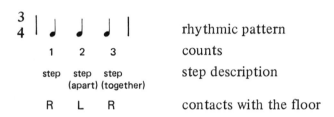

The quality of movement is smooth and flowing. (See pages 87-90 for Variations of the Waltz.)

4. **Two-step**

Despite its name, the two-step consists of three smooth steps. In the first and third steps the feet are apart, while in the second step the feet come together in a closed position. There are three transfers of weight in the two-step. Successive two-steps are taken on alternate feet. The rhythm is even, the meter 2/4 and occasionally 4/4.

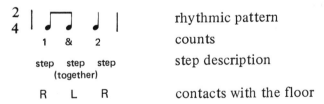

The quality of movement is lively and quick, but in the best two-step the quickly changing foot pattern occurs in so smooth a fashion that the body seems to glide across the floor. Beginners may tend to do a two-step to waltz time. After studying the foregoing step description and rhythmic pattern, the reason becomes evident. It is only a matter of being one count behind the 3/4 waltz rhythm that the waltz will become a two-step. The second step in the foot pattern is the all important one: in the waltz the feet are apart on count 2; if performing the two-step to waltz time the feet will come together on count 2. (See pages 90-92 for Variations of the Two-step.)

5. **Polka**

   The polka is a two-step preceded by a hop. The hop begins on the upbeat as did the hop in the skipping step. The hop is followed by three quick steps, the second of which brings the feet together. There are three transfers of weight in a polka. Successive polka steps are taken on alternate feet. The rhythm is uneven, the meter 2/4.

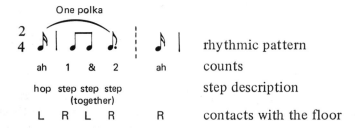

   The quality of movement is spirited and brisk.    (See pages 92-94 for Variations of the Polka.)

6. **Mazurka**

   The mazurka is a combination of a glide-step, leap, and hop. Following the glide-step, the non-supporting foot leaps in to replace the supporting foot, which swings forward from the hip, leg straight and low. As a hop is taken on the supporting foot, the free leg bends up in front. There are two transfers of weight in a mazurka. Successive mazurka steps are taken on the same foot. Although the rhythmic pattern is uneven, the actual mazurka step is done to the three underlying beats of the 3/4 meter with a marked accent on the second beat.

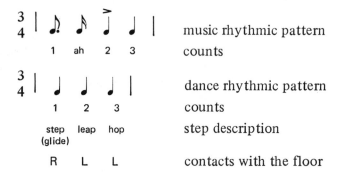

   The quality of movement is energetic, forceful, and lively. The following rhythmic pattern, frequently found in typical mazurka music, presents a rhythmic base on which the dancer may develop many variations.

(See pages 94-95 for Variations of the Mazurka.)

## NON-LOCOMOTOR MOVEMENTS

A variety of non-locomotor movements characterize the human body in daily activities. Bending, stretching, swinging, swaying, turning, twisting, striking, lifting, pushing, pulling, sitting, falling, and rising are examples of the many motions experienced. Since non-locomotor movements tend to be limited in the use of space, they become identified according to the manner in which energy is released. The variations of exerted energy determine the changing quality or effectiveness of any movement in this category. Specifically, energy release consists of an initial impulse or impetus, a possible or well-defined course of action, and a termination with a comparative degree of follow-through. It may proceed in continuous harmony of connecting impulses, or it may be arrested temporarily at any point preceding its termination.

The following classification establishes non-locomotor movement types and variations both in relation to the specific impetus applied and to the continuity or arrestment of force effected.

### Flexions, Extensions, and Rotations

When any part of the body bends to decrease the size of the angle between the respective parts, flexion results. When any part of the body straightens to increase the size of the angle between the respective parts, extension results. When any part of the body turns or twists on or around one or more axes and in one or more planes, rotation results.

Flexion, extension, and rotation are basic ways in which the body moves generally. Normally the body bends, stretches, turns, and twists as a part of any number of activities in everyday life. Dance movement involves controlled flexions, extensions, and rotations that are developed and distorted in many different ways depending upon the manner in which energy is released and expended. (See pages 100-109 for Variations.)

### Contractions and Releases

A tensing of muscle groups with the momentum arrested by the balancing of all forces involved may be called contraction. Release, which must follow contraction, is the relaxation of the tensed muscle groups. The contraction and the release may be abrupt, gradual, contrastingly sharp or smooth. Controlled power is a characteristic quality of both contractions and releases. Usually contractions and releases originate in the torso and may emanate to the extremities as a follow-through. (See pages 110-113 for Variations.)

### Falls and Recoveries

Falling is marked by a downward descent of the body from one plane to another. In dance, whether the descent is partial or complete, fast, gradual, or slow, it requires that controlled balance be maintained. (See Chapter 3, pages 31-32, Levels.) (See pages 113-122) for Lead-ups and examples of Falls and Recoveries.) (See pages 151-152 for Variations.)

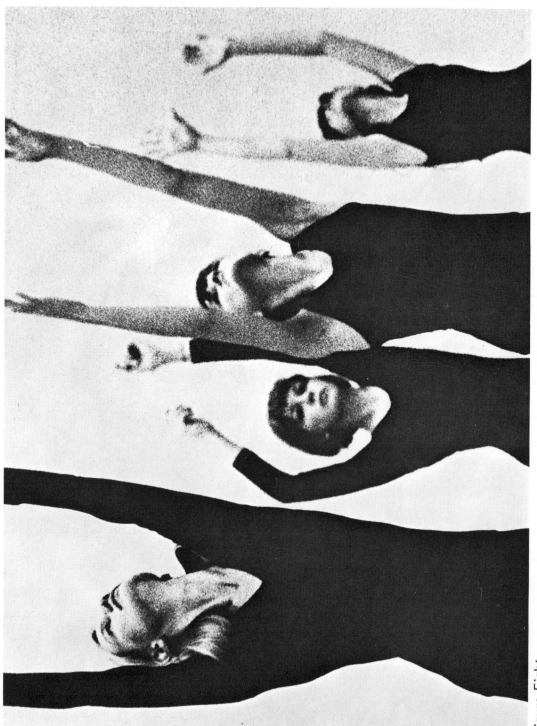

Figure Eight

# APPROACHES TO DANCE PATTERNS

A dance pattern may be a sequence, combination, or progression of basic movements developed significantly in space, force, and time. As listed, the patterns ranging from the simple to the more difficult offer only a sampling of the many variations possible.

Patterns represent the middle ground between basic movements and composition. When the basic movements are taught creatively and progressively leading to the development of simple dance patterns, the gap separating techniques from composition tends to become bridged. When the basic movements are not taught creatively, they resolve into an imitative effort to copy that which has been originated by someone else.

There are many ways of teaching basic movements creatively. Whatever the point of departure employed, there should be a sincere effort to challenge creative endeavor with tangible and concrete suggestions.

As basic movements are elaborated into specific movement units, the resulting variation becomes a dance pattern or study, the stepping stone to dance composition. A true dance pattern should stress logical and ordered progression with the choice of movements related in quality.

In order to show the development of basic movements into dance patterns, the following variations are deliberately organized to progress from the simple to the more complex.

## SYMBOLIC MARKINGS AND ABBREVIATIONS

L = left with respect to direction and to weight transference

R = right with respect to direction and to weight transference

X = times with respect to the number of times a movement is done

Wt. = weight

St. = start or starting

Fd. = forward

Bk. = backward or back

Sd. = sideward or side

Sds. = sides

Dn. = downward or down

ct. = count

cts. = counts

No. = number

meas. = measure

= facing front

= facing right

= facing left

= facing forward with back to the front

## SAMPLE VARIATIONS BUILT FROM FUNDAMENTAL LOCOMOTOR MOVEMENTS

WALK

1. **Walking Forward**

   Facing forward, with arms swinging freely in opposition to legs, move across the floor stressing the correct position and body line in a dance walk. The movement progresses smoothly with controlled power by pushing off from the supporting foot and catching the weight with the toes of the leading foot, letting the weight roll down to the heel. The rear leg trails slightly.

2. **Walking on a Square Facing in the Line of Direction**

   4/4 meter

| | cts. | meas. |
|---|---|---|
| With arms swinging in opposition, walk Fd. 4 X, St. L - - - - - - - - - - - - - - - - - - - - - - - - - - - - - - - - - - - - - | 1 2 3 4 | 1 |
| 1/4 turn L and walk Fd. 4 X, St. L- - - - - - - - - - - - - - - - - | 1 2 3 4 | 1 |
| 1/4 turn L and walk Fd. 4 X, St. L- - - - - - - - - - - - - - - - | 1 2 3 4 | 1 |
| 1/4 turn L and walk Fd. 4 X, St. L- - - - - - - - - - - - - - - - | 1 2 3 4 | 1 |
| | total - - | 4 |

Floor Pattern:

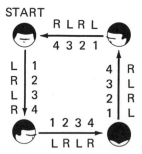

3. **Walking on a Square Facing Forward**

   4/4 meter

| | cts. | meas. |
|---|---|---|
| A. With arms extended low Sd. palms Fd., Walk Fd. 4 X, St. L - - - - - - - - - - - - - - - - - - - - - - - | 1 2 3 4 | 1 |

|  | cts. | meas. |
|---|---|---|
| Keeping knees and feet turned outward, walk Sd. L 4 X: step L to Sd. ct. 1, step R across in front of L ct. 2, and repeat cts. 3, 4 ------------------------------------------ | 1 2 3 4 | 1 |
| Swinging the leg Bk. from the hip, walk Bk. 4 X, St. L ------------------------------ | 1 2 3 4 | 1 |
| Walk Sd. R 4 X: step L across in front of R ct. 1, step R to Sd. ct. 2, and repeat cts. 3, 4 ------ | 1 2 3 4 | 1 |
|  | total -- | 4 |

Floor Pattern:

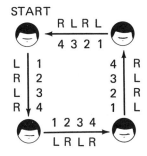

B. Try the above pattern beginning on the right foot changing the sideward direction to the right.
C. Combine "A" and "B" as follows:
   At the completion of "A", take a quick step left on the final "ah" count, freeing the right foot to repeat "B".

4. **Walking to Various Meters**
   A. With arms swinging freely, walk forward while stamping to the primary accents of each of the following meters: 5/4, 4/4, 3/4, 2/4.
   B. Combine two measures of each of the above meters to form a rhythmic sequence of 5, 5, 4, 4, 3, 3, 2, 2.

5. **Walking Distortedly**
   A. Walk with stiff knees.
   B. Walk with an exaggerated bend of the knees.
   C. Combine "A" and "B" using four of each; two of each.
   D. Walk on heels, on tip-toes, with a toe-heel rolling step. Combine four walks on heels with four walks on tip-toes; try two of each. Combine four toe-heel rolling steps with four heel-toe rolling steps; try two of each.

6. **Creative Clues**
   To assist individuals in creating original variations, have the entire class begin walking in a circle to a chosen meter. While they continue to move to the underlying beat, give each of the following suggestions in sequence allowing each one to be tried a number of times before proceeding to the next:
   A. Stamp and clap hands on the primary accent.

B. Stamp and clap hands on the primary accent of each measure and continue walking to the underlying beat.

C. Stamp and move an arm forcibly on the primary accent of each measure.

D. Stamp to the side and experiment with a different arm movement on the primary accent of each measure.

E. Let the free leg show the primary accent by a kick, with a straight knee, in any direction.

F. Try "E" with a bent knee kick.

G. Turn the head sharply in any direction on the primary accent.

H. Combine any leg or arm movement on the primary accent.

I. Combine any leg, arm, and head movement on the primary accent.

J. Each half of the class watch the individual creations of the other half and select several movements that appeal to them particularly. Let everyone in the class experience these.

## RUN

1. Using all the walk variations described, substitute the run in place of the walk.

2. **Running Forward and Backward with Changing Direction**

   4/4 meter

   |  | cts. | meas. |
   |---|---|---|
   | Run Fd. 8 X, St. L - - - - - - - - - - - - - - - - - - - - - - - - - - - - - | 1 - 8 | 2 |
   | Run Bk. 8 X, St. L - - - - - - - - - - - - - - - - - - - - - - - - - - - | 1 - 8 | 2 |
   | 1/2 turn L and run Fd. 8 X, St. L - - - - - - - - - - - - - - - - - | 1 - 8 | 2 |
   | 1/2 turn L and run Bk. 8 X, St. L - - - - - - - - - - - - - - - - - | 1 - 8 | 2 |
   |  | total - - | 8 |

3. **Running with Partner**

   A. Standing side by side hands joined, weight on the right foot, the partner on the left runs in place two times left and right, and then runs forward two times left and right while the partner on the right runs forward two times left and right and then runs in place two times left and right. Continue alternately across the floor. Repeat with both partners reversing the movement.

   B. Start with the partner on the left two steps ahead of the partner on the right. Left partner runs in place four times, then runs forward four times while right partner runs forward four times and then in place four times. Continue alternately across the floor, with each leading person giving a tug to the trailing partner.

4. **Running to Syncopated Beat**

   Rhythmic Pattern:

   Clap, step, and then run to the above syncopated rhythmic pattern, holding the encircled counts.

|  | cts. | meas. |
|---|---|---|
| With arms extended Dn. slightly away from sides of body, run Fd. R - - - - - - - - - - - - - - - - - - - - - - | 1 | |
| Run Fd. L. bending body to L Sd. while bending L arm diagonally upward with palm of hand toward face - - - - - - - - - - - - - - - - - - - - - - - - - - | 2 | |
| Hold - - - - - - - - - - - - - - - - - - - - - - - - - - - - - - - - - - - - | ③ | |
| Maintaining body and arm position, run Fd. quickly 2 X, R L - - - - - - - - - - - - - - - - - - - - - - - - - | & 4 | 1 |
| Repeat all 2 more X - - - - - - - - - - - - - - - - - - - - - - - - | 1 2 ③ 4 | 1 |
| | 1 2 ③ 4 | 1 |
| St. R, run 4 X completing a turn R in place with R arm sweeping wide around leading the body with L arm following in a slightly lower plane - - - - - - - - - - - - - - - - - - - - - - - - - - - - - - - - | 1 & 2 & | |
| Run Fd. R reversing arm positions used in ct. 2 of meas. 1, 2, and 3 - - - - - - - - - - - - - - - - - - - - - - - - | 3 | |
| Extend arms Dn. to original position as in ct. 1, meas. 1 - - - - - - - - - - - - - - - - - - - - - - - - - - - - - - - - | ④ | 1 |
| | total - - | 4 |

Repeat all on the opposite side.

5. **Running Distortedly**
   A. Lock hands and extend arms straight above head, framing the face between the arms. Starting left, run in place eight times with exaggerated knee bend kicking free leg back.
   B. Arms extended sideward waist level, palms forward, start left, run in place eight times kicking free leg forward without bending the knee.
   C. Repeat "A" traveling across the floor with wide runs and with the body inclined forward.
   D. Repeat "B" traveling across the floor with high straight leg kick and body inclined backward.
   E. Combine "C" and "D": eight of each; four of each; two of each.

6. **Creative Clues**
   A. Utilizing the syncopated rhythmic pattern for running (No. 4 above) have small groups work out a different ending for the fourth measure.
   B. Have the class run for one measure of 3/4 meter. On the next measure each person develops his own turn, partial or complete, in any direction. Continue alternating the above run and turn.
   C. Have the group run across the floor as though they were late for class, or rushing to catch a bus. Choose one or two that best express hurriedness; have these demonstrated.
   D. Runs expressing different personalities.
      Try running like a sophisticated lady who is endeavoring to recapture her hat that has just blown down the street. What about the typical show-off? The shy girl?

HOP

1. **Hopping in Place and Traveling**
   A. Hop in place eight times left, travel forward eight times left. Try on the right foot.
   B. Step left and hop seven times, then step right and hop seven times, first in place and then forward. As the step is taken left, slap the left thigh with an upward movement of the left hand. As the hops are taken, allow the hand to slowly move in a circle away from the body and back to the side.
   C. Try decreasing one hop each time until a step-hop results. Continue to repeat the leg slap on every step.
   D. Try hopping to the side instead of forward using a combination of "B" and "C."

2. **Hopping Combined with Stepping and Turning**
   A. Step forward left, hop forward left three times. Repeat right.
   B. Stamp forward left, make a complete turn left with three hops left. Step forward right, hop forward right three times. Try all beginning right with a right turn.
   C. Step forward right, hop forward right three times. Step forward left, hop forward left three times. Stamp forward right, make a complete turn right with three hops right. Stamp forward left, make a complete turn left with three hops left. Repeat all.

3. **Creative Clues**
   A. Experiment with movements of the free leg while hopping.
   B. Partners face each other. No. 1 experiment with hops at a high level. No. 2 experiment with hops at a low level. This may assume a humorous or grotesque quality.
   C. Partners experiment with hops of varying force.

JUMP

1. **Jumping Twice as Fast**
   Jump four times. Double the time and jump twice as fast. Repeat all moving forward.

2. **Jumping with Aerial Splits**
   Jump in place four times. On the last jump, whip the legs sideward into an aerial split-jump.

3. **Jumping Combined with a Lunge**
   A. Jump in place two times. Lunge forward on the left foot with arms moving in opposition, body held straight, left knee bent, right leg slightly bent in back. Repeat jumps and lunge right. Progress forward on jumps.
   B. Add a decided forward body lean on the forward lunge. Change the arm position so that on the left lunge the left arm extends forward in a sharp line. Extend the right leg so that the body line accents the directional line.
   C. Continue to let the jumps carry the body forward, but let the lunge fall directly to the left side. The left arm extends left as the line of the body bends laterally. The right leg straightens to the right. Repeat all with lunge falling to the right.
   D. Lunge backward left, extending the right leg forward, body leaning backward with both arms pushing low beside lifted right leg. The jumps continue to be used alternately with the lunge so that the contrast between the straight body line of the jump and the backward lean of the body in the lunge is exceedingly marked.

E. Combine "B", "C", and "D" alternating two of each: jump two times, lunge forward left; jump two times, lunge forward right; jump two times, lunge sideward left; jump two times, lunge sideward right; jump two times, lunge backward left; jump two times, lunge backward right.

4. **Creative Clues**
   A. Jump two times and run two times. After learning this pattern, vary the jumps directionally. This can be done with a body lean, a turn in place, or moving with a resulting floor pattern.
   B. Jump three times and run two times to 5/4 meter. Vary the jumps dimensionally. This can be done by gradually letting the legs spread farther apart, or by covering more or less space while moving across the floor.
   C. While the body is in the air, experiment with various leg positions. Choose several and all try.

## COMBINED STUDIES USING THE FOUR FUNDAMENTAL LOCOMOTOR MOVEMENTS

The quality of the first three movement patterns should be vigorous, gay, and lifted.

1. **Rhythmic pattern:**

$\frac{4}{4}$ | ♩ ♩ ♩ 𝄽 | ♩ ♩ ♩ 𝄽 | ♩ ♩ ♩ ♩ | ♩ ♩ ♩ 𝄽 |
   1  2  3 ④    1  2  3 ④    1  2  3  4    1  2  3 ④

|  | cts. | meas. |
|---|---|---|
| Jump 1/2 turn L to face opposite direction - - - - - - - - - - | 1 | |
| Jump in place - - - - - - - - - - - - - - - - - - - - - - - - - - - - - | 2 | |
| Lunge Fd. L with body bent Fd. and L arm extended straight Fd., R. leg is low and straight Bk. giving a strong directional Fd. line to the body - - - - - - - - - - - - - - - - - - - - - - - - - - - - - - | 3 | |
| Hold - - - - - - - - - - - - - - - - - - - - - - - - - - - - - - - - - | ④ | 1 |
| Repeat all - - - - - - - - - - - - - - - - - - - - - - - - - - - - - | 1  2  3 ④ | 1 |
| Step R, hop R - - - - - - - - - - - - - - - - - - - - - - - - - - - | 1  2 | |
| Step L, hop L - - - - - - - - - - - - - - - - - - - - - - - - - - - - | 3  4 | 1 |
| Run 2, R L - - - - - - - - - - - - - - - - - - - - - - - - - - - - - | 1  2 | |
| Lunge Fd. R with R arm extended Fd. and L leg straight and low in Bk. - - - - - - - - - - - - - - - | 3 | |
| Hold - - - - - - - - - - - - - - - - - - - - - - - - - - - - - - - - - | ④ | 1 |
| | total - - | 4 |

Try turning right on jump-turn and lunging on the right foot with step-hops and runs beginning left.

2. **Rhythmic Pattern:**

|  | cts. | meas. |
|---|---|---|
| St. facing Fd. heels together, arms at sides. Jump 3 X gradually widening the dimension -------- | 1  2  3 |  |
| Throw body Wt. to L extending L arm straight up by side of head, palm flat and turned inward with R leg extended Sd. R in straight line, R arm close to R side, hop L --------------------- | 4 |  |
| Maintaining the same body position, hop L --------- | 5 |  |
| Hold (returning to vertical position) -------------- | ⑥ | 1 |
| Step Sd. R -------------------------------- | 1 |  |
| Step L across in front of R -------------------- | 2 |  |
| Lean Sd. L extending L arm by head and straightening R leg to R, hop L 2 X --------------- | 3  4 |  |
| Drop R shoulder and stamp R ------------------- | 5 |  |
| Hold ------------------------------------- | ⑥ | 1 |
| Run Fd. 3 X, L R L, with exaggerated knee bend kicking free leg Bk., arms low, hands clasped in Bk. --------------------------- | 1  2  3 |  |
| Run Fd. 3 X, R L R, kicking free leg Fd. without knee bend, arms extended Sd. waist level, palms Fd. --------------------------- | 4  5  6 | 1 |
| Drop L shoulder sharply and stamp L ------------- | 1 |  |
| Hold ------------------------------------- | ② |  |
| Stamp 3 X, R L R, dropping shoulders alternately --------------------------------- | 3  4  5 |  |
| Hold ------------------------------------- | ⑥ | 1 |
|  | total -- | 4 |

3. **Combining Fundamental Locomotor Movements Stressing Directional Changes**
   4/4 meter

|  | cts. | meas. |
|---|---|---|
| Heels together, toes turned out, jump 2 X ----------- | 1  2 |  |
| Run Fd. 2 X, L R -------------------------- | 3  4 | 1 |
| Turn slightly to L and run diagonally Fd. 3 X, L R L ------------------------------------ | 1  2  3 |  |

|  | cts. | meas. |
|---|---|---|
| 1/4 turn R and step Bk. R - - - - - - - - - - - - - - - - - - - - - - | 4 | 1 |
| 1/4 turn L and step Sd. L - - - - - - - - - - - - - - - - - - - - | 1 | |
| Step R across in front of L - - - - - - - - - - - - - - - - - - - - | 2 | |
| Leap low and wide Sd. L - - - - - - - - - - - - - - - - - - - - | 3 | |
| 1/4 turn R, supporting Wt. on L toe, lifting R leg, knee bent Fd. close to body - - - - - - - - - - - - - - - - - - | 4 | 1 |
| Run Fd. 3 X, R L R - - - - - - - - - - - - - - - - - - - - - - - - | 1  2  3 | |
| 1/2 turn L and step Bk. crossing L in Bk. of R - - - - - - | 4 | 1 |
| 1/4 turn R and step Sd. R - - - - - - - - - - - - - - - - - - - - | 1 | |
| Step L across in front of R - - - - - - - - - - - - - - - - - - - - | 2 | |
| Leap low and wide Sd. R - - - - - - - - - - - - - - - - - - - - | 3 | |
| 1/4 turn L, suspend Wt. on R toe, lifting L leg, knee bent Fd. close to body - - - - - - - - - - - - - - - - - - - | 4 | 1 |
| Run Fd. 2 X, L R - - - - - - - - - - - - - - - - - - - - - - - - - | 1  2 | |
| Leap low and wide Fd. L - - - - - - - - - - - - - - - - - - - - | 3 | |
| 1/2 turn R, suspend Wt. on L toe, lifting R leg, knee bent Fd. - - - - - - - - - - - - - - - - - - - - - - - - - - - - - | 4 | 1 |
| Run Fd. 2 X, R L - - - - - - - - - - - - - - - - - - - - - - - - - | 1  2 | |
| Leap low and wide Fd. R - - - - - - - - - - - - - - - - - - - - | 3 | |
| 1/2 turn L, suspend Wt. on R toe, lifting L leg, knee bent Fd. - - - - - - - - - - - - - - - - - - - - - - - - - - - - - | 4 | 1 |
| Leap low and wide Fd. L - - - - - - - - - - - - - - - - - - - - | 1 | |
| 1/2 turn R, suspending body as before - - - - - - - - - - - - | 2 | |
| Leap low and wide Fd. R - - - - - - - - - - - - - - - - - - - - | 3 | |
| 1/2 turn L, suspending body as before - - - - - - - - - - - - | 4 | 1 |
| 1/4 turn R to face Fd., stepping L into stride - - - - - - - - | 1 | |
| Hold - - - - - - - - - - - - - - - - - - - - - - - - - - - - - - - - - - | 2 | |
| Bend both knees as place R foot in Bk. and to the L of L foot, arms low to Sd. focus Dn. - - - - - - - - - - | 3 | |
| 1/2 turn R, pivoting on balls of feet, ending in high relevé, heels together, toes and knees turned out - - - - - - - - - - - - - - - - - - - - - - - - - - - - - - | 4 | 1 |
| | total - - | 9 |
| Repeat all facing opposite direction - - - - - - - - - - - - - - - - - - - - - - - - - - - - - - - - - | | 9 |
| | total - - | 18 |

Divide the group, having one group face the other, and do the pattern through four times. Have both groups face forward. One group begin the runs with the left foot as given; the other start the runs with the right foot so that both groups are moving in directional opposition to one another.

The quality of the following pattern should be one of sorrow and loneliness. Still using fundamental locomotor movements, the feeling becomes more serious by the use of circular directional lines, slower tempo, and by keeping the movements close to the floor.

| 4/4 meter, slow | cts. | meas. |
|---|---|---|
| St. arms at Sd., small stride. Making 1/2 large semi-circular turn R with wide low strides, step 4 X, R L R L | 1 2 3 4 | 1 |
| Jump Bk. 2 X | 1 2 | |
| Low runs Fd. 4 X, L R L R | 3 & 4 & | 1 |
| Step Fd. L | 1 | |
| 1/2 turn L as hop 2 X | 2 3 | |
| Twisting body toward R, step R | 4 | 1 |
| Repeat last meas. | 1 2 3 4 | 1 |
| Standing in small stride, hands locked low in Bk. of body, sway L | 1 2 | |
| Sway R | 3 4 | 1 |
| Arms at Sd., 1/4 turn L, step L | 1 | |
| Hop L | 2 | |
| Rock Bk. stepping R | 3 | |
| Step L | 4 | 1 |
| Hop L 2 X | 1 2 | |
| 1/4 turn R, step R | 3 | |
| 1/4 turn L, step L | 4 | 1 |
| Hop L | 1 | |
| 1/4 turn R, step R | 2 | |
| Balance Wt., lock hands low in Bk. | 3 | |
| Throw focus high | 4 | 1 |
| | total -- | 8 |
| Repeat all beginning L | | 8 |
| | total -- | 16 |

Experiment with a number of groups facing in different directions and starting to move at one measure intervals.

## SAMPLE VARIATIONS BUILT FROM INTERMEDIATE LOCOMOTOR MOVEMENTS

LEAP

1. **Leaping Forward and Turning**
   A. Leap Fd. 4 X, R L R L. Make 1/2 turn R and repeat in opposite direction.
   B. Travel on a straight line. Leap forward right making one-half turn right. Leap backward left to complete the turn. Continue across the floor, keeping each stride leap wide in dimension.

2. **Leaping with Varied Force**

   | 3/4 meter | cts. | meas. |
   |---|---|---|
   | Leap Fd. 3 X, L R L  -------------------------- | 1  2  3 | 1 |
   | Leap-lunge R with supporting knee bent, trailing leg bent Bk., body inclined Fd. and R hand thrusting Dn. as though striking something - - - - - - - - - - | 1 | |
   | Hold - - - - - - - - - - - - - - - - - - - - - - - - - - - - - - - - - - - - - - | 2 | |
   | Short Leap L in place - - - - - - - - - - - - - - - - - - - - - - - - - | 3 | 1 |
   | | total - - | 2 |

   Repeat all St. R.

3. **Leaping Combined with Running**
   A. As a lead-up to a leap-run, do a cut-step in place. Cut-step: a short reaching step backward and forward. The right foot cuts backward to replace the left foot as it cuts out backward; then the left foot cuts forward to replace the right foot as it cuts forward. The knees flex appreciably to create a rocking motion.

   | 4/4 meter | cts. | meas. |
   |---|---|---|
   | St. Wt. L. Cut-step 4 X, R L, R L, R L, R L ------ | 1 & 2 & 3 & 4 & | 1 |
   | Progress Fd. with 4 wide range leap-steps, R L, R L, R L, R L - - - - - - - - - - - - - - - - - - - - - - - - - - - | 1 & 2 & 3 & 4 & | 1 |
   | | total - - | 2 |

   B. 4/4 meter

   | | cts. | meas. |
   |---|---|---|
   | Repeat "A" with 4 cut-steps in place - - - - - - - - - - - - | 1 & 2 & 3 & 4 & | 1 |
   | Progress Fd. with 4 wide range leaps, R L R L - - - - - - - - - - - - - - - - - - - - - - - - - - - - - - - - - - - - - - - - - - - | 1 2 3 4 | 1 |
   | | total - - | 2 |

   C. Vary the number of running steps combined with the leap.

   2/4 meter:  Leap run

   3/4 meter:  Leap run run; or, run run leap; or, run leap run

4/4 meter:  Leap run run run; or, run run run leap

6/8 meter:  Leap run run run run run; or, run run run run run leap

Many interesting and intricate combinations may be devised from leaps and runs.
One example follows:

| 6/8 meter | cts. | meas. |
|---|---|---|
| Leap R ------------------------------------------------- | 1 | |
| Hold ------------------------------------------------- | 2 | |
| Run L, R, L ------------------------------------------------- | 3  4  5 | |
| Leap R ------------------------------------------------- | 6 | 1 |
| Repeat beginning L ------------------------------------------------- | | 1 |
| | total -- | 2 |

## 4. Leaping with Changing Accents

Rhythmic Pattern:

| | cts. | meas. |
|---|---|---|
| A.  Leap high L ------------------------------ | 1 | |
| Leap low and wide R L R -------------------- | 2  3  4 | 1 |
| Leap low and wide L---------------------- | 1 | |
| Leap high R ---------------------------- | 2 | |
| Leap low and wide L R --------------------- | 3  4 | 1 |
| Leap low and wide L R ----------------------- | 1  2 | |
| Leap high L ---------------------------- | 3 | |
| Leap low and wide R ---------------------- | 4 | 1 |
| Leap low and wide L R L --------------------- | 1  2  3 | |
| Leap high R ------------------------------ | 4 | 1 |
| | total -- | 4 |

B.  Using the above rhythmic pattern, divide the class into four groups, side by side,
and numbered 1, 2, 3, 4 consecutively. All groups move at the same time. Group 1
travels to the movement pattern of the first measure accenting count one with a
high leap; group 2 the second measure accenting count two; group 3 the third
measure accenting count three; and group 4 the fourth measure accenting count
four. Re-number all groups permitting each one to experience the movement
sequence in each of the four measures. Then have the entire class try the complete
pattern of the four measures in sequence.

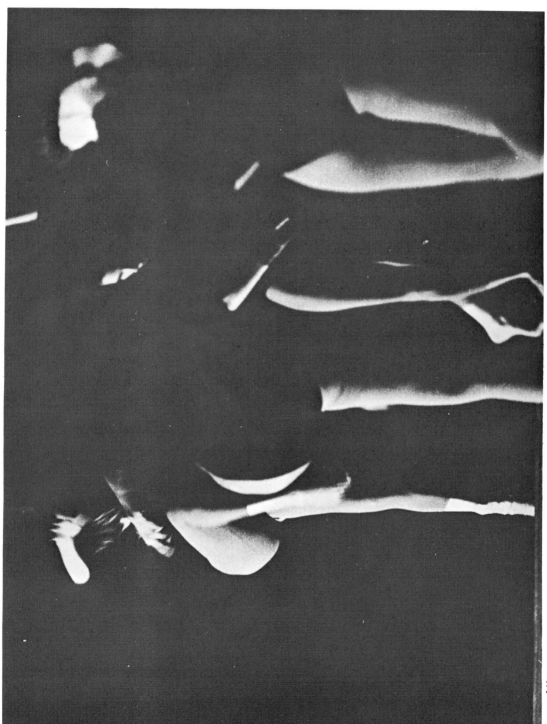

Figure Nine

5. **Leaping with Directional Change**

A. 8/4 meter

|  | cts. | meas. |
|---|---|---|
| Leap Sd. R ------------------------------- | 1 | |
| Step L Bk. of R ------------------------------- | 2 | |
| Repeat 3 X ------------------------------- | 3 4 5 6 7 8 | |
| Quick catch-step R ------------------------ | ah | 1 |
| Repeat all St. L, traveling L ------------------------------- | | 1 |
| | total -- | 2 |

B. Leap-lunge turning right in place.

Fling right arm back to right as body whips around to complete one turn with leap-lunge right and step left. The movement is literally one of throwing the body in the direction of the turn. Repeat three times in the same direction. Take a quick catch-step right and repeat starting left and turning left.

6. **Leaping Combined with Step-hop and Run**

2/4 meter

|  | cts. | meas. |
|---|---|---|
| Arms swing in opposition.  Leap R ---------------- | 1 | |
| Hop R swinging L leg Fd. ---------------------- | ah | |
| Run Fd. L, R ------------------------------- | 2 & | 1 |
| Repeat St. L ------------------------------- | 1 ah 2 & | 1 |
| | total -- | 2 |

7. **Leaping Distortedly**
A. While leaping, bend the leading leg inward to kick front thigh of trailing leg.
B. While leaping, flex the ankle of the leading leg and swing the arms in opposition pushing the heel of the hand strongly forward.
C. Try "B" swinging the same arm and leg forward.

8. **Creative Clues**
A. Run rapidly toward a chosen focal point; terminate the momentum with an individually styled leap.
B. Try self-styled leaps while focusing toward the directional line, away from the directional line; alternate the above. First, while focusing alternately toward and away from the directional line try a slow change of focus; and second, use a rapid change of focus.

SKIP

1. **Skipping Forward and Turning**
Start with weight on right foot. Skip four times making one complete turn left in place, whipping left arm around to the left. Try the above making two complete turns left in place to four skips.

2. **Skipping in Place and Through Space**
Skip in place four times starting left. Skip forward four times starting left to cover

considerable space. Repeat skipping in place four times starting left. Skip backward four times starting left by stepping directly behind the other foot, knees turned outward. Repeat the above sequence emphasizing the force to give greater height and dimension.

3. **Skipping Sideward**
   A. Skip sideward cross-stepping the free foot in front of the other foot.
   B. Repeat "A" cross-stepping the free foot in back of the other foot.
   C. Travel sideward right: start with weight on left foot. Continue by cross-stepping in front of the supporting foot. Double the time on the next two skips. Repeat all skipping sideward left.

4. **Skipping Directionally to Mixed Meter**

   Rhythmic pattern:

   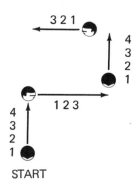

   Floor pattern:

   |  | cts. | meas. |
   |---|---|---|
   | St. Wt. L, skip Fd. 4X - - - - - - - - - - - - - - - - - - - - - | ah 1 ah 2 ah 3 ah 4 | 1 |
   | Sharp 1/4 turn R and skip Fd. 3 X St. R - - - - - - - - | ah 1 ah 2 ah 3 | 1 |
   | Sharp 1/4 turn L and skip Fd. 4 X St. L - - - - - - - - | ah 1 ah 2 ah 3 ah 4 | 1 |
   | Sharp 1/4 turn L and skip Fd. 3 X St. L - - - - - - - - | ah 1 ah 2 ah 3 | 1 |
   |  | total - - | 4 |

   Sharp 1/4 turn R and repeat all.
   Continue across the floor.

5. **Skipping Distortedly**
   Start with weight on left foot, arms bent out to sides with forearms hanging downward, backs of hands forward.
   A. Hop left to greatest height swinging right leg and both arms high sideward right with body leaning sideward left. Stamp right across in front of left. Repeat right on opposite side and continue alternating left and right while traveling forward. This gives the body a grotesque side to side rocking effect.

B. Try traveling backward reversing the body plane and whipping the arms alternately forward and backward with the forward arm in opposition to the extended rear leg.

C. Combine "A" and "B."

6. **Creative Clues**

A. Form a number of small groups each with a leader. With respective groups following the movement, each leader invents an individually styled series of skips for a phrase of eight beats; then devises a different skip for each succeeding eight beats. Every leader chooses a new leader and the same procedure continues. The interest may be heightened by having the leaders change the direction, level, or focus at the beginning of each phrase of eight beats.

B. Partners facing each other, stand about ten to twelve long paces apart. Move toward each other gradually increasing the dimension of four skipping steps. On the fourth skip, the widest in range, partners clap right hands two times in passing. Repeat with partners experimenting with various ways and styles of passing each other; such as, a sudden stop with a marked change of focus, a movement showing a feeling of greeting or boredom, or a sudden turn away from each other as though showing disinterest or a desire to avoid the other person.

## SLIDE

1. **Sliding Forward and Backward**

Slide forward eight times starting right. Slide backward eight times starting right. Repeat sliding forward four times and backward four times starting right. Repeat sliding forward two times and backward two times starting right.

2. **Sliding with a Partner**

A. Partners face each other with both hands joined across.

| 2/4 meter | cts. | meas. |
|---|---|---|
| Slide to one side 4 X  - - - - - - - - - - - - - - - - - - - - | 1 ah 2 ah 1 ah 2 ah | 2 |
| Continue in the same direction with 4 steps while completing 2 turns under raised arms ("wring the dish rag")  - - - - - - - - - - - - - - - - - - | 1 2 1 2 | |
| Shift Wt. quickly to free foot - - - - - - - - - - - - - - | ah | 2 |
| | total - - | 4 |

Repeat all in opposite direction.

B. Partners in exaggerated knee-bend position with hands across on each other's shoulders. Slide seven times gradually increasing the level to the highest reach off the floor. Jump on count eight. Repeat in the opposite direction gradually reducing the level to that of the original.

3. **Sliding Sideward with Half Turns**

Group start in a circle facing the center. 2/4 meter.

A. Slide to the right in the circle. Change weight and slide left in the circle.

B.  2/4 meter                                                            <u>cts.</u>        <u>meas.</u>

With arms extended Sd. waist level, slide Sd.
counter-clockwise with 7 slides, St. R - - - - - - - -        1 ah 2 ah
                                                              1 ah 2 ah
                                                              1 ah 2 ah
                                                              1 ah

Step R  - - - - - - - - - - - - - - - - - - - - - - - - - - - -   2

Make 1/2 turn R to face outward in the
circle by hopping on R foot and whipping
the arms high above head - - - - - - - - - - - - - - - - -    ah                    4

Repeat the movement traveling counter-
clockwise to the L and ending with a
step-hop L, 1/2 turn L to face inward  - - - - - - - - - - - - - - - - - - - - - - - - -                  4

Repeat sliding 3 X R  - - - - - - - - - - - - - - - - - - - -   1 ah 2 ah
                                                              1 ah

Step R, hop R with 1/2 turn R - - - - - - - - - - - - -        2 ah                  2

Slide 3 X L - - - - - - - - - - - - - - - - - - - - - - - - - - -   1 ah 2 ah
                                                              1 ah

Step L, hop L with 1/2 turn L - - - - - - - - - - - - -        2 ah                  2

Slide 1 X R - - - - - - - - - - - - - - - - - - - - - - - - - - -   1 ah

Step R, hop R  - - - - - - - - - - - - - - - - - - - - - - - -   2 ah                  1

Slide 1 X L - - - - - - - - - - - - - - - - - - - - - - - - - - -   1 ah

Step L, hop L - - - - - - - - - - - - - - - - - - - - - - - - -   2 ah                  1
                                                                         total --   14

4.  **Sliding to Changing Phrases and Direction**
    Divide class into two groups, one on each side of the room in scattered formation
    facing opposite group. After the initial pause for Group I, both groups move
    simultaneously for the remainder of the sequence. Note that it requires ten total
    measures to complete the pattern. While Group I is finishing the last two measures of
    the sequence, Group II will be silent.

    Arm movements for slides:

    Sideward – extended sideward waist level.
    Forward  – right slide, right hand leads forward with a strong pushing movement. Left
                slide in reverse.
    Backward – both hands push straight forward.

    Group I

    4/4 meter

    St. Wt. R. facing front, arms extended Sd. waist
    level

| | cts. | meas. |
|---|---|---|
| Silent - - - - - - - - - - - - - - - - - - - - - - - - - - - - - - - - - - - - - - - - - - - - - - - - - - | | 2 |
| Slide Sd. L 7 X St. L - - - - - - - - - - - - - - - - - - - - | 1 ah 2 ah 3 ah 4 ah<br>1 ah 2 ah 3 ah | |
| Step L, hop L - - - - - - - - - - - - - - - - - - - - - - - - - | 4 ah | 2 |
| Slide Sd. R 7 X St. R - - - - - - - - - - - - - - - - - - - | 1 ah 2 ah 3 ah 4 ah<br>1 ah 2 ah 3 ah | |
| 1/4 turn L and step R, hop R - - - - - - - - - - - - - - - | 4 ah | 2 |
| Slide Fd. 3 X St. L - - - - - - - - - - - - - - - - - - - - - | 1 ah 2 ah 3 ah | |
| Step L, Hop L - - - - - - - - - - - - - - - - - - - - - - - - | 4 ah | 1 |
| Slide Bk. 3 X St. R - - - - - - - - - - - - - - - - - - - - - | 1 ah 2 ah 3 ah | |
| 1/4 turn R to face front and step R, hop R - - - - - - | 4 ah | 1 |
| Slide Fd. 1 X St. L - - - - - - - - - - - - - - - - - - - - - | 1 ah | |
| Step Fd. L, hop L - - - - - - - - - - - - - - - - - - - - - - | 2 ah | |
| Slide Bk. 1 X St. R - - - - - - - - - - - - - - - - - - - - - | 3 ah | |
| 1/4 turn L and step Bk. R, hop R - - - - - - - - - - - - | 4 ah | 1 |
| Slide Fd. 1 X St. L - - - - - - - - - - - - - - - - - - - - - | 1 ah | |
| Step Fd. L, hop L - - - - - - - - - - - - - - - - - - - - - - | 2 ah | |
| Step Bk. 1 X St. R - - - - - - - - - - - - - - - - - - - - - | 3 ah | |
| Step Bk. R to end facing opposite group - - - - - - - - | 4 | 1 |
| | total - - | 10 |

Group I Floor Pattern:

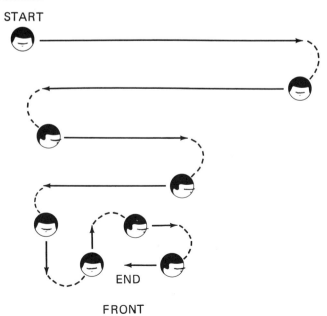

Group II

| | cts. | meas. |
|---|---|---|
| 4/4 meter | | |
| St. Wt. L facing front, arms extended Sd. waist level | | |
| Slide Sd. R 7 X St. R - - - - - - - - - - - - - - - - - - - - - - - | 1 ah 2 ah 3 ah 4 ah 1 ah 2 ah 3 ah | |
| Step R, hop R - - - - - - - - - - - - - - - - - - - - - - - - - | 4 ah | 2 |
| Slide Sd. L 7 X St. L - - - - - - - - - - - - - - - - - - - - - | 1 ah 2 ah 3 ah 4 ah 1 ah 2 ah 3 ah | |
| 1/4 turn R and step L, hop L - - - - - - - - - - - - - - - - | 4 ah | 2 |
| Slide Fd. 3 X St. R - - - - - - - - - - - - - - - - - - - - - - - | 1 ah 2 ah 3 ah | |
| Step R, hop R - - - - - - - - - - - - - - - - - - - - - - - - - | 4 ah | 1 |
| Slide Bk. 3 X St. L - - - - - - - - - - - - - - - - - - - - - - - | 1 ah 2 ah 3 ah | |
| Step L, hop L - - - - - - - - - - - - - - - - - - - - - - - - - | 4 ah | 1 |
| 1/4 turn L to face front and slide Fd. 1 X St. R - - | 1 ah | |
| Step R, hop R - - - - - - - - - - - - - - - - - - - - - - - - - | 2 ah | |
| Slide Bk. 1 X St. L - - - - - - - - - - - - - - - - - - - - - - - | 3 ah | |
| 1/4 turn R and step L, hop L - - - - - - - - - - - - - - - - | 4 ah | 1 |
| Slide Fd. 3 X St. R - - - - - - - - - - - - - - - - - - - - - - - | 1 ah 2 ah 3 ah | |
| Step R to end facing opposite group - - - - - - - - - - - | 4 | 1 |
| Hold - - - - - - - - - - - - - - - - - - - - - - - - - - - - - - - - - - - - - - - - - - - - - - - - - - - - - - - - - - | | 2 |
| | total - - | 10 |

Group II Floor Pattern:

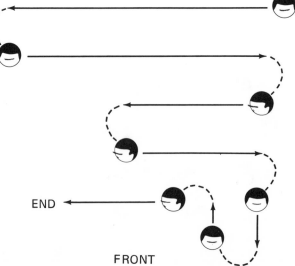

5. **Sliding Distortedly**
    A. Exaggerate the slide by clicking the heels together in the air.

| | cts. | meas. |
|---|---|---|
| 4/4 meter | | |
| Face Fd., arms at sides. Step R Sd., legs in medium stride, knees turned out, plié - - - - - - - | 1 | |
| Straighten knees springing into air, bringing heels together extending toes - - - - - - - - - - - - - | ah | |
| Repeat 3 X with the last spring carrying the body into 1/2 turn R - - - - - - - - - - - - - - - - - - - | 2 ah 3 ah 4 ah | 1 |
| Repeat 4 slides to L - - - - - - - - - - - - - - - - - - - - - - - - - - - - - - - - - - - - - - - - | | 1 |
| total - - | | 2 |

   Try two slides right, one-half jump-turn right and two slides left. Vary the arm position from sides to shoulder level.

    B. Combine a distorted slide with stamping,

| | cts. | meas. |
|---|---|---|
| 4/4 meter | | |
| Stand with arms akimbo (hands at waist with backs of hands facing Fd.). Step diagonally Fd. on R heel as R arm flings out Sd. R with palm up - - - - - - - - - - - - - | 1 | |
| Bring L foot up to and displace the R with a stamp as R hand whips sharply Bk. to waist position - - - - - - - - - - - - - - - - - - - - - - - - - - - - - | 2 | |
| Repeat 2 X - - - - - - - - - - - - - - - - - - - - - - - - - | 3 4 1 2 | |
| Stamp in place R, L, R kicking bent knees Bk. while focusing Bk. over L shoulder - - - - - - - | 3 & 4 | 2 |
| Repeat all reversing arm positions - - - - - - - - - - - - - - - - - - - - - - - - - - - - | | 2 |
| total - - | | 4 |

6. **Creative Clues**
    A. Travel across a pre-determined distance with as few sliding steps as possible. Work for wide dimension slides.
    B. Travel across space using as many sliding steps as possible. Work for great height.
    C. Two groups experiment with sliding movement used to convey contrasting ideas such as "hello" and "good-bye", or work and play. Variations in timing, force, and different aspects of space should be evidenced in such a study.

## SAMPLE VARIATIONS BUILT FROM COMBINED LOCOMOTOR MOVEMENTS

STEP-HOP

1. **Lead-up to the Step-hop**
    A. Step left and hop left seven times; repeat right. Work for low even bounces. The change from one foot to the other should be hardly noticeable.

B. Step left and hop left seven times; repeat right. Repeat all with six hops and five hops. Continue to decrease a hop each time until finally a step-hop results.

2. **Step-hop Forward and Turning**
    A. Step-hop forward four times. Step-hop four times making one complete turn right. Work for much flexion in the knees and ankles on the step-hops. The free foot should be in back and not extended forward.
    B. Step-hop forward four times. Step-hop four times making two complete turns right. Keep the knees and legs well apart as the turns are made. The body completes a one-half circle on each step-hop.
    C. Step-hop forward four times. Step-hop four times completing a turn left. Keep the knees and legs close together on this turn so that a larger circular floor pattern results.
    D. Try combining the turns of "A", "B", and "C" in consecutive order alternating each with four step-hops forward.
    E. Partners face, placing hands on each other's waist. Try the right turns of "A" and "B" together.
    F. Try "C" type turn with partners moving away from each other as each completes an individual turn. The person on the left turns left; the person on the right turns right.

3. **Side-to-side Step-hop**
    Leap sideward right, hop right as left leg sweeps far in back and toward the right. Repeat to the left. The focus follows the direction of the leap with the arms swinging from side to side just below shoulder level.

4. **Step-hopping to Shifting Accents**

    Rhythmic Pattern:

    The pattern is built on a 4 measure phrase. The shifting accents result from emphasizing movements on the two beats of the first measure of the entire phrase, then the second measure, the third, and so on.
        The sequence is rather difficult, but a challenge rhythmically and fun to do. First, try repeating the four measure phrase accenting only the beats of the first measure until the group becomes familiar with double accents. Then, try the following shifting accent combination.

    First time through:

    |                                               | cts.        | meas. |
    |-----------------------------------------------|-------------|-------|
    | Stamp Fd. L, stamp Fd. R - - - - - - - - - - - | 1 2         | 1     |
    | St. L, step-hop 3 X - - - - - - - - - - - - - | 1 2 1 2 1 2 | 3     |

Second time through:

Rhythmic Pattern:

|                                              | cts. | meas. |
|----------------------------------------------|------|-------|
| St. R, step-hop - - - - - - - - - - - - - - - - - - - - - - - - - - - - - - - - | 1 2 | 1 |
| Stamp Fd. L, stamp Fd. R - - - - - - - - - - - - - - - - - - | 1 2 | 1 |
| St. L, step-hop 2 X - - - - - - - - - - - - - - - - - - - - - - - | 1 2 1 2 | 2 |

Third time through:

Rhythmic Pattern:

|                                              | cts. | meas. |
|----------------------------------------------|------|-------|
| St. L, step-hop 2 X - - - - - - - - - - - - - - - - - - - - - - - | 1 2 1 2 | 2 |
| Stamp Fd. L, stamp Fd. R - - - - - - - - - - - - - - - - - - | 1 2 | 1 |
| St. L, step-hop - - - - - - - - - - - - - - - - - - - - - - - - - - - - - | 1 2 | 1 |

Fourth time through:

Rhythmic Pattern:

$$\frac{2}{4}\ |\ \text{♩}\ \text{♩}\ |\ \text{♩}\ \text{♩}\ |\ \text{♩}\ \text{♩}\ |\ \overset{>}{\text{♩}}\ \overset{>}{\text{♩}}\ |$$

|                                              | cts. | meas. |
|----------------------------------------------|------|-------|
| St. R, step-hop 3 X - - - - - - - - - - - - - - - - - - - - - | 1 2 1 2 1 2 | 3 |
| Stamp Fd. L, stamp Fd. R - - - - - - - - - - - - - - - - - - | 1 2 | 1 |
|                                              | total - - | 16 |

Repeat all.

Vary the pattern by stamping sideward instead of forward. Add a shoulder drop and a sharp head movement on sideward stamps.

5. **Step-hop Phrase Pattern**
   There should be a heavy, bouncing, throbbing quality to the whole pattern with a built-in excitement or intensity to the end of the phrase.

Floor Pattern:

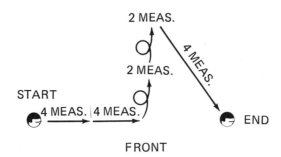

2/4 meter                                                                                           meas.

Focus straight ahead, arms gradually lifting from Sd. to
shoulder level as St. L, step-hop 4X - - - - - - - - - - - - - - - - - - - - - - - - - - - - - - - - -        4

Focus very high, arms reaching from shoulders to accent every
step, continue step-hop 4 X - - - - - - - - - - - - - - - - - - - - - - - - - - - - - - - - - - - - - -        4

Lower focus to floor, dropping arms to Sd., progress L,
step-hop 4 X completing 2 L turns - - - - - - - - - - - - - - - - - - - - - - - - - - - - - - - - -        4

Lift focus, gradually raise arms in pulsing rhythm high over
head, progress diagonally R step-hop 4 X with greater force - - - - - - - - - - - - -        4
                                                                                            ———
                                                                     total - -    16

Repeat all.

6. **Step-hop Distortedly**
   A. Exaggerate the step into a low stamp, emphasizing the hop so that the body
      rebounds high into the air. The free leg extends backward, and the arms swing in
      opposition. A gay vigorous strutting effect should result.
   B. Exaggerate the stamp, but check the dynamic rebound so that a small hop follows.
      The effect becomes more flirtatious.
   C. Stamp with the free leg extended in back. Hop landing on the toes and ball of foot
      with the knee locked, free leg swinging forward.
   D. Step on the toes with the knee locked, free leg extended backward. Hop
      exaggerating the knee bend on the drop. As the body drops from the high knee
      locked position into the low hop, the free leg swings forward.

7. **Creative Clues**
   A. Start a bouncing easy step-hop. Encourage the group to try various arm
      movements as they move. Change the arm movements every four measures; two
      measures.
   B. Try a directional change every four measures.
   C. Accent various beats in a series of four measures with stamps, turns and arm
      movements.
   D. Have a leader move for four measures improvising a step-hop variation. The group
      follows the movement on the next four measures. At the same time the leader
      tries a new movement which will be picked up by the group in a canon type study.
      Have half the group watch as others move. Then change groups so all may see the
      interesting floor patterns and group relationships that result.

SCHOTTISCHE

1. **Lead-ups to the Schottische**
   A. Walk to the following rhythm:

   $$\frac{4}{4} \quad | \quad \downarrow \quad \downarrow \quad \downarrow \quad \xi \quad |$$
   1   2   3   ④
   Step  Step  Step  Hold

   B. Swing the free leg forward from the hip with straight knee on the fourth count. Be sure the kick is low. Point the toes slightly.
   C. Carry the walks into an easy jog run. Keep the body relaxed. The same bouncing quality found in the step-hop should be present in the schottische.

2. **Schottische Combined with Step-hops**
   A. Follow two running schottische steps with four step-hops.
   B. Vary the step-hops each time to include left, right, and double turns.
   C. Try "A" and "B" with partners, running side by side on the schottische steps and closing together on the step-hops.

3. **Zigzag Schottische**
   A. Run left, cross right over left, run left, hop left, swing right leg low across in front of left leg. Repeat to the opposite side. This is sometimes called the "drunken schottische" because of the staggering effect it produces as it works in diagonals across the floor.
   B. Try three runs forward right, left, right swinging left leg out sideward to the left side, hop right completing one-quarter turn right. Repeat to opposite side turning left. Progress in zigzag across the floor.

4. **Syncopated Schottische**
   A. Rhythmic Pattern

   $$\frac{4}{4} \quad | \quad \downarrow \quad \downarrow \quad \downarrow \quad \gamma \quad \downarrow \quad |$$
   1   2   3   ④  &

|  | cts. | meas. |
|---|---|---|
| Run L - - - - - - - - - - - - - - - - - - - - - - - - - - - - - - - - - - - - | 1 | |
| Run R - - - - - - - - - - - - - - - - - - - - - - - - - - - - - - - - - - - - | 2 | |
| Run L - - - - - - - - - - - - - - - - - - - - - - - - - - - - - - - - - - - - | 3 | |
| Hold - - - - - - - - - - - - - - - - - - - - - - - - - - - - - - - - - - - - - | ④ | |
| Hop L - - - - - - - - - - - - - - - - - - - - - - - - - - - - - - - - - - - - | & | 1 |
| Repeat Beginning R - - - - - - - - - - - - - - - - - - - - - - - - - - - - - - - - - - - - | | 1 |
| | total - - | 2 |

B. Rhythmic Pattern:

|                                                    | cts. | meas. |
|----------------------------------------------------|------|-------|
| Run L -------------------------------------------- | 1    |       |
| Run R -------------------------------------------- | 2    |       |
| Hold --------------------------------------------- | ③    |       |
| Run L -------------------------------------------- | 4    |       |
| Hop L -------------------------------------------- | &    | 1     |
| Repeat all beginning R -------------------------------------------- | | 1 |
|                                          total - - | | 2 |

C. Rhythmic Pattern:

$$\frac{4}{4}\ |\ \quarternote\ \quarterrest\ \quarternote\ \eighthnote\eighthnote\ |$$
1  ②  3  4  &

|                                                    | cts. | meas. |
|----------------------------------------------------|------|-------|
| Run L -------------------------------------------- | 1    |       |
| Hold --------------------------------------------- | ②    |       |
| Run R -------------------------------------------- | 3    |       |
| Run L -------------------------------------------- | 4    |       |
| Hop L -------------------------------------------- | &    | 1     |
| Repeat all beginning R -------------------------------------------- | | 1 |
|                                          total - - | | 2 |

D. Rhythmic Pattern:

$$\frac{4}{4}\ |\ \quarterrest\ \quarternote\ \quarternote\ \eighthnote\eighthnote\ |$$
①  2  3  4  &

|                                                    | cts. | meas. |
|----------------------------------------------------|------|-------|
| Hold --------------------------------------------- | ①    |       |
| Run L -------------------------------------------- | 2    |       |
| Run R -------------------------------------------- | 3    |       |
| Run L -------------------------------------------- | 4    |       |
| Hop L -------------------------------------------- | &    | 1     |
| Repeat all beginning R -------------------------------------------- | | 1 |
|                                          total - - | | 2 |

Try each of the above rhythmic patterns adding a sharp hand clap on the held beats.

Divide the group into four sections. Have each section perform one of the above rhythmic patterns as all move across the floor. Allow first group four measures before second group starts across. Then four more measures before next group follows.

A drum beat sounding the basic rhythmic pattern will help hold the groups

together. Each group will be clapping on a different beat. The beats should sound even and clear.

5. **Schottische Distortedly**
   A. Bend the knee of the free leg high forward on the hop keeping the arms straight by sides pushing toward floor.
   B. Bend the knee of the free leg high sideward on the hop keeping the knee well turned out. Arms are straight pushing toward opposite side, shoulder level; focus follows arms.
   C. Bend the knee of the free leg high backward on the hop keeping the knee turned out. Arms are straight pushing forward shoulder level.
   D. Try combining four of each of the above variations. Divide the group into three sections and start them across the floor at intervals of four measures. Later, give the group an opportunity to see the pattern which results by having half the class move while the other half observes.

6. **Creative Clues**
   Divide the class into small groups of three or four. Using the schottische as the common step for all, limit each group to one main emphasis of variation. For example, primarily a rhythmical variation of the basic schottische step; primarily a dimensional variation; a directional variation.

   If the class is large enough it is interesting to have two different groups work on the same aspect. The usefulness comes when the entire group sees the different approaches that are possible to the same problem. A friendly critical appraisal and discussion by the entire group should always be a part of studies of this type.

WALTZ

1. **Lead-ups to the Waltz**
   A. Walk to the following rhythmic pattern:

   $$\frac{3}{4}$$

   B. Accent the first beat with a slight stamp.
   C. Shorten the last step gradually until the feet come together on the third beat.
   D. Step diagonally sideward on the second count bringing the feet together on the third count — the forward waltz results. Reverse the procedure to arrive at a backward waltz. Keep weight on balls of feet gliding smoothly across the floor.

2. **Double Hesitation Waltz**
   A. Step forward, backward or sideward on count 1. Hold counts 2, 3. The free foot may swing low forward on forward double hesitation, backward on backward double hesitation, or across on sideward double hesitation. Or, the free foot may pause close to the supporting foot on counts 2, 3.
   B. Partners standing side by side with inside hands joined start on outside foot. Step forward pivoting away from partner swinging inside foot through and pointing it close to the floor in line of direction. Hold counts 2, 3. Step on pointing foot pivoting one-half turn to face partner and swing the outside foot forward to point in line of direction. As the hesitations are taken, the arms swing down on count 1, and up to hold sideward shoulder level on counts 2, 3.

3. **Waltz Run**
   A. Run forward in long strides accenting the first beat with a leap. Gradually increase the tempo.
   B. Leap low and wide on the first count, and run very high on counts 2, 3.
   C. Try "B" accenting the lift of count 2. This seems to eliminate any element of heaviness. The whole movement becomes more gay, light and exciting. Gradually increase the tempo so that the feet seem barely to touch the floor.

4. **Combined Waltz Run and Double Hesitation**

   A. 3/4 meter

   | | cts. | meas. |
   |---|---|---|
   | St. Wt. R. 2 waltz runs Fd. accenting lift on ct. 2 - - - - - - - - - - - - - - - - - - - - - - - - - - - - - - - - - - - - - - - - - - - - - - - - - - | | 2 |
   | Leap Fd. L turning body 1/4 L and extending R toe Sd. - - - - - - - - - - - - - - - - - - - - - - - - | 1 | |
   | Hesitate - - - - - - - - - - - - - - - - - - - - - - - - - - - - - - - | 2  3 | 1 |
   | Step Sd. R. pivoting Bk. 1/2 turn swinging L leg Sd. L - - - - - - - - - - - - - - - - - - - - - - - - - - - - - - - | 1 | |
   | Hesitate - - - - - - - - - - - - - - - - - - - - - - - - - - - - - - - | 2  3 | 1 |
   | | total - - | 4 |

   1/4 turn to face Fd. and repeat waltz runs.

   Gradually increase the tempo.

   Have partners move together—partner on left starts left; partner on right starts right.

   B. Rhythmic Pattern:

Floor Pattern:

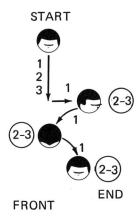

3/4 meter

| | cts. | meas. |
|---|---|---|
| St. Wt. L. Waltz run Fd. R - - - - - - - - - - - - - - - - - - - - - | 1 2 3 | 1 |
| 1/4 turn L, step Fd. L bringing R foot up close to instep of L foot - - - - - - - - - - - - - - - - - - - | 1 | |
| Hold - - - - - - - - - - - - - - - - - - - - - - - - - - - - - - - - - - | 2 3 | 1 |
| 1/4 turn L step Bk. R swinging L leg Sd. and extending L toe - - - - - - - - - - - - - - - - - - - - - - - | 1 | |
| Hold - - - - - - - - - - - - - - - - - - - - - - - - - - - - - - - - - - | 2 3 | 1 |
| 1/2 turn L step L swinging R leg Sd. and extending R toe - - - - - - - - - - - - - - - - - - - - - - - | 1 | |
| Hold - - - - - - - - - - - - - - - - - - - - - - - - - - - - - - - - - - | 2 3 | 1 |
| | total - - | 4 |

Repeat all.

Add these simple arm movements:

| | meas. |
|---|---|
| Let the R arm swing Bk. and reach upward in a circular movement - - - - - - - - - - - - - - - - - - - - - - - - - - - - - - - - - - - - - - - - - - - | 1 |
| Hold high arm reach lifting focus high - - - - - - - - - - - - - - - - - - - - - - - - | 1 |
| Drop the arm and focus sharply - - - - - - - - - - - - - - - - - - - - - - - - - - - - | 1 |
| Bring focus Bk. to normal position, arms held at Sd. - - - - - - - - - - - - - - - - | 1 |
| | total - - 4 |

C. Rhythmic Pattern:

$$\frac{3}{4}$$

1 2 3 | 1 ② 3 | 1 (2-3) | 1-2-3

Floor Pattern:

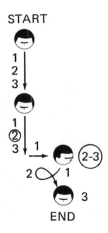

| Slow 3/4 meter | cts. | meas. |
|---|---|---|
| St. Wt. L. Waltz run Fd. R - - - - - - - - - - - - - - - - - - - - - | 1 2 3 | 1 |
| Step L - - - - - - - - - - - - - - - - - - - - - - - - - - - - - - - - | 1 | |
| Hold - - - - - - - - - - - - - - - - - - - - - - - - - - - - - - - - - | ② | |
| Step R - - - - - - - - - - - - - - - - - - - - - - - - - - - - - - - - | 3 | 1 |
| 1/4 turn L step Fd. L bringing R foot up close to instep of L foot - - - - - - - - - - - - - - - - - - - | 1 | |
| Hold - - - - - - - - - - - - - - - - - - - - - - - - - - - - - - - - - | ②③ | 1 |
| 1 complete turn plus 1/4 turn. Step Fd. R sweeping L leg far out in circular pattern - - - - - - - - - | 1 2 3 | 1 |
| | total - - | 4 |

Repeat all beginning left.

5. **Creative Clues**
    A. Two waltz runs forward, improvise one measure turning.
    B. Two waltz runs forward, improvise two measures of non-locomotor movement.
    C. Sit on floor. Experiment with movements of the body, head, arms to show circular or swaying quality of waltz time. Accent the movement of the first beat of each measure; second beat; third beat.
        Divide the group into three sections with each section accenting different beats of the measure. The same movement may be used by all sections and later a different movement for each section developed.

TWO-STEP

1. **Lead-ups to the Two-step**
    A. Slide forward right seven times. Step forward right on count eight. Hop right quickly on the up-beat count "ah". Repeat all starting left. Decrease the slides by two each time until one slide and a step-hop is taken on each side. The latter is a polka step. Now eliminate the hop and a two-step results: step close step.

B. Walk to the following rhythmic pattern:

$$\frac{4}{4} \;|\; \underset{1}{\quad} \;\; \underset{2}{\quad} \;\; \underset{3\text{-}4}{\quad} \;|$$

Glide the foot along the floor on count one. On count two bring the feet together. Keep the weight forward over the balls of the feet. Gradually increase the tempo until the rhythmic pattern is:

$$\frac{2}{4} \;|\; \underset{1 \;\; \&}{\quad} \;\; \underset{2}{\quad} \;|$$
Step Close Step

2. **Two-step Forward and Turning**
   A. Start with weight on right foot. Two-step forward two times. Complete right turn in two two-steps.
   B. Start with weight on right foot. Two-step forward one time. Complete left turn in two two-steps. Two-step forward right once to end a four measure phrase.
   C. Combine "A" and "B" into an 8 meas. phrase.

| 2/4 meter | cts. | meas. |
|---|---|---|
| St. Wt. R. Two-step Fd. 2 X - - - - - - - - - - - - - - - - - - - | 1 & 2<br>1 & 2 | 2 |
| Complete R turn in 2 two-steps - - - - - - - - - - - - - - - - | 1 & 2<br>1 & 2 | 2 |
| Two-step Fd. L - - - - - - - - - - - - - - - - - - - - - - - - - | 1 & 2 | 1 |
| Complete L turn in 2 two-steps - - - - - - - - - - - - - - - - | 1 & 2<br>1 & 2 | 2 |
| Two-step Fd. R - - - - - - - - - - - - - - - - - - - - - - - - - | 1 & 2 | 1 |
| | total - - | 8 |

Repeat all.

Try with partners in social dance position.

3. **Two-step Distortedly**
   A. Kick the feet backward as a quick leap is taken on the first and last step. The movement should be rapid, bouncy and gay.
   B. Lead with an exaggerated heel movement on the first and last step. Allow the body to tuck forward and then backward so a rocking motion results.

4. **Two-step Combined with Step**

Rhythmic Pattern:

|  | cts. | meas. |
|---|---|---|
| St. Wt. R. Two-step Sd. L ------------------------- | 1 & 2 | 1 |
| Stamp R, L -------------------------------------- | 1 2 | 1 |
| Two-step Sd. R ---------------------------------- | 1 & 2 | 1 |
| Stamp L, R -------------------------------------- | 1 2 | 1 |
| Two-step Sd. L ---------------------------------- | 1 & 2 | 1 |
| Two-step Sd. R ---------------------------------- | 1 & 2 | 1 |
| 1/2 turn L, stamp L, R -------------------------- | 1 2 | 1 |
| 1/2 turn L, stamp L, R -------------------------- | 1 2 | 1 |
| Two-step Fd. L ---------------------------------- | 1 & 2 | 1 |
| Step Fd. 2 X ------------------------------------ | 1 2 | 1 |
| Two-step Fd. R ---------------------------------- | 1 & 2 | 1 |
| 1/2 turn L, step L ------------------------------ | 1 | |
| Step in place R --------------------------------- | 2 | 1 |
| Two-step Fd. 2 X, L R --------------------------- | 1 & 2 | |
|  | 1 & 2 | 2 |
| Stamp L, R -------------------------------------- | 1 2 | 1 |
| 1/2 turn L, stamp L, R -------------------------- | 1 2 | 1 |
|  | total -- | 16 |

Experiment with different qualities of movement throughout. For example, distort the two-step as in "3 A" to make it lively and bouncy — kicking the feet backward on the steps. Try the whole combination exaggerating a heel lead on the two-step and stamps. Try the bouncing two-steps with a heel stamp.

5. **Creative Clues**
   A. Two-step changing direction at the end of each phrase of four measures.
   B. Have partners work out sixteen measures of 2/4 time using the two-step as their basic movement, the purpose being primarily to show phrasing. The phrase length may be two or four measures. They may work in unison, or in contrast, but an abrupt change should be noted at the beginning of each new phrase.

POLKA

1. **Lead-ups to the Polka**
   A. Slide to changing phrases as follows:
      Slide sideward right seven times to a phrase of seven beats. Step sideward right on count eight, hop right quickly on the upbeat count "ah." Repeat the phrase traveling sideward left. Repeat the above to four beats traveling first sideward right and second sideward left. Repeat again to two beats first to the right and then to the left. The latter is the polka.
   B. Repeat "A" traveling forward and backward.

C. Repeat "A" traveling right and left in a circle.

D. The two-step may also be used as a lead-up to the polka. After the two-step is well established, precede each two-step with a quick hop on the up-beat.

2. **Polka in Place and Moving Forward**
Start with weight on the left foot. Polka in place two times left and right. Repeat two polkas forward left and right to cover a wide amount of space. Continue across the floor.

3. **Polka Forward and Sideward with Variation**
Start with weight on the left foot. Polka forward two times left and right. Polka sideward right as follows: Hop left, step right, close left up to right, place right heel forward toe up without taking the weight. Repeat.

4. **Open-and-close Polka with Partners**
Partners stand side by side, with inside hands joined, weight on outside feet. Hop on outside feet and polka forward turning back-to-back as inside arms swing high toward the line of direction.

Hop on inside feet and polka forward turning to face each other as inside arms swing high away from the line of direction. Continue this gay, lifted movement across the floor.

5. **Polka Distortedly**
A. Start with weight on the left foot. Try hop-step-close-leap. Take the leap diagonally forward keeping it low and wide in dimension with supporting knee bent, and right arm thrust out percussively to the right side. Move the body as a unit. Repeat on opposite foot.

B. 2/4 meter

| | cts. | meas. |
|---|---|---|
| St. Wt. L. Polka Fd. L substituting a leap R for the final step cutting L leg Bk., palms of both hands pushing straight Fd. ---------------- | ah 1 & 2 | 1 |
| Repeat polka Bk. R bringing arms Dn. to Sd. --------------------------------------- | ah 1 & 2 | |
| 1/2 turn R, hop L ------------------------ | ah | 1 |
| Progress Fd. with 7 steps, R L R L R L R, keeping the R foot in the lead and closing the L in to the R -------------------------- | 1 & 2 &<br>1 & 2 | 2 |
| Repeat all facing in opposite direction and retrace original path with 1/2 turn L to end facing as in the beginning ------------------------------------------ | | 4 |
| | total -- | 8 |

6. **Creative Clues**
Form groups of two, three or four. Each develop a polka variation using folk songs (not folk dance music) as a starting support. Sources of this kind of music may stem from sea chanties, work and play songs, mountain songs, cowboy songs, and the various traditional folk songs from many countries. Give each study a title in keeping

with its respective quality. Suggested titles may include Nautical Polka, International Polka, Mountaineer's Polka, and Polka Jamboree.

## MAZURKA

1. **Mazurka Forward**
   A. Start with weight on the left foot. Mazurka forward three times right. Walk forward three times right, left, right. Repeat all starting left.
   B. Repeat "A" substituting three stamp steps, forward right, left, right for the three walks. Give style to the latter part of the movement by placing backs of hands at waist.

2. **Mazurka Sideward**
   Start with weight on the left foot. Mazurka sideward right three times. Do three runs in place right, left, right with free leg cutting out sideward. Repeat starting left.

3. **Partners Mazurka Combined with Leap and Hop**
   A. Partners stand side by side, hands joined across as in skating position. Start with weight on the left foot. Mazurka forward three times right. Leap right, hop two times right. Repeat to opposite side.
   B. Repeat "A" completing one-half turn right on the leap, hop, hop. Repeat all moving in opposite direction.

4. **Mazurka Distortedly**
   A. Try mazurkas substituting a stamp forward for the slide.
   B. Try mazurkas substituting a leap for the final hop.
   C. 3/4 meter

| | cts. | meas. |
|---|---|---|
| St. Wt. R. Hop Fd. R, clicking L heel Bk. against inner border of R heel - - - - - - - - - - - - - - - - - | 1 | |
| Stamp Fd. L - - - - - - - - - - - - - - - - - - - - - - - - - - - - - - | 2 | |
| Step Fd. R - - - - - - - - - - - - - - - - - - - - - - - - - - - - - - - | 3 | 1 |
| Repeat all 2 X - - - - - - - - - - - - - - - - - - - - - - - - - - - | | 2 |
| Run in place 3 X, L R L - - - - - - - - - - - - - - - - - - - - | 1 2 3 | 1 |
| Repeat all St. Wt. L - - - - - - - - - - - - - - - - - - - - - - - - - - - - - - - - - - - - - - - - | | 4 |
| | total - - | 8 |

D. St. Wt. L, arms bent reaching upward out to the sides. Travel diagonally Fd. R hopping off L foot as R heel clicks back against inner border of L heel - - - - - - - - - - - - - - - - - - - - - - - - - - | 1 | |
| Repeat - - - - - - - - - - - - - - - - - - - - - - - - - - - - - - - - | 2 | |
| Stamp Fd. R, rotating L forearm inward with accented movement - - - - - - - - - - - - - - - - - - - | 3 | 1 |
| Repeat on opposite foot clicking L foot against inner border of R heel 2 X - - - - - - - - - - - - - | 1 2 | |
| Stamp Fd. L - - - - - - - - - - - - - - - - - - - - - - - - - - - - - - | 3 | 1 |

|                                                               | cts.    | meas. |
|---------------------------------------------------------------|---------|-------|
| Hop L and click R to L 3 X - - - - - - - - - - - - - - - - - - - - | 1 2 3   | 1     |
| Stamp in place 3 X, R L R - - - - - - - - - - - - - - - - - - - | 1 2 3   | 1     |
| Repeat all St. Wt. R - - - - - - - - - - - - - - - - - - - - - - - - - - - - - - - - - - - - - |         | 4     |
|                                                               | total - - | 8     |

## 5. Creative Clues

A. Teach the following pattern emphasizing a mazurka variation:

|                                                               | cts.    | meas. |
|---------------------------------------------------------------|---------|-------|
| St. Wt. L. Slide Fd. R - - - - - - - - - - - - - - - - - - - - - - | 1       |       |
| Cut L in to replace R - - - - - - - - - - - - - - - - - - - - - - | 2       |       |
| 1/2 turn R hopping L to face in opposite direction - - - - - - - - - - - - - - - - - - - - - - - - - - - - - - - - | 3       | 1     |
| Repeat all to end in original position - - - - - - - - - - - | 1 2 3   | 1     |
| Slide Sd. R - - - - - - - - - - - - - - - - - - - - - - - - - - - | 1       |       |
| Hop 2 X R traveling Sd. R - - - - - - - - - - - - - - - - - - - | 2 3     | 1     |
| Wide elevated step L Sd. L - - - - - - - - - - - - - - - - - - | 1       |       |
| Carry this into a sustained whole turn L - - - - - - - - - - | 2 3     |       |
| Leap-lunge Fd. R - - - - - - - - - - - - - - - - - - - - - - - - - | &       | 1     |
| Repeat all St. L - - - - - - - - - - - - - - - - - - - - - - - - - - - - - - - - - - - - - - - - - |         | 4     |
|                                                               | total - - | 8     |

B. Divide class into small groups. Give each group a card on which is indicated the specific manner in which the above pattern is to be varied further in quality. Examples:

1) Vary the floor pattern such that one part of the group will be moving in opposition and in contrast to the other.
2) Vary the timing to show normal speed; twice as fast; or twice as slow.
3) Vary the directional line in relation to changing focus.
4) Vary the quality of the movement by making it swinging, sustained or percussive.
5) Vary the dimension to show a wide margin of contrast; by a gradual building up or building down of the size of the movement.
6) Vary the level to give the movement a feeling of submission or aggression.

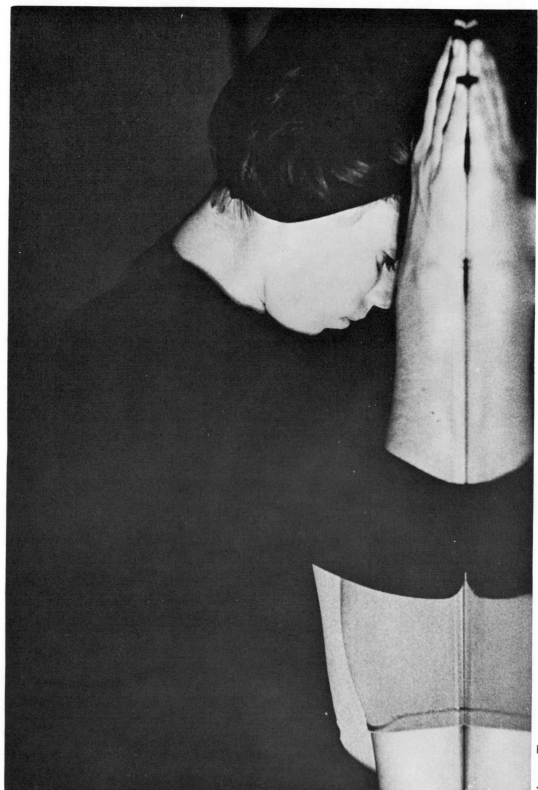

Figure Ten

# Chapter 6

# EXAMPLES OF CREATIVE MOVEMENT PATTERNS

The sample variations thus far presented have been concerned primarily with established locomotor movements. Expanded development of these basic steps has been explored, and specific examples of ways to vary these movements have been offered.

The other large category of movement involves non-locomotor movement. This is movement occurring within the body regardless of floor pattern. Movement performed in one place—standing, sitting or lying—is referred to as stationary, axial or non-locomotor movement.

## VARIATIONS BUILT FROM NON-LOCOMOTOR MOVEMENTS

Before the dancer can begin to move in a dance sense, his instrument must be put in a physical state of readiness. All areas of the body must be tested and tried, pulled and pushed, stretched and bent, and in general attuned to the business to be done. Preparative activities are necessary as a safety measure and should precede the more vigorous technical and creative work.

There are many exercises available for the dance teacher to employ in conditioning the dance student. A fine dancer is a fine athlete in the sense that his body is flexible, has strong muscle tone, can endure great physical demands, and can respond quickly and accurately. Many of the dance techniques are designed to meet the general aims of body conditioning.

Dance work goes beyond mere conditioning, however, and for this reason every dance technique should be performed with rhythmic cognizance and specific recognition of dynamic stress. To dance is to be aware of the way a movement is performed. The aesthetics of dance involve line, shape, form, relationships, and over-all design. These factors become more and more important as the dancer deals with abstract ideas. Kinesthetic involvement along with projection and communication to an audience are intricate and complex elements which are vital to the dance art. By promoting and demanding pride in performance of even the simplest technique from the very beginning of dance work, over a period of time the awareness of the complex qualities which are intrinsic to the dance art is allowed to germinate and grow. The finished dance is the result of the maturation of a great many factors all developing concurrently.

### FLEXIONS, EXTENSIONS AND ROTATIONS

The following series of movement patterns involving flexions, extensions, and rotations have been designed to use almost every part of the body. They may serve as a continuous sequence to start a class. Again, certain sections may fulfill the needs of one particular group more than another. Therefore, although the entire pattern is related, it has been divided into small units with transitions and breaks for the convenience of the teacher.

When the series is performed dynamically and continuously, it may serve as a beginning for a dance demonstration. A group of stationary dancers moving precisely together and to count with clear, strong movements can be exhilarating to do and exciting to watch. The demonstration group could follow the non-locomotor series by moving across the floor in simple, clearly defined spatial patterns using various fundamental and combined locomotor movements. The program could be climaxed by displaying a few choice individual and group creative efforts.

A simple "three-part" dance program of this type is satisfying to the teacher, the dancers and the audience. For the audience it offers an easily observable progression from stationary movement to active locomotor movement across the floor to more complex creative work. For the student dancers, by utilizing material that has developed in class, they are more natural in their presentation, and the stress and strain of performing is minimized. And for the teacher — how can he resist the opportunity to inform an audience as to the meaning of dance, the educational goals he is trying to attain through dance by helping the student discover his own potential?

There are innumerable and varied ways in which the following non-locomotor movement patterns may be utilized. Therefore, each teacher should seek the approaches that best suit the interests of his particular class.

This technique series is available on the film, Focus On Control. (See Appendix D, Films for Dance.) The viewing of this film may serve to inspire students before they begin to learn the series. Later, a re-viewing of the film may provide a self-evaluative measure. Accompanying music for this series has been recorded on side two, band one, of "Music by Cola Heiden for Keynotes To Modern Dance." (See Appendix B, Selected Recordings for Teaching Modern Dance.)

## Section A

### Unit I

4/4 meter

| | cts. | meas. |
|---|---|---|
| Sitting back straight, knees bent, soles of feet together, arms inside legs, hands touching lower legs. | | |
| Drop Fd. as far as possible with hands resting on ankles. Take 8 quick, small bobs — movement orginating from the base of the spine --------- | 1 & 2 & 3 & 4 & | 1 |
| Bounce 4 X with slower, larger movement letting body rebound vigorously (Fd. bounces on underlying beats; rebound on the "and" cts.) ------------------------------ | 1 & 2 & 3 & 4 & | 1 |
| Repeat 8 quick, small bobs -------------------- | 1 & 2 & 3 & 4 & | 1 |
| Grasp ankles, and flattening back from base of spine to top of head, pull Fd. through legs ----------- | 1 2 3 4 | 1 |
| Return to original high sitting position while pulling feet close to body -------------------- | 1 2 3 4 | 1 |
| Brace elbows on upper leg just above knees letting body weight push knees toward the floor with 8 quick, small bobs ------------------ | 1 & 2 & 3 & 4 & | 1 |
| Bounce 4 X with slower, larger movement ----------- | 1 & 2 & 3 & 4 & | 1 |

|  | cts. | meas. |
|---|---|---|

Slowly straighten legs Fd. to full extension (no turn-out of legs) and sit high with finger tips touching just above knees - - - - - - - - - - - - - - - - - - - - - -  1 2 3 4        1

                                                          A Unit I - - total - -    8

## Unit II

With ankles extended, round back, dropping Fd. as far as possible with hands holding ankles. Take 8 quick, small bobs - - - - - - - - - - - - - - - - - - - - - - 1 & 2 & 3 & 4 &   1

Straighten back, head lifted, ankles flexed, hands sliding to just below knees, and bounce 4 X with slower larger movement letting body rebound vigorously - - - - - - - - - - - - - - - - - - - - - - 1 & 2 & 3 & 4 &   1

Repeat 8 quick, small bobs - - - - - - - - - - - - - - - - - - - - 1 & 2 & 3 & 4 &   1

Grasp ankles, flattening back from base of spine to top of head and pull Fd. close to legs - - - - - - - - - - - 1 2

Return to original high sitting position - - - - - - - - - - - - 3 4               1

Repeat 8 quick, small bobs - - - - - - - - - - - - - - - - - - - - 1 & 2 & 3 & 4 &   1

Repeat 4 slow, large bounces - - - - - - - - - - - - - - - - - - - 1 & 2 & 3 & 4 &   1

Repeat 8 quick, small bobs - - - - - - - - - - - - - - - - - - - - 1 & 2 & 3 & 4 &   1

Repeat the pull Fd. close to legs - - - - - - - - - - - - - - - - - 1 2

Sit high - - - - - - - - - - - - - - - - - - - - - - - - - - - - - - - - - - - 3

Spread legs extended to wide stride, opening arms with fingers touching legs below knees - - - - - - - - - 4               1

                                                          A Unit II - - total - -   8

## Unit III

With ankles extended, round back dropping Fd. as far as possible with hands holding ankles. Take 8 quick, small bobs - - - - - - - - - - - - - - - - - - - - - - 1 & 2 & 3 & 4 &   1

Straighten back, head lifted, ankles flexed and bounce 4 X with slower, larger movement letting body rebound vigorously - - - - - - - - - - - - - - - - - - 1 & 2 & 3 & 4 &   1

Repeat 8 quick, small bobs - - - - - - - - - - - - - - - - - - - - 1 & 2 & 3 & 4 &   1

Flatten back from base of spine to top of head and pull Fd. through legs close to floor - - - - - - - - - - - - 1 2

Return to high sitting position - - - - - - - - - - - - - - - - - - 3 4               1

Repeat last 4 meas. - - - - - - - - - - - - - - - - - - - - - - - - - - - - - - - - - - - - - -   4

                                                          A Unit III - - total - -  8

Unit IV

|  | cts. | meas. |
|---|---|---|
| Drop head Bk., focusing upward, flex ankles and swing arms circularly Dn., Bk., up and around - - - - - - - - - - - - - - - - - - - - - - - - - - - - - - - | 1  2  3 |  |
| Bend body far Fd. and slap hands on floor - - - - - - - - - - | & |  |
| Rebound - - - - - - - - - - - - - - - - - - - - - - - - - - - - - - - - - - - - - | 4 | 1 |
| Clasp hands, straightening arms, flattening back, extending knees and ankles, pull Fd. close to floor - - - - - - - - - - - - - - - - - - - - - - - - - - - - - - - - | 1 |  |
| Lift arms and body up to high sitting position with clasped hands reaching up above head and focus following hands - - - - - - - - - - - - - - - - - - - - - | 2 |  |
| Drop hands, unclasped, behind head - - - - - - - - - - - - - - | 3 |  |
| Open arms Sd. just below shoulder level, palms Dn. - - - - - - - - - - - - - - - - - - - - - - - - - - - - - - - - - - - - - - - | 4 | 1 |
| Repeat the last 2 meas. 3 X - - - - - - - - - - - - - - - - - - - - - - - - - - - - - - - - - - - - |  | 6 |

A Unit IV - - total - -  $\overline{8}$

Section A    total - -  32

Break:

| Bring legs together with arms extended Fd. above legs - - - - - - - - - - - - - - - - - - - - - - - - - - - - - - - - - | 1  2 |  |
| Bend knees to chest, soles of feet on floor, arms encircling legs, body relaxed Fd. - - - - - - - - - - - - - - - - - - | 3  4 | 1 |
| Hold relaxed position - - - - - - - - - - - - - - - - - - - - - - - - - - - - - - - - - - - - - - - - - - - - |  | 2 |

Break    total - -  $\overline{3}$

Transition:

| Extend legs Fd., straighten back as hands touch knees - - - - - - - - - - - - - - - - - - - - - - - - - - - - - - - - - | 1 |  |
| Hold sitting high - - - - - - - - - - - - - - - - - - - - - - - - - - - - - - - - | 2 |  |
| Shift Wt. to R hip bending both legs to L in L pretzel position (L leg bent Bk. and R leg bent front), arms Sd. palms Fd. fingers touching floor - - - - - - - - - - - - - - - - - - - - - - - - - - - - - - - - - - - | 3 |  |
| Hold - - - - - - - - - - - - - - - - - - - - - - - - - - - - - - - - - - - - - - - - | 4 | 1 |

Transition    total - -  $\overline{1}$

Section B

Unit I

|  | cts. | meas. |
|---|---|---|
| Rotate body to R - - - - - - - - - - - - - - - - - - - - - - - - - - - - | 1 2 | |
| Sit high on R hip, lift L arm up over head, Bk. of R hand on floor near R hip, focus on R hand - - - - - - - | 3 4 | 1 |
| Stretching body laterally R, bob 4 X - - - - - - - - - - - - - - | 1 2 3 4 | |
| Drop L hand Bk. of head - - - - - - - - - - - - - - - - - - - - - | & | 1 |
| Whip L hand across front of body beyond R knee, with body bending Fd., keeping R hand low in Bk. - - - - - - - - - - - - - - - - - - - - - - - - - - - - - - - | 1 | |
| Extend L arm circling around to L close to floor, body rotating in same direction with R arm following - - - - - - - - - - - - - - - - - - - - - - - - - - - - - | 2 3 | |
| Clasp hands and drop behind head - - - - - - - - - - - - - - - - | 4 | 1 |
| Repeat last meas. to end with body rotated to face R - - - - - - - - - - - - - - - - - - - - - - - - - - - - - - - - - - | 1 2 3 4 | 1 |
| Lower hands to floor - - - - - - - - - - - - - - - - - - - - - - - - | 1 2 | |
| Sit high on R hip, lift L arm up over head, Bk. of R hand on floor near R hip, focus on R hand - - - - - - | 3 4 | 1 |
| Repeat lateral bobs 4 X - - - - - - - - - - - - - - - - - - - - - | 1 2 3 4 | 1 |
| Repeat body rotation to L as in meas. 3 - - - - - - - - - - - - | 1 2 3 4 | 1 |
| Whip L hand across front of body beyond R knee, with body bending Fd., keeping R hand low in Bk. - - - - - - - - - - - - - - - - - - - - - - - - - - - - - - - | 1 | |
| Clasp hands far Fd. - - - - - - - - - - - - - - - - - - - - - - - - | 2 | |
| Bend knees close to chest bringing clasped hands to drop behind head - - - - - - - - - - - - - - - - - - - - | & | |
| Drop bent knees to floor L while extending arms Sd. shoulder level - - - - - - - - - - - - - - - - - - - - - | 3 | |
| Lower arms Sd. to touch finger tips on floor, palms Fd. - - - - - - - - - - - - - - - - - - - - - - - - - - - - - - - - - - | 4 | 1 |
| | total - - | 8 |
| Repeat all 3 X alternating Sd. to end finally facing Fd. in original L pretzel position - - - - - - - - - - - - - - - - - - - - - - - - - - - - | | 24 |
| | B Unit I    total - - | 32 |

Unit II

| | cts. | meas. |
|---|---|---|
| Rotate body 1/4 turn R - - - - - - - - - - - - - - - - - - - - - - - | 1  2 | |
| Rotate body to face Fd. - - - - - - - - - - - - - - - - - - - - - - | 3  4 | 1 |
| Rotate body 1/4 turn L - - - - - - - - - - - - - - - - - - - - - - | 1  2 | |
| Rotate body to face Fd. - - - - - - - - - - - - - - - - - - - - - - | 3  4 | 1 |
| Rotate body 1/4 turn R - - - - - - - - - - - - - - - - - - - - - - | 1  2 | |
| Take Wt. on R hand close to R hip, pushing heel of L hand straight upward close to the face to full arm extension, focus on L hand - - - - - - - - - - - - | 3  4 | 1 |
| Swing L arm Dn. to place in Bk. of L hip, rotating body 1/2 turn L - - - - - - - - - - - - - - - - - - - - - | 1  2 | |
| Take Wt. on L hand close to L hip, pushing heel of R hand straight upward close to the face to full arm extension, focus on R hand - - - - - - - - - - - - - | 3  4 | 1 |
| Swing R arm Dn. to place in Bk. of R hip, rotating body 1/2 turn R - - - - - - - - - - - - - - - - - - - - - | 1  2 | |
| Take Wt. on R hand pushing body up on knees extending L arm straight upward, focus following L hand - - - - - - - - - - - - - - - - - - - - - - - - - - - - - | 3 | |
| Hold - - - - - - - - - - - - - - - - - - - - - - - - - - - - - - - - - - - - - - | 4 | 1 |
| Lower body to R hip Swing L arm Dn. to place in Bk. of L hip, rotating body 1/2 turn L - - - - - - - - - - - - - - - - - - - - - | 1  2 | |
| Take Wt. on L hand pushing body up on knees extending R arm straight upward, focus following R hand - - - - - - - - - - - - - - - - - - - - - - - - - - - - - | 3 | |
| Hold - - - - - - - - - - - - - - - - - - - - - - - - - - - - - - - - - - - - - - | 4 | 1 |
| Arms swing Dn. to Sd., rotate body 1/2 turn R - - - - - - - - - - - - - - - - - - - - - - - - - - - - - - - - - - - - | 1 | |
| Hold - - - - - - - - - - - - - - - - - - - - - - - - - - - - - - - - - - - - - - | 2 | |
| Rotate body 1/2 turn L - - - - - - - - - - - - - - - - - - - - - - - | 3 | |
| Swing body and arms laterally L and up onto knees - - - - - - - - - - - - - - - - - - - - - - - - - - - - - - - - - - - | 4 | 1 |
| Stretch laterally to finger tips and describe large semi-circle up overhead to the R sustaining the movement - - - - - - - - - - - - - - - - - - - - - - - - - - - - - | 1  2  3  4 | 1 |
| Drop body suddenly to R Sd. breaking the fall by catching Wt. on both hands and R knee, lifting L leg in air and focusing on floor - - - - - - - - - - - - | >  1  2 | |

|  | cts. | meas. |
|---|---|---|
| Push off from floor in a rebound 1/4 turn L opening L leg to high, toe-on-floor position, R knee on floor with Wt. on ball of R foot, R hand close to R hip and L arm bent in toward body - - - - - - - - - - - - - - - - - - - - - - - - - - - - - - - - - - - - - - - - | 3 |  |
| Push off floor, rolling Wt. on L foot, into deep Fd. L lunge, R leg straight. Extend L arm Fd. close to head, focus Dn.- - - - - - - - - - - - - - - - - - - - - | 4  1 | 1 |
| Lift body to upright stride stand 1/4 turn L, focus Fd. with hands at Sd. - - - - - - - - - - - - - - - - - - - - - | 2 |  |
| Lift arms and clasp hands straight up above head - - - - - - - - - - - - - - - - - - - - - - - - - - - - - - - - - - - - - - - - - - | 3  4 | 1 |
| Pivot-twist 1/4 turn L - - - - - - - - - - - - - - - - - - - - - - - - - - - | 1 |  |
| Lower body to reverse pretzel position as follows: descend with R knee touching floor, then L hand, L hip - - - - - - - - - - - - - - - - - - - - - - - - - - - - - - - | 2  3 |  |
| With L hand on floor diagonally Bk. L, extend R arm upward - - - - - - - - - - - - - - - - - - - - - - - - - - - - - - - - | 4 | 1 |
| Reach straight upward L with L arm - - - - - - - - - - - - - - | 1 |  |
| Drop clasped hands behind head - - - - - - - - - - - - - - - - - | 2 |  |
| Extend arms Sd. and Dn. to floor - - - - - - - - - - - - - - - - - | 3  4 | 1 |
| Repeat all 3 X alternating Sd. - - - - - - - - - - - - - - - - - - - - - |  | 36 |
| B Unit II - - total - - |  | 48 |
| Section B    total - - |  | 80 |

Transition:

|  | cts. | meas. |
|---|---|---|
| St. L pretzel position (R leg bent front L leg bent Bk.), arms Sd. fingers touching floor, palms Fd. |  |  |
| Swing arms Fd. up over head with hands clasped, lifting body to knees - - - - - - - - - - - - - - - - - - - - | 1 |  |
| Drop hands behind head - - - - - - - - - - - - - - - - - - - - - - - - | 2 |  |
| Open arms Sd. and sit - - - - - - - - - - - - - - - - - - - - - - - - - - | 3 |  |
| Hold - - - - - - - - - - - - - - - - - - - - - - - - - - - - - - - - - - - - - - - - - - - | 4 | 1 |
| Repeat lift movement to knees - - - - - - - - - - - - - - - - - - - | 1  2 |  |
| Fall Fd. prone, hands breaking fall, knees in stride on floor, feet together and up close to hips - - - - - - - - - - - - - - - - - - - - - - - - - - - - - - - - - - - - - - - - - - - | 3 |  |
| Hold - - - - - - - - - - - - - - - - - - - - - - - - - - - - - - - - - - - - - - - - - - - | 4 | 1 |

|  | cts. | meas. |
|---|---|---|

Roll body 1/2 turn R to sit on L hip, facing in opposite direction, L leg bent front sole of L foot on floor, R leg bent Bk., Wt. supported on L hand close to L hip - - - - - - - - - - - - - - - - - - - - - - - - - - - `1 2`

Lift to kneel on R knee, L foot taking Wt. front, R arm reaching upward, L arm Bk. low to L - - - - - - - - - - - - - - - - - - - - - - - - - - - - - - - - - - `3`

Hold - - - - - - - - - - - - - - - - - - - - - - - - - - - - - - - - - `4`          1

Flex body Fd. with R elbow bent in front of body and close to chest, L knee bent, R knee straight, Wt. on both feet - - - - - - - - - - - - - - - - - - - - - `1`

Hold - - - - - - - - - - - - - - - - - - - - - - - - - - - - - - - - - `2`

Extend R arm Fd. body reaching Fd. lifting R leg extended Bk. (forming long straight line from R hand through R foot) - - - - - - - - - - - - - - - - - - `3`

Hold - - - - - - - - - - - - - - - - - - - - - - - - - - - - - - - - - `4`          1

Step Bk. R carrying the movement into 1/2 turn R (pivoting on ball of R foot ending with heels together, toes, and knees turned out, now facing in original direction) dropping clasped hands behind head - - - - - - - - - - - - - - - - - - - - - - - - `1 2`

Open arms to Sd. - - - - - - - - - - - - - - - - - - - - - - - - - - - `3`

Hold - - - - - - - - - - - - - - - - - - - - - - - - - - - - - - - - - `4`          1

Transition   total - -   5

## Section C

### Unit I

Stand tall, heels together, toes and knees turned out, arms slightly out from Sd.

Plie' (keeping hips turned out bend knees as far as possible with heels on floor) - - - - - - - - - - - - - - - - - - `1 2`

Straighten knees - - - - - - - - - - - - - - - - - - - - - - - - - - - - `3 4`          1

Releve' (hips turned out, lift body as high as possible, Wt. on balls of feet, heels off the floor, heels pushing Fd.) - - - - - - - - - - - - - - - - - - - - - - `1 2`

Lower to heels - - - - - - - - - - - - - - - - - - - - - - - - - - - - `3 4`          1

Repeat all - - - - - - - - - - - - - - - - - - - - - - - - - - - - - - - - - - - - - - - - - -          2

Plie' - - - - - - - - - - - - - - - - - - - - - - - - - - - - - - - - - - `1`

Straighten knees - - - - - - - - - - - - - - - - - - - - - - - - - - - `2`

|  | cts. | meas. |
|---|---|---|
| Releve' - - - - - - - - - - - - - - - - - - - - - - - - - - - - - - - - - - - - - - - - - - - - | 3 |  |
| Lower to heels - - - - - - - - - - - - - - - - - - - - - - - - - - - - - - - - - | 4 | 1 |
| Repeat last meas. - - - - - - - - - - - - - - - - - - - - - - - - - - - - - - - - - - - - - - - - |  | 1 |
| Plie' - - - - - - - - - - - - - - - - - - - - - - - - - - - - - - - - - - - - - - - | 1 |  |
| Releve' - - - - - - - - - - - - - - - - - - - - - - - - - - - - - - - - - - - - - - - | 2 |  |
| Plie' - - - - - - - - - - - - - - - - - - - - - - - - - - - - - - - - - - - - - - - | 3 |  |
| Releve' - - - - - - - - - - - - - - - - - - - - - - - - - - - - - - - - - - - - - - - | 4 | 1 |

Combine plie's and releve's into aerial jumps as follows:

|  | cts. | meas. |
|---|---|---|
| Plie' quickly - - - - - - - - - - - - - - - - - - - - - - - - - - - - - - - | & |  |
| Jump, extending legs and feet - - - - - - - - - - - - - - - - | 1 |  |
| Land in plie' - - - - - - - - - - - - - - - - - - - - - - - - - - - - - - - | & |  |

Repeat jump-land 3 X ending in a medium stride, with knees bent, feet turned outward, heels on floor - - - - - - - - - - - - - - - - - - - - - - - - - - - - - 2 & 3 & 4 &      1

C Unit I - - total - -    $\dfrac{1}{8}$

## Unit II

|  | cts. | meas. |
|---|---|---|
| Straighten knees slowly - - - - - - - - - - - - - - - - - - - - - - - | 1  2  3  4 | 1 |
| Releve' - - - - - - - - - - - - - - - - - - - - - - - - - - - - - - - - - - - - - - | 1  2 |  |
| Lower to heels - - - - - - - - - - - - - - - - - - - - - - - - - - - - - - - - - | 3  4 | 1 |
| Plie' - - - - - - - - - - - - - - - - - - - - - - - - - - - - - - - - - - - - - - - | 1  2 |  |
| Straighten knees - - - - - - - - - - - - - - - - - - - - - - - - - - - - - - - | 3  4 | 1 |
| Releve' - - - - - - - - - - - - - - - - - - - - - - - - - - - - - - - - - - - - - - | 1  2 |  |
| Lower to heels - - - - - - - - - - - - - - - - - - - - - - - - - - - - - - - - - | 3  4 | 1 |
| Plie' - - - - - - - - - - - - - - - - - - - - - - - - - - - - - - - - - - - - - - - | 1 |  |
| Straighten knees - - - - - - - - - - - - - - - - - - - - - - - - - - - - - - - | 2 |  |
| Releve' - - - - - - - - - - - - - - - - - - - - - - - - - - - - - - - - - - - - - - | 3 |  |
| Lower to heels - - - - - - - - - - - - - - - - - - - - - - - - - - - - - - - - - | 4 | 1 |
| Repeat last meas. - - - - - - - - - - - - - - - - - - - - - - - - - - - - - - - - - - - - - |  | 1 |
| Plie' - - - - - - - - - - - - - - - - - - - - - - - - - - - - - - - - - - - - - - - | 1 |  |
| Releve' - - - - - - - - - - - - - - - - - - - - - - - - - - - - - - - - - - - - - - | 2 |  |
| Plie' - - - - - - - - - - - - - - - - - - - - - - - - - - - - - - - - - - - - - - - | 3 |  |
| Releve' - - - - - - - - - - - - - - - - - - - - - - - - - - - - - - - - - - - - - - | 4 | 1 |

|                                                                                      | cts.              | meas.        |
|--------------------------------------------------------------------------------------|-------------------|--------------|
| Combine pliés and relevés into aerial jumps as follows:                              |                   |              |
|   Plié quickly - - - - - - - - - - - - - - - - - - - - - - - - - - - -               | &                 |              |
|   Jump, extending legs and feet  - - - - - - - - - - - - - - -                       | 1                 |              |
|   Land in stride-plié - - - - - - - - - - - - - - - - - - - - - - - - -              | &                 |              |
| Repeat jump-stride land 3 X - - - - - - - - - - - - - - - - - -                      | 2 & 3 & 4 &       | 1            |
|                                                                                      | C Unit II - - total - - | 8      |

## Unit III

|                                                                                      | cts.       | meas. |
|--------------------------------------------------------------------------------------|------------|-------|
| Rotate body 1/4 turn R - - - - - - - - - - - - - - - - - - - - - -                   | 1          |       |
| Bend R knee  - - - - - - - - - - - - - - - - - - - - - - - - - - - -                 | 2          |       |
| Rotate body 1/4 turn L with both knees bent equalizing Wt. between both feet - - - - - - - - - - - - - - - - | 3 | |
| Straighten knees - - - - - - - - - - - - - - - - - - - - - - - - - - -               | 4          | 1     |
| Repeat all to opposite Sd. - - - - - - - - - - - - - - - - - - - -                   | 1 2 3 4    | 1     |
| Rotate body 1/4 turn R bending R knee - - - - - - - - - - -                          | 1          |       |
| With slight rebound, rotate body 1/4 turn L with both knees bent, equalizing Wt. between both feet - - - - - - - - - - - - - - - - - - - - - - - - - - - - - - | 2 | |
| Repeat rotation 1/4 turn L  - - - - - - - - - - - - - - - - - - -                    | 3 4        | 1     |
| Repeat last meas. keeping movement alive with strong, but controlled rebounds - - - - - - - - - - - - - - - - - - | 1 2 3 4 | 1 |
| Straighten knees - - - - - - - - - - - - - - - - - - - - - - - - - - -               | 1 2        |       |
| Rotate body 1/4 turn R - - - - - - - - - - - - - - - - - - - - - -                   | 3          |       |
| Lift L arm up over head - - - - - - - - - - - - - - - - - - - - - -                  | 4          | 1     |
| Lifting body high, bob laterally R 4 X  - - - - - - - - - - - -                      | 1 2 3 4    | 1     |
| Drop L hand behind head flexing R knee - - - - - - - - - - -                         | &          |       |
| Push L hand across in front of body to R rotating body 1/4 turn R - - - - - - - - - - - - - - - - - - - - - | 1 | |
| Rotate body 1/4 turn L, knees bent equalizing Wt. between feet, arms extended front, heels of hands pushing Fd. - - - - - - - - - - - - - - - - - - - - - - - - | 2 | |
| L leg in plié, R leg straight, swing arms to L and clasp hands - - - - - - - - - - - - - - - - - - - - - - - - - - - - - - - - - | 3 | |
| Straighten legs as clasped hands swing up over head and body rotates 1/4 turn R - - - - - - - - - - - - - - - - | 4 | 1 |

|  | cts. | meas. |
|---|---|---|
| Repeat last meas. - - - - - - - - - - - - - - - - - - - - - - - - - - - | 1 2 3 4 | 1 |
| Drop clasped hands behind head - - - - - - - - - - - - - - - - - | & | |
| Lower arms to Sd. - - - - - - - - - - - - - - - - - - - - - - - - - | 1 | |
| Lift L arm up over head - - - - - - - - - - - - - - - - - - - - - | 2 | |
| Lifting body high, bob laterally 2 X - - - - - - - - - - - - - - | 3 4 | 1 |
| Drop L hand behind head flexing R knee - - - - - - - - - - | & | |
| Push L hand across in front of body to R, rotating body 1/4 turn R - - - - - - - - - - - - - - - - - - - - - - - | 1 | |
| Rotate body 1/4 turn L, knees bent equalizing Wt. between feet, arms extended front, heels of hands pushing Fd. - - - - - - - - - - - - - - - - - - - - - - - - - | 2 | |
| L leg in plié, R leg straight, swing arms to L and clasp hands - - - - - - - - - - - - - - - - - - - - - - - - - - - - - - | 3 | |
| Straighten legs as clasped hands swing up over head and body rotates 1/4 turn R - - - - - - - - - - - - - - - - - | 4 | 1 |
| Repeat last meas. - - - - - - - - - - - - - - - - - - - - - - - - - - - | 1 2 3 4 | 1 |
| Walk, L R L, in wide semi-circle L, L arm leading the movement - - - - - - - - - - - - - - - - - - - - - - - - | 1 2 3 | |
| Step R in medium stride, arms Sd., now facing in opposite direction - - - - - - - - - - - - - - - - - - - - - - - - | 4 | 1 |
| Repeat last 12 meas. beginning rotation L - - - - - - - - - - - - - - - - - - - - - - - - - | | 12 |
| | C Unit III - - total - - | 24 |
| | Section C    total | 40 |

## CONTRACTIONS AND RELEASES

It has been said that the real "stuff" of the dance begins and ends with contractions and releases. Certainly a gathering together of inner tensions and concentration on controlled movement happens before movement which we term dance can begin. Contractions are complex in nature and should be experienced only after the teacher has made known exactly what is happening in the body. As in falls, if not taught with care and precaution, the body may be injured.

Contraction alters the normal alignment of the body — lying, sitting or standing. The initial action starts in the pelvis. The hips are tucked under, the abdomen is flattened, the spine is rounded, and the shoulders come forward. The chest and abdomen form a concave line. Release position brings the body back into normal alignment. Controlled power is a characteristic of both contractions and releases.

In teaching contractions and releases, care must be taken to stress the constant lift of the torso and the controlled execution of movement.

Contractions and releases are important movements to the dancer. They most closely relate to deep breathing movements. Breath is life giving — the rise and fall of the chest occurs with rhythmic certainty. In body contractions the body mass is affected profoundly. The line is distorted so that the visual impact is dramatically disquieting. When the action center or life area is involved, response is compelling and arresting. It is hard to imagine how any deep emotional experience could be expressed without the use of contractions and releases. As man becomes more and more aware of life and its complexities, the search for new ways of moving to express these truths continues. The dancer is limited only by the confines of his physical body and his creative imagination. Any way he can use his body as an expressive instrument is open to exploration.

1. **Contractions and Releases Lying Down**
   A. Start lying on the back. Tense only the lower abdomen so that the natural curve of the back rests against the floor. The knees will bend, shoulders come forward and the head fall back. This is the basic pelvic contraction and should be learned before other more complicated movement contractions and combinations are attempted. Release the tensions and return to the long stretch position. Do these in slow, sustained movement phrases first.

| Slow 4/4 meter | cts. | meas. |
|---|---|---|
| Contract in sustained - - - - - - - - - - - - - - - - - - - - - - - | 1 2 3 4 | 1 |
| Release out sustained - - - - - - - - - - - - - - - - - - - - - - | 1 2 3 4 | 1 |
| Contract percussively in - - - - - - - - - - - - - - - - - - - | 1 | |
| Hold - - - - - - - - - - - - - - - - - - - - - - - - - - - - - - - - - - - | 2 3 4 | 1 |
| Release percussively out - - - - - - - - - - - - - - - - - - | 1 | |
| Hold - - - - - - - - - - - - - - - - - - - - - - - - - - - - - - - - - - - | 2 3 4 | 1 |
| Contract percussively - - - - - - - - - - - - - - - - - - - - | 1 | |
| Release sustained - - - - - - - - - - - - - - - - - - - - - - - - | 2 3 4 | 1 |
| Contract sustained - - - - - - - - - - - - - - - - - - - - - - - | 1 2 3 | |
| Release percussively - - - - - - - - - - - - - - - - - - - - - | 4 | 1 |
| Tie altogether for dance phrase - - - - - - - - - - - - - - - - - - - - - - - - - | total - - | 6 |

   B. St. lying on Bk.

| | cts. | meas. |
|---|---|---|
| Contract emphasizing pull into L hip. Only come up 2 or 3 inches. Focus L with palms up, wrists close to hips - - - - - - - - - - - - - - - - - - - | 1 2 | |
| Release and lie Dn. centered - - - - - - - - - - - - - - - - | 3 4 | 1 |
| Repeat contracting hard and lifting about 6 inches - - - - - - - - - - - - - - - - - - - - - - - - - - - - - - | 1 2 | |
| Release - - - - - - - - - - - - - - - - - - - - - - - - - - - - - - - - - | 3 4 | 1 |
| Repeat contracting almost to sit - - - - - - - - - - - - - - - | 1 2 | |
| Release - - - - - - - - - - - - - - - - - - - - - - - - - - - - - - - - - | 3 4 | 1 |
| Contract to high as possible still holding onto contraction in L hip - - - - - - - - - - - - - - - - - | 1 2 | |

|                                                                                   | cts. | meas. |
|-----------------------------------------------------------------------------------|------|-------|
| Release - - - - - - - - - - - - - - - - - - - - - - - - - - - - - - - - - - -     | 3 4  | 1     |
| Repeat entire build-up contracting on R hip - - - - - - - - - - - - - - - - - - - |      | 4     |
| total - -                                                                         |      | 8     |

## 2. Contractions and Releases Sitting

A. Sit with the soles of the feet together, knees bent. Try contractions and releases in this position.

B. Sit with the knees straight. Extend the feet with the legs together. Hold the chest high with the fingertips touching knees. Contract suddenly, flexing the feet. Lift the focus up, turn palms up and hold three counts. Release slowly to a high sit in four counts.

C. 4/4 meter

|                                                                                                                 | cts.      | meas. |
|-----------------------------------------------------------------------------------------------------------------|-----------|-------|
| Sit with legs in wide stride, arms shoulder level at Sd., palms Dn. Contract suddenly, flexing ankles, focus up, palms turned up - - - - - - - - - | >1 2 3 4  | 1     |
| Release slowly  - - - - - - - - - - - - - - - - - - - - - - - - - - -                                           | 1 2 3 4   | 1     |
| Contract suddenly into R hip, twisting upper body L, focus up and L.- - - - - - - - - - - - - -                 | >1 2 3 4  | 1     |
| Release slowly  - - - - - - - - - - - - - - - - - - - - - - - - - - -                                           | 1 2 3 4   | 1     |
| Contract into L hip  - - - - - - - - - - - - - - - - - - - - - -                                                | >1 2 3 4  | 1     |
| Release - - - - - - - - - - - - - - - - - - - - - - - - - - - - - -                                             | 1 2 3 4   | 1     |
| total - -                                                                                                       |           | 6     |

D. St. sit on R hip with both feet tucked to L. Knees are about 18 inches apart, L hip is off the floor. Arms held at Sd. with fingers touching floor by hips. Contract into the L hip so that the Wt. is on both hips, lower focus L - - - - - - - - - - - - - - - - - - - - - - - - - - - - -   1 2 3 4   1

Release with a strong lift of head and chest - - - - - -   1 2 3 4   1

Repeat contract and release  - - - - - - - - - - - - - - - - - - - - - - - - - - - - - -   2

Let R arm come low across to join L hand as repeat contraction into L hip - - - - - - - - - - - - - - -   1 2 3 4   1

Strong release as R hand lifts and circles up and out to R, then returns to Sd. on last ct. - - - - - -   1 2 3 4   1

Repeat with R arm movement  - - - - - - - - - - - - - - - - - - - - - - - - - - - - - -   2

Bring L arm up to join R hand at shoulder level, focus to R as take the contraction into L hip - - - - - - - - - - - - - - - - - - - - - - - - - - - - -   1 2 3 4   1

|  | cts. | meas. |
|---|---|---|
| Release and circle L hand up around and lower both hands to original position - - - - - - - - - - - - | 1 2 3 4 | 1 |
| Repeat L arm movement  - - - - - - - - - - - - - - - - - - - - - - - - - - - - - - - - - - - - - - - - | | 2 |
| total - - | | 12 |

Transition:

|  | cts. | meas. |
|---|---|---|
| Contract into L hip, gradually bringing knees up to chest and circling arms around knees, head Dn. in tucked position- - - - - - - - - - - - - - - | 1 2 3 4 | 1 |
| Release lowering knees to L, chest and focus lifting, arms at Sd., Wt. on L hip - - - - - - - - - - - - - - - - | 1 2 3 4 | 1 |
| total - - | | 2 |

Repeat entire sequence on the other side.

3. **Contractions and Releases Standing**

4/4 meter

| | cts. | meas. |
|---|---|---|
| Stand in small stride with arms Dn. by Sd. Contract letting knees bend, focus low, elbows rotate out  - - - - - - - - - - - - - - - - - - - - - - - - - - - - - - - - - - - | 1 2 3 4 | 1 |
| Release straightening body - - - - - - - - - - - - - - - - - - - - - - - | 1 2 3 4 | 1 |
| Contract into R hip - - - - - - - - - - - - - - - - - - - - - - - - - - | 1 2 3 4 | 1 |
| Release  - - - - - - - - - - - - - - - - - - - - - - - - - - - - - - - - - | 1 2 3 4 | 1 |
| Contract into L hip - - - - - - - - - - - - - - - - - - - - - - - - - - | 1 2 3 4 | 1 |
| Release  - - - - - - - - - - - - - - - - - - - - - - - - - - - - - - - - - | 1 2 3 4 | 1 |
| Contract into R hip turning L, deepening movement to twist 1/2 turn L with R arm crossing low to clasp L hand - - - - - - - - - - - - - - - - - - - - - - - - - - | 1 2 3 4 | 1 |
| Release and unwind to open arms high over head and return to original position - - - - - - - - - - - - - - - - | 1 2 3 4 | 1 |
| total - - | | 8 |

4. **Contractions and Releases Moving**

| | cts. | meas. |
|---|---|---|
| A. Contract as take 4 steps Bk. - - - - - - - - - - - - - - - - - - - | 1 2 3 4 | 1 |
| Release as take 4 steps Fd. - - - - - - - - - - - - - - - - - - - | 1 2 3 4 | 1 |
| Contract as take 2 steps Bk. - - - - - - - - - - - - - - - - - - - | 1 2 | |
| Release as take 2 steps Fd. - - - - - - - - - - - - - - - - - - - | 3 4 | 1 |
| Contract stepping Bk. - - - - - - - - - - - - - - - - - - - - - - | 1 | |
| Release stepping Fd. - - - - - - - - - - - - - - - - - - - - - - - | 2 | |

|                                                                    | cts. | meas. |
|--------------------------------------------------------------------|------|-------|
| Repeat stepping Bk. and Fd. - - - - - - - - - - - - - - - - - - -  | 3 4  | 1     |
|                                                           total - - |      | 4     |

B. Walk across the floor slowly contracting on four counts, then slowly releasing on four counts.

C. Run quickly forward six runs. Contract suddenly to stop the forward movement. Release quickly to run forward again, and so on across the floor.

5. **Creative Clues**
   A. Standing, contract into one shoulder and let the movement push the body backward into a turn.
   B. Contract into one hip to twist the body into the floor. Let the release bring the dancer lifting back to the starting position.
   C. From a kneeling position experiment contracting to sit on one hip; to tuck into a small ball and release to a high kneel; to effect a controlled fall to the floor.

## FALLS AND RECOVERIES

Falling is not just an act, it is a dramatic process controlled in harmonious form. The starting point may begin from a standing, kneeling or sitting position. The downward descent may be gradual or sudden and may end in a prone, supine or side position. The chosen impetus affects the dramatic quality of the fall. For instance, a slow lowering of level may suggest a feeling of sustained emotion, whereas a sudden falling may inspire a response of vivid excitement. Again, the effect may vary according to the degree of falling – partial or complete.

In order to protect the body from injury, safety precautions must be observed. It is important that the body be as close as possible to the floor before the weight is transferred from the feet to the buttocks, the thigh or the side of the leg. In this way the base of the spine, the elbows and knees will be safeguarded from sudden and forceful contact with the floor. The use of relaxation is another principle of falling. The novice dancer, due to a real fear of moving from a standing to a prone position, may be very tense. By starting with very slow falls and having the body parts relax sequentially (ankles, knees, shoulders, head, arms), the beginner will be able to gain self-confidence in this down-and-up environment.

A fall may be considered a preparation for rising. Thus it is followed by a recovery – incomplete or total. To convey certain dance ideas the fall may be consummated without a recovery. In such cases the dancer, in order to avoid total collapse and to keep the dance from losing form, still maintains a certain amount of muscle tension. Since falls are obvious and dramatic, they must have real purpose in becoming an integral part of a dance study. Whenever and however they are woven into a continuing movement pattern, the intent must be significant.

1. **Lead-up Falls and Recoveries**
   These simple falls may be introduced first for the purpose of "feeling at home" with the sensation of dropping the body to an extremely low level.

   A. 4/4 meter

|                                                         | cts.      | meas. |
|---------------------------------------------------------|-----------|-------|
| Walk upright 8 steps in any chosen direction - - - - - -| 1 2 3 4   |       |
|                                                         | 1 2 3 4   | 2     |

|                                                                                      | cts.                  | meas. |
|--------------------------------------------------------------------------------------|-----------------------|-------|
| Walk 8 steps gradually lowering the body to a complete slump in any manner on the floor - - - - - - - - - - - - - - - - - - - - - - - - - - - - - - - - - - - - - - - | 1 2 3 4 <br> 1 2 3 4 |  <br> 2 |
| Recover to stand upright in any desired fashion 8 cts.- - - - - - - - - - - - - - - - - - - - - - - - - - - - - - - - - | 1 2 3 4 <br> 1 2 3 4 |  <br> 2 |
| Walk Fd. 8 cts. - - - - - - - - - - - - - - - - - - - - - - - - - - - - - | 1 2 3 4 <br> 1 2 3 4 |  <br> 2 |
|                                                                                      |            total - -  | 8 |

Repeat walking and falling using a sequence of 6, 4, 2, 1 counts for each part respectively. Try starting individuals at different time intervals.

B. Drum and Gong

| 4/4 meter      With Partners                                                          | cts.     | meas. |
|--------------------------------------------------------------------------------------|----------|-------|
| To drum beats partners walk 4 steps toward each other - - - - - - - - - - - - - - - - - - - - - - - - - - - - - - - | 1 2 3 4  | 1 |
| To a sudden sound of a gong fall away from each other to the floor - - - - - - - - - - - - - - - - - - - - | 1        |   |
| Hold - - - - - - - - - - - - - - - - - - - - - - - - - - - - - - - - - - | 2 3 4    | 1 |
| Recover in any manner to 8 slow drum beats - - - - - - - - - - - - - - - - - - - - - - - - - - - - - - - | 1 2 3 4 <br> 1 2 3 4 |  <br> 2 |
|                                                                                      | total - - | 4 |

C. Lower the body to a kneeling position. Shift the weight to one hip and let the body slide sideward in the corresponding direction along the floor. Recover in any chosen manner.

D. Start in a stride position toeing out with the heels on the floor. Lower the body to a deep squat, sit down on the floor, and fall sideward or backward. Recover slowly in any fashion.

E. 6/8 meter

|                                                                                      | cts.   | meas. |
|--------------------------------------------------------------------------------------|--------|-------|
| Stand with weight on L foot, hands pushing Dn. close to sides of body. Swing R leg Fd. as torso tucks low close to free leg - - - - - - - - - - - - - | 1 2 3  |   |
| Hands contact the floor first to break the impact as the body lowers to sitting position with the supporting L leg remaining bent and R leg extended Fd. on the floor - - - - - - - - - - - - - | 4 5 6  | 1 |

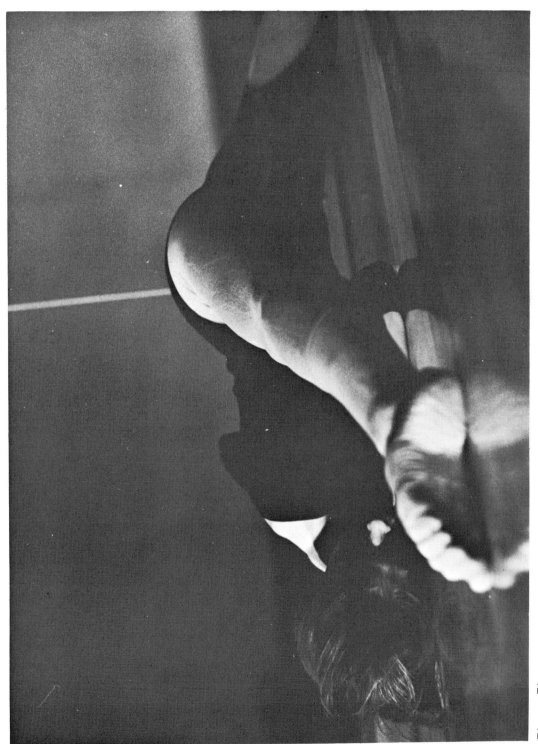

Figure Eleven

| | cts. | meas. |
|---|---|---|

To recover, push off with both hands pro-
pelling the tucked body Fd. to step L and R
into original upright position - - - - - - - - - - - - - - - - -    1 2 3
4 5 6                              1

total - -      2

Repeat on the opposite side. For a variation repeat with a preliminary step-hop
lifting the body.

2. **Backward Fall and Recoveries**

   A. Backward Fall

| 4/4 meter | cts. | meas. |
|---|---|---|
| St. Wt. L. Tuck torso Fd. bending R knee Bk. to maintain Wt. Fd. on L foot - - - - - - - - - - - - - - | 1 | |
| Lower to kneeling position on R knee (foot extended with toes uncurled to avoid injury) with palms of hands on floor - - - - - - - - - - - - - | 2 | |
| Using R knee as a pivot, turn R foreleg inward toward L, sit Bk. on R hip as hands slide Bk. along floor at sides - - - - - - - - - - - - - - - - - - | 3 | |
| Lower body to back-lying position as R leg remains bent under L leg with L leg extended Fd. on floor - - - - - - - - - - - - - - - - - - - - - - - | 4 | 1 |
| Repeat on opposite side - - - - - - - - - - - - - - - - - - - - - - - - - - - - - - - - - - - - - | | 1 |

total - -      2

   B. Recoveries
   1) Roll-over
      Without using the hands as a continuing support, flex both knees to the chest
      as the body tucks forward rolling onto the right side and over into a kneeling
      position to face the opposite direction. Step forward left and right to an
      upright position.
   2) Push-forward
      Contract the abdominal muscles, give one push-off from the floor with both
      hands, tuck the torso throwing the weight forward as the arms shoot forward
      strongly beyond the body. The forward momentum brings the weight onto the
      right knee. Step forward left and right to an upright position.
   3) Kick-down
      Raise the extended left leg to a vertical position. Kick down vigorously tucking
      and propelling the body forward to step left as the weight rolls onto the right
      bent knee. Step forward right to an upright position.

   C. Sample Variations of Backward Falls
   1) Increase the initial elevation with a preliminary swing of the arms while
      jumping upward, landing with the weight on the left foot to continue the
      backward fall described above.

2) 4/4 meter                                                  cts.        meas.

St. in stride stance. Sustain a lowering of
the body to a deep knee bend - - - - - - - - - - - - - -      1 2 3 4        1

At the lowest level do 1/4 turn L to sit
with arms extended Fd. - - - - - - - - - - - - - - - - - -    1 2

Reach upward and Bk. with R arm, slide
R hand along floor as body extends Bk.
into a slow fall - - - - - - - - - - - - - - - - - - - - - - -  3 4           1

Recover with a "roll-over" - - - - - - - - - - - - - - - -    1 2 3 4
                                                              1 2 3 4         2
                                                       total - -             4

3) 4/4 meter

St. in Fd. stride with L leg leading.
Thrust hips Fd. (See "Percussive Hip
Whip" page 134) - - - - - - - - - - - - - - - - - - - - - -    1

Raise R arm Fd.-Up-Bk. lowering body
slowly to R knee turning it to L under
body while pushing R hand Bk. along
floor to slide into a backward fall - - - - - - - - - - - -    2 3 4          1

Recover in an improvised manner - - - - - - - - - - -         1 2 3 4        1
                                                       total - -             2

4) 4/4 meter

St. in upright stance. Thrust hips Fd.
keeping body in a straight line from
knees to head - - - - - - - - - - - - - - - - - - - - - - - -  1

Sustain this position to a low level Bk.
until upper back and shoulders contact
floor - - - - - - - - - - - - - - - - - - - - - - - - - - - - -  2 3 4        1

Push Bk. to full extension along floor - - - - - - - - -      1 2 3 4        1

Recover by rolling over facing Dn.,
placing hands on floor at sides of body - - - - - - -         1 2

Bend L leg Bk. over body to step L as
body continues to roll over 1/2 turn L to
face upward with Wt. supported on R
hand and R foot - - - - - - - - - - - - - - - - - - - - - -    3 4            1

With back toward floor, place Wt. on L
foot, push off with R hand, propel Wt.
Fd. over L foot and step R to upright
position - - - - - - - - - - - - - - - - - - - - - - - - - - -  1 2 3 4       1
                                                       total - -             4

3. **Sideward Fall and Recovery**

   A. 6/8 meter                                                         cts.        meas.

   St. with Wt. on L foot. Tuck torso Fd. while
   bending R knee and maintaining Wt. on Fd.
   L foot - - - - - - - - - - - - - - - - - - - - - - - - - - - - - - - - - - - - -     1

   Lower to kneeling on R knee with R foot
   extended and toes uncurled - - - - - - - - - - - - - - - - - -     2  3

   Shift Wt. to R hip reaching to R Sd. with
   both hands as they slide with the body to
   stretch Sd. along the floor - - - - - - - - - - - - - - - - - -     4  5  6              1

   To recover, arch the R Sd. of torso, pulling
   body toward L while swinging arms to L
   with Wt. moving onto R knee and L foot - - - - - - - - -     1  2  3

   Swing arms toward R Sd. and step R and L
   into upright position - - - - - - - - - - - - - - - - - - - - - -     4  5  6              1

   Repeat fall and recover to opposite side - - - - - - - - - - - - - - - - - - - - - -                2

                                                                       total - -             4

   B. Sample Variations of Sideward Falls
      1) Swing both arms Sd. L and fall Sd. to R. Recover as indicated for "sideward
         fall." Repeat with a preliminary hop on the supporting foot.
      2) 6/8 meter

         Repeat "1" to 6/8 meter increasing the
         number of preliminary arms swings.
         Swing arms to L - - - - - - - - - - - - - - - - - - - - - - - -     1  2  3

         Swing arms to R - - - - - - - - - - - - - - - - - - - - - - - -     4  5  6              1

         Swing arms to L - - - - - - - - - - - - - - - - - - - - - - - -     1  2  3

         Fall suddenly Sd. R - - - - - - - - - - - - - - - - - - - - -     4

         Hold - - - - - - - - - - - - - - - - - - - - - - - - - - - - - - -     5  6              1

         Recover with a "roll-over" - - - - - - - - - - - - - - - - - - - - - - - - - - - -                1

         Repeat all on the opposite side - - - - - - - - - - - - - - - - - - - - - - - - - -                3

                                                                       total - -             6

      3) 6/8 meter

         Progress Sd. R with 2 slides arms ex-
         tended Sd. shoulder level - - - - - - - - - - - - - - - - -     1  2  3
                                                                       4  5  6              1

         Step-hop R lifting body to full extension
         upward - - - - - - - - - - - - - - - - - - - - - - - - - - - - -     1  2  3

         Fall Sd. L - - - - - - - - - - - - - - - - - - - - - - - - - - -     4  5  6              1

         Recover with a "roll-over" - - - - - - - - - - - - - - - - - - - - - - - - - - - -                1

                                                                       total - -             3

| | cts. | meas. |
|---|---|---|

4) 2/4 meter

St. with R arm extended Sd. R, palm
Dn. and focus to the R. Step R across
in front of L as R arm swings sharply
Dn., up and around to R. Body leans
far R - - - - - - - - - - - - - - - - - - - - - - - - - - - - - - - - - -    1

Fall to the L - - - - - - - - - - - - - - - - - - - - - - - - - -    2

Recover with a "roll-over" in 2 cts. - - - - - - - - - - - - - - - - - - - - - -             1

total - -    2

5) 6/8 meter

Step L across in front of R swinging
arms diagonally upward L and stretching
R leg out Sd. horizontally as body bends
Sd. L - - - - - - - - - - - - - - - - - - - - - - - - - - - - - -    1 2 3

Fall to the R by bending R leg behind L
along the floor toward the L Sd. lowering the body until R thigh and hip take
the Wt., gradually stretching the body
along the floor to the R - - - - - - - - - - - - - - - - - -    4 5 6             1

Recover as desired - - - - - - - - - - - - - - - - - - - - - - - - - - - - - - - - -             1

Repeat on the opposite side - - - - - - - - - - - - - - - - - - - - - - - - - - -             2

total - -    4

## 4. Forward Fall and Recovery

### A. Forward Fall      4/4 meter

St. Wt. on L foot. Bend body to a Fd.
horizontal position extending R leg Bk.,
arms reaching toward floor, palms Dn. - - - - - - - - - - -    1

Bend L knee lowering body to take Wt. on
both hands placed at Sds. and close to hips - - - - - - -    2

Bend elbows and kick L leg Bk. beside R to
land on toes (curled) of L and R foot - - - - - - - - - - -    3

Fall prone keeping body in a straight line - - - - - - - - -    4             1

### B. Recovery

Straighten arms, bend R knee and step Fd. tucking torso. Step L coming to
upright position.

### C. Sample Variations of Forward Falls and Recoveries

1) 4/4 meter

Lower body to kneeling position - - - - - - - - - - - - -    1 2 3 4             1

|  | cts. | meas. |
|---|---|---|
| Reach far Fd. along floor with R hand as L leg stretches Bk. - - - - - - - - - - - - - - - - - - - - - - - - | 1 2 3 4 | 1 |
| Slide L hand Fd. along floor and slowly stretch body Fd. into prone position - - - - - - - - - - | 1 2 3 4 | 1 |
| Recover by suddenly contracting body into kneeling position - - - - - - - - - - - - - - - - - - - - | 1 | |
| Hold - - - - - - - - - - - - - - - - - - - - - - - - - - - - - - - - - | 2 3 4 | 1 |
| | total - - | 4 |

2) Step-hop left forward bending right and raising left arm upward. Lower the body to a half kneel position on right knee while continuing the momentum forward as in the latter part of "1" above.

5. **Roll Fall and Recovery**
This type of fall may start from various levels. Due to the momentum involved, it includes a built-in recovery. Therefore, it is unnecessary to list recoveries separately.
A. Roll Fall and Recovery
   Lower body to half kneel position on the right knee with the left foot diagonally forward on the floor, knee bent, and the body tucked forward. Swing the right arm low across in front bending the body sideward to take the weight on the right hip. Roll toward the right shifting the weight successively onto the right shoulder, back, left shoulder, and hip to end in original half kneel position facing in the original direction with the legs in reversed starting position.
   To give the necessary momentum to the roll, the left leg bends toward the chest and is followed by a sudden kick upward of the right leg.
B. Sample Variations
   1) Repeat a roll fall from a sitting position. Sit on the right hip with both legs bent, right leg close to the body on the floor. Sole of left foot flat on the floor in front of the right foot. Roll on upper back toward the right end with legs in reverse position now facing the original direction. Try in half kneel position.
   2) Repeat the roll fall from a standing position. Weight on left foot, tuck the body forward to the lowest possible bend, sliding the free right foot across and behind the supporting left foot. Otherwise the technique is identical with that of the roll fall described initially. The roll must maintain sufficient dynamic momentum to lift the body into a final upright standing position.
   3) Repeat "2" above ending in a downward position. At the completion of the roll, finalize the movement in a left pretzel position (left leg bent in front, right leg bent in back) with the forehead touching the floor in front and the arms stretching sideward with the palms flat on the floor.
   4) Repeat "3" in variation. Stand with the weight on the right foot. Swing the left leg forward, backward, and forward, step forward left. Do a right roll fall to end in a stride sitting position. Shift to a right pretzel. Do a left roll fall to end in a half kneel position, weight on the right knee. Repeat a right roll fall to end in an upright position stepping right and then left.

6. **Creative Clues**
   A. Whirl in a spiral pathway using the center of the axis as a fixed point of focus. Repeat whirling in a spiral with the periphery as the given focal point. Suspend the body in full elevation and do a slow sustained fall. Improvise a recovery.
   B. From a hyperextended position, twirl in place — corkscrew fashion — gradually lowering the body. At the greatest speed, arrest the momentum. Create a sideward fall bringing the body into full extension on the floor.
   C. Run through a given distance. Stop suddenly and fall sharply backward, sideward, or in opposition to the running line of direction.
   D. Run through a given distance. Twist the body one-half turn and fall with one arm extended toward the moving line of direction.
   E. Sequential Falls
      1) Form a circle facing inward. Number in clockwise succession a group of from 6 to 16 dancers. Each one in sequence contracts torso, tucking upper body forward with arms held forward and rotated inward and palms facing sideward. Sustain a 4-beat fall backward and outward from the circle.
      2) Repeat "1" as follows: number one tucks and sustains a 4-beat fall. Number two repeats with a 3-beat fall. Number three continues with a 2-beat fall. Number four and all others in succession tuck and fall suddenly in 1-beat falls respectively.
      3) Repeat "1" as follows: sound a given number of beats on one or more drums to coincide with the respective falls. Each dancer should know in advance on what beat he is to fall. To lend variety, scatter the order of falling. For example, number six may go first; numbers one and seven may be second; numbers four, five and nine may be third with the remainder following according to a prearranged plan.
      4) Repeat "1," "2," and "3" above with one-half turn to face outward as body tucks forward. Fall back toward the center of the circle. Have all recover in unison.

## VARIATIONS BUILD FROM QUALITIES OF MOVEMENT

### SWINGING MOVEMENT

Swings are fun to do! Beginners right up through advanced dancers enjoy doing them. The throbbing, pulsing quality is pleasing rhythmically and stimulating physically. Swings should be characterized by power and vigor. Soft and lilting swings quickly nullify and destroy the dynamic drive inherent in swinging movement.

Pendular movement permits the arms and legs to swing freely through various size arcs or circles around a stationary axis. The torso and head may respond in more limited swinging arcs.

Swinging combinations and patterns may be used effectively to illustrate how various movements or parts of dances may be woven together smoothly and tightly. The swing itself with its easily discernible initial impulse and its moment of suspension at completion demonstrates graphically what is expected from transitions and phrasing in movement.

Figure Twelve

2-BEAT SWINGS — 6/8 meter

1. **Arm Swings**
   A. Stand in wide stride with hands crossed low in front of body. Swing arms out sideward and up over head. Return to original position. Stress the power and freedom that is necessary to all swings.
   B. Swing the arms in opposition starting with the right arm forward and left arm sideward left shoulder level. Swing both arms down sideward and out to reverse starting position. Care should be taken to prevent hunching of shoulders. The swings should start from the back with the shoulders pushing down into the back.

2. **Leg Swings**
   A. Start with weight on left foot and right leg extended backward. Swing the right leg forward and backward. Reverse the starting position and swing left forward and backward. A barre may be used for support at first, or partners may work together with one acting as a support.
   B. Three people join hands (or shoulders if easier). Start facing front, weight left and right leg back. Swing forward and back for seven counts. On the eighth count step forward right. Repeat swinging left leg. Try swinging forward and backward for three counts and stepping on count four. Try alone with arms swinging in opposition.
   C. Start with weight on left foot and right leg extended to the side. Swing the right leg across in front of body and out to original position. Hold arms sideward shoulder level for balance. Swing for seven counts and step right across in front of left extending left leg sideward on count eight. Repeat all. Try swinging for three counts and stepping across on count four.

3. **Body Swings**
   Body swings are big, powerful movements requiring a great deal of strength. Do not repeat any of these movements too long.
   A. Perpendicular Plane
      1) Start in small stride with arms reaching high above head. Swing the entire body forward and downward with arms swinging to outside of legs as hands brush the floor. Legs flex and then extend on counts one, two, three. Then swing up to original position on counts four, five, six.
      2) Let the powerful upward movement carry the body high on the toes; off the floor; finally into a high jump with the body hyperextended.
      3) Let the upward swing carry the body forward three steps.
   B. Lateral Plane
      1) Start in wide stride lunging sideward left. Both arms are shoulder level and to the left. Swing far to the right, arms reaching laterally, body twisting right to lunge sideward right. Focus follows hands on counts one, two, three. Repeat to left on counts four, five, six.
      2) After two swings right and left, let the third carry the body into a complete three-step turn right. Repeat two swings left and right and turn left in three-step turn.
   C. Combined Perpendicular and Lateral Swing
      1) Start in side stride with deep lunge to the left with arms over head, body twisted laterally to face forward. Drop arms and body to swing down and across to low right lunge. Body then rotates laterally to face forward. Arms form a frame to the face at the beginning and end of the swing, but drop low and relaxed as body swings across.

2) Swing two times right and left, then let the swing carry the body into a complete three-step turn right. Repeat all. Be sure to keep the body very low on both the swings and the turn.

4.  **Combined Swings in a Building Phrase Pattern**

6/8 meter                                                                    cts.              meas.

St. in medium stride with hands clasped low in
Bk. Sway 4 X, R L R L, allowing 3 cts. for each
sway - - - - - - - - - - - - - - - - - - - - - - - - - - - - - - - - - - - - - - - - - - - - - -             1 2 3
                                                                             4 5 6
                                                                             1 2 3
                                                                             4 5 6                    2

Reaching arms far out, lunge R and swing
laterally 4 X, R L R L - - - - - - - - - - - - - - - - - - - - - - - - -          1 2 3
                                                                             4 5 6
                                                                             1 2 3
                                                                             4 5 6                    2

Drop R arm Dn. in Bk. twisting body far R - - - - - - - - - -           1 2 3

Swing R arm Fd. across in front of body
completing a figure 8 pattern with the arm  - - - - - - - - - -          4 5 6                    1

Repeat figure 8, Bk. and Fd. As the R arm
swings in front of the body on the last swing,
let the arm carry the body into 1/4 turn L - - - - - - - - - - -          1 2 3
                                                                             4 5 6                    1

Swing entire body Fd. and Dn. with arms
swinging outside legs and brushing the floor - - - - - - - - - -         1 2 3

As the body swings up, let the movement carry
the body Fd. 3 quick steps - - - - - - - - - - - - - - - - - - - - - - -          4 5 6                    1

Repeat the big body swing and the runs finish-
ing with feet apart in medium stride  - - - - - - - - - - - - - -          1 2 3
                                                                             4 5 6                    1
                                                                                                   ___
                                                                                                     8

Repeat entire phrase 3 X to complete a square
floor pattern  - - - - - - - - - - - - - - - - - - - - - - - - - - - - - - - - - - - - - - - - - -          24
                                                                                                   ___
                                                                        total - -   32

Vary the pattern by substituting a three-step turn on the last two lateral swings. The three-step turn will be to the right. The left arm will then drop in back of the body to describe the figure eight. The turn at the end of the figure eight will be to the right thus making the square floor pattern to the right instead of to the left.

Divide the group into two parts. One group make the left square omitting the three-step turn on the lateral swing. The second group make a right square by substituting the three-step turn.

Now alternate first a left square, then a right square.

Experiment with different groupings.

Note the build within the phrase and the sense of completion at the end of each phrase of eight measures.

## 3-BEAT SWINGS — 9/8 meter

Unlike the 2-beat swing which stresses counts one and four in 6/8 meter taking two impulses for completion, the 3-beat swing stresses counts one, four and seven in 9/8 meter and takes three impulses for completion. Many 3-beat swings are nothing more than a 2-beat swing plus a push, a lift, or a thrust. They are sometimes more interesting to perform than the monotonous repeating of solid 2-beat swings. Though they may be more difficult, they should flow together with a true swinging quality or they do not deserve the name 3-beat swing.

1. Stand with arms reaching above head. Swing the entire body forward and downward, counts one, two, and three. Swing up to original position on counts four, five, six. Circle both arms from right to left side across in front of body to end in lateral horizontal extension of the body left with right leg extended hip level to the right side, counts seven, eight, nine. Repeat extending to the opposite side.

2. Stand in a wide stride. Swing the entire body forward and downward with arms swinging backward between legs, counts one, two, three. Swing arms forward to slap floor with palms, counts four, five, six. Turn arms out and circle them backward and up over head as hips thrust forward and body unrolls to its original standing position, counts, seven, eight, nine.

3. Combined 3-Beat Swings in a Building Phrase Pattern

| 9/8 meter | cts. | meas. |
|---|---|---|
| St. medium stride, arms stretched diagonally above head. Swing both arms Dn. to cross hands low in front of body, plié, focus straight ahead - - - - - - - - - - - - - - - - - - - - - - - - - - - - - - - - | 1 2 3 | |
| Swing arms up to original position straightening knees - - - - - - - - - - - - - - - - - - - - - - - - - - - - - - | 4 5 6 | |
| Circle both arms Dn. and push Fd. away from body, plié - - - - - - - - - - - - - - - - - - - - - - - - - - - - | 7 8 9 | 1 |
| Repeat all - - - - - - - - - - - - - - - - - - - - - - - - - - - - - - - - - - - - - - - - | | 1 |
| Swing both arms Dn. to cross hands low in front of body, plié - - - - - - - - - - - - - - - - - - - - - - - - | 1 2 3 | |
| Swing both arms up to original position - - - - - - - - - - - | 4 5 6 | |
| Circle both arms Dn. and push Sd. away from body, plié - - - - - - - - - - - - - - - - - - - - - - - - - - - - | 7 8 9 | 1 |
| Repeat the last meas. - - - - - - - - - - - - - - - - - - - - - - - - - - - - - - - - - - | | 1 |
| Swing both arms Dn. to cross hands low in front of body, plié - - - - - - - - - - - - - - - - - - - - - - - - | 1 2 3 | |
| Swing arms up to original position - - - - - - - - - - - - - - | 4 5 6 | |

|  | cts. | meas. |
|---|---|---|

Thrusting the L hip Sd. L, circle L arm Dn. close to L Sd. R arm crosses in front of body so that both arms push together Sd. L. Focus follows hands - - - - - - - - - - - - - - - - - - - - - - - - - - - - - - - - -     7 8 9       1

Repeat the last meas. to the R - - - - - - - - - - - - - - - - - - - - - - - - - - - - - - - - - -        1

Drop both arms and body to swing Dn. and across toward L. Let the swing carry the body into 1/2 turn L pivoting on the L foot - - - - - - - - - - - - -     1 2 3

Swing the arms and body Dn. and across to the R - - - - - - - - - - - - - - - - - - - - - - - - - - - - - - - - - -     4 5 6

Thrusting the R hip Sd. R, circle R arm Dn. close to R Sd., R arm crossing in front of body so that both arms push together Sd. R - - - - - - - - - - - - - -     7 8 9       1

Repeat the body swing turning again to the L - - - - - -     1 2 3

Swing the arms and body Dn. and across to the R - - - - - - - - - - - - - - - - - - - - - - - - - - - - - - - - - -     4 5 6

As a quick plié is taken, circle both arms Dn. to Sd. and push diagonally upward to strong overhead position. Focus high - - - - - - - - - - - - - - - - - - - -     7 8 9       1

                                              total - -    8

## 4-BEAT SWINGS – 12/8

4-Beat swings stress counts 1, 4, 7, 10 in 12/8 meter taking four impulses for completion. Most often they are composed of two different 2-beat swings; however, they may be almost any four movements containing a swinging quality and seeming to flow together.

1. Stand in wide stride, arms above head. Swing the entire body forward and downward with arms swinging backward between legs, counts one, two, three. Swing arms forward to slap floor with palms, counts four, five, six. Swing body down with arms swinging backward between legs, counts seven, eight, nine. Swing up to original standing position, counts ten, eleven, twelve.
2. Stand in medium stride, arms reaching diagonally upward. Swing both arms down to cross hands low in front of body, counts one, two, three. Swing arms up to original position, counts four, five, six. Plié as left arm drops and pushes downward close in front of body and right arm pushes upward close by side of ear, counts seven, eight, nine. Drop right arm in circular movement down across body and out to right side as left arm swings out to left side to end in original starting position, counts ten, eleven, twelve. Repeat with right arm pushing downward and left arm pushing upward.

## 5-BEAT SWINGS – 15/8 meter

5-Beat swings take five impulses for completion stressing counts 1, 4, 7, 10, and 13 in 15/8 meter. They may be built from any 2- and 3-beat swing combination; or, like the

4-beat swing they may be composed of any five swinging movements that seem to fit together.

1. Stand in small stride, arms high above head. Swing both arms down and out to side, counts one, two, three. Swing arms back to original position bringing them first in close to the body and then up, counts four, five, six. Drop entire body forward and downward with arms swinging to outside of legs and brushing floor. Legs flex and then extend, counts seven, eight, nine. Swing up to original position, counts ten, eleven, twelve. Thrust hips forward as arms circle down to side open and back up to high beginning position, counts thirteen, fourteen, fifteen.

2. Stand in medium stride with arms reaching above head. Swing entire body forward and downward, counts one, two, three. Swing up to original position, counts four, five, six. Circle both arms from right to left sideward across in front of body to end in lateral horizontal extension of the body left with right leg extended hip level to right side, counts seven, eight, nine. Lower right leg to wide stride and drop body downward swinging across to low right lunge, arms relaxed and close to head, counts ten, eleven, twelve. Turn body forward, thrust hips forward opening arms backward and circling them outward and upward to original starting position, counts thirteen, fourteen, fifteen.

## 2-BEAT, 3-BEAT, 4-BEAT, 5-BEAT SWING COMBINED STUDY

|  | cts. | meas. |
|---|---|---|
| Stand in medium stride with arms stretched diagonally upward.   Swing both arms Dn. to cross hands low in front of body - - - - - - - - - - - - - - - - - - | 1 2 3 | |
| Swing arms up to original position - - - - - - - - - - - - - - - - - | 4 5 6 | 1 |
| Repeat 2-beat swing - - - - - - - - - - - - - - - - - - - - - - - - - - - - - - - - - - - - - - - - - | | 1 |
| Repeat 2-beat swing again - - - - - - - - - - - - - - - - - - - - - - | 1 2 3 4 5 6 | |
| Circle both arms Dn. and push Fd. away from body, plie' - - - - - - - - - - - - - - - - - - - - - - - - - - - - - - - - | 7 8 9 | 1 |
| Repeat 3-beat swing - - - - - - - - - - - - - - - - - - - - - - - - - - | 1 2 3<br>4 5 6<br>7 8 9 | 1 |
| Repeat 2-beat swing - - - - - - - - - - - - - - - - - - - - - - - - - - | 1 2 3<br>4 5 6 | |
| Plie' as L arm drops and pushes Dn. close in front of body, R arm pushes upward close by Sd. of ear - - - - - - - - - - - - - - - - - - - - - - - - - - - - - - - - - - | 7 8 9 | |
| Drop R arm in circular movement Dn. across body and out to R Sd. as L arm swings out to L Sd. to end in original St. position - - - - - - - - - - - - - - - | 10 11 12 | 1 |

| | cts. | | | meas. |
|---|---|---|---|---|

Repeat 4-beat swing with R arm pushing Dn.,
L arm pushing upward - - - - - - - - - - - - - - - - - - - - - - - - -      1  2  3
                                                                      4  5  6
                                                                      7  8  9
                                                                      10  11  12          1

Swing both arms Dn. to cross hands low in
front of body - - - - - - - - - - - - - - - - - - - - - - - - - - - - -      1  2  3

As arms swing up to original open position,
pivot 1/2 turn L suspending R leg Sd. R - - - - - - - - - - -      4  5  6

Lower R leg and swing arms Dn. to cross hands
low in front of body  - - - - - - - - - - - - - - - - - - - - - - -      7  8  9

Thrust hips Fd., drop focus, lower arms close to
Sd. of body and swing them Bk. and out away
from Sd. - - - - - - - - - - - - - - - - - - - - - - - - - - - - - - - - - -      10  11  12

Push hands Dn. and circle Fd. and up, unrolling
body to straighten to original position with
arms diagonally over head - - - - - - - - - - - - - - - - - - - -      13  14  15          1

Repeat 5-beat swing  - - - - - - - - - - - - - - - - - - - - - - - -      1  2  3
                                                                      4  5  6
                                                                      7  8  9
                                                                      10  11  12
                                                                      13  14  15          1
                                                                               total - -   8

## CREATIVE CLUES FOR SWINGS

1. Give the group five minutes to think of a swing variation which they have not done in class. Divide the group into sections of five or six people. Number each member of each group. Have all the No. 1's stand in front of their respective groups and demonstrate their own variation of a swing which they have devised. As soon as the small section behind each No. 1 learns the variation, they join the leader in performing it. When the No. 1's have finished showing their swings, the No. 2's stand in front, and so on until all have had a turn. It is interesting to see how many, many swings may be created by even beginning groups.

2. Have the class form in groups of four. Using a swing as a basis for forming movement, create one mood or quality. Names for such studies might be "Joy in Living," "Youthful Vigor," "Harvest Time," "Lament." The study should sustain a mood for approximately eight measures. Note that the examples given are solid in nature using work themes, growth — things with strength, feeling and depth. This type of quality should be encouraged, for it is only too easy for the beginner to wax sentimental when using swings or waltz rhythms and after much laborious effort come forth with "The Wanderings of a Butterfly on a Summer's Day" or something equally as trite.

## SUSTAINED MOVEMENT

Sustained movement gives a feeling of continuity and smoothness – the result of releasing and expending the energy in an equalized or proportioned manner. Due to the demanding controlled muscle tension required, it is difficult to perform this quality of movement for prolonged periods of time. To be effective, sustained movement must be executed against resistence. When Marcel Marceau, the celebrated French Pantomimist, does his slow walk in place, the discipline and control of his sustained movement hypnotizes the audience into believing that he is crossing space. The illusion is even more astonishing when he leans into a heavy wind.

1. **Sustained Walks**
   Walk as evenly and slowly as possible across the floor. Think of a slow motion movie to aid in getting the correct feeling.

2. **Sustained Walks with Turns**
   Very slow 4/4 meter
   A. Start weight right. Sustained walk forward two times left and right, counts one, two. One-quarter turn left step left as right leg swings out from body in low sustained lift, counts three, four. Repeat starting right and turning right.
   B. Repeat "A" turning one-half turn; now a whole turn.

3. **Head and Torso Rotation**
   Stand in wide stride. Slowly lower head to left side, counts one, two. Let it roll forward, counts three, four. Then to right side, counts five, six. And back, counts seven, eight. Repeat. Repeat allowing the body to bend with the head movement, arms relaxed at side. Repeat. Reverse the turns to rotate right. Keep the movement controlled and sustained.

4. **Arm Reaching and Pulling**

   4/4 meter

   | | <u>cts.</u> | <u>meas.</u> |
   |---|---|---|
   | St. sitting on R hip with both legs bent toward L, arms at Sd. Slowly lift R arm to extend Sd. R, focus following hand - - - - - - - - - - - - - - - - - - - - - - - - | 1 2 3 4 | 1 |
   | Pull R arm in close to body, tucking the body low over R fist - - - - - - - - - - - - - - - - - - - - - - - - | 1 2 3 4 | 1 |
   | Extend R arm reaching Fd., focus following hand - - - - - - - - - - - - - - - - - - - - - - - - - - - - - - | 1 2 3 4 | 1 |
   | Pull R arm in and tuck body low over R fist - - - - - - - - - | 1 2 3 4 | 1 |
   | Twist body L and reach R arm across body to extend far L, focus following hand - - - - - - - - - - - - - - - | 1 2 3 4 | 1 |
   | Pull R arm in and tuck body low over R fist - - - - - - - - - | 1 2 3 4 | 1 |
   | Uncurl body and sit very high lifting focus up as far as possible, arms remaining at Sds. - - - - - - - - - - - - | 1 2 3 4 | 1 |
   | Hold - - - - - - - - - - - - - - - - - - - - - - - - - - - - - - - - - - - - - | 1 2 3 4 | 1 |
   | | total - - | 8 |

To vary the pattern:

A. Try the entire pattern moving percussively on every first beat. Use great power and sharpness on each movement.
B. On all the reaching movements, use sustained movement; on the pulling movements, use percussive movement.
C. Use percussive movement on the reaches, sustained movement on the pulls.
D. Use the last four held counts to shift the weight onto the left hip and repeat the pattern to the opposite side.
E. Half of the group move using only sustained movement; the other half use only percussive movement. Experiment with any number of group variations — with partners, directional variations, and dimensional changes.

5. **Sustained Movement Combined with Percussive to Give a Primitive Quality**

| 4/4 meter, slow | cts. | meas. |
|---|---|---|
| St. in small stride, both knees bent in slight crouch, Bk. straight, focus Fd., arms at Sds. with palms Fd., elbows bent slightly toward Bk. Step Fd., L R, on cts. 1 and 3 as both arms circle Dn., Bk., and up with Bk. of hand leading the movement. Keep knees bent and body low on walks - - - - - - - - - - - - - - - - - - - - - - - - - - - - | 1 2 3 4 | 1 |
| Turn palms sharply toward face and step Fd. L - - - - - - | 1 | |
| Lower hands slowly Dn. to Sd., Bk. of hand leading. Step Sd. R in medium stride, knees bent, ct. 3 - - - - - - - - - - - - - - - - - - - - - - - - - - - - - - - | 2 3 4 | 1 |
| Clap hands 2 X in front of chest, focus Dn. - - - - - - - - - - | 1 2 | |
| Arms drop to Sd., palms Fd., elbows bent Bk. as focus lifts very high - - - - - - - - - - - - - - - - - - - - - - - - | 3 | |
| Hold - - - - - - - - - - - - - - - - - - - - - - - - - - - - - - - - - - - - - - | 4 | 1 |
| Repeat the last meas. - - - - - - - - - - - - - - - - - - - - - - - - - - - - - - - - - - - - | | 1 |
| Lower head Sd. L, ct. 1, Bk. ct. 2, Sd. R, ct. 3, and Fd. ct. 4 - - - - - - - - - - - - - - - - - - - - - - - - - - - - - - - | 1 2 3 4 | 1 |
| Allow body to bend far Sd. L, Bk., Sd. R, and Fd. as head again rotates - - - - - - - - - - - - - - - - - - - - - - | 1 2 3 4 | 1 |
| Drop head and body Sd. L and make 1/2 turn L - - - - - - | 1 | |
| Straighten to small crouching stride - - - - - - - - - - - - - - - - | 2 | |
| Raising arms diagonally upward focus high, jump 2 X keeping close to the floor - - - - - - - - - - - - - - - - | 3 4 | 1 |
| Repeat the last meas. turning again to the L, building the intensity of the movement to climax the sequence - - - - - - - - - - - - - - - - - - - - - - - - - - | 1 2 3 4 | 1 |
| | total - - | 8 |

6. **Creative Clues**
    A. Experiment with any swinging movement to make it sustained. The sensation is quite different and sometimes very amusing. Show several and all try.
    B. Walk briskly to 4/4 meter across floor. When the music stops (unexpectedly) all look slowly and pointedly at the piano, record player or drum. Allow about four counts for the sustained "look" and continue brisk walk.
    C. Descend from a normal standing position to the lowest plane possible in eight counts using sustained movement. Ascend to the highest possible level in eight counts using sustained movement.

## PERCUSSIVE MOVEMENT

Percussive movement is the drama and excitement of modern dance. The sharp, harsh, distorted movement is a device to capture attention, to add dash and color, and to hold one's audience. Too much emphasis on percussive movement in a dance may result in the dancers' projecting a nervous, fidgety quality; or if performed slower, a morbid, unbalanced, sinister quality. Like anything else, and of course depending on the purpose of the dance, percussive movement must be used wisely and sparingly to make its greatest contribution.

1. **Percussive Strikes**
    Experiment with striking types of movement in various planes and directions. Try hitting with fists clenched, lashing with elbows leading, and kicking with the heel of the foot leading.

2. **Percussive Strikes with Partners**

| | cts. | meas. |
|---|---|---|
| A. 4/4 meter | | |
| Partners facing each other stand in elevated Fd. stride with L foot and L Sd. leading and R arm raised high Bk. of head. Propel body Fd. to heavy leap R lifting L leg bent Bk. as R arm whips Fd. to strike with body bending Fd.- - - - - - - - - - - - - - - - - - - - - - - - - - - - - - - - | 1 | |
| Step Bk., L R L, high on balls of feet - - - - - - - - - - - | 2  3  4 | 1 |
| Repeat 3 X - - - - - - - - - - - - - - - - - - - - - - - - - - - - - - - - - - - - - | | 3 |
| | total - - | 4 |
| B. 4/4 meter | | |
| Repeat "A" as follows: | | |
| Heavy leap Fd. R as in "A" - - - - - - - - - - - - - - - - - - | 1 | |
| Step Bk. L high on ball of foot - - - - - - - - - - - - - - - - | 2 | |
| 1/4 turn R stepping R, L elevated - - - - - - - - - - - - - - | 3  4 | 1 |
| Repeat all facing new direction - - - - - - - - - - - - - - - - - - - - - - - - - - - | | 1 |
| Repeat 2 X to complete a square - - - - - - - - - - - - - - - - - - - - - - - - - - | | 2 |
| | total - - | 4 |

C. 3/4 meter

| | cts. | meas. |
|---|---|---|
| Repeat heavy leap R as in "A" - - - - - - - - - - - - - - - - | 1 | |
| 1/4 turn R stepping Bk., L R - - - - - - - - - - - - - - - - - | 2  3 | 1 |
| Repeat St. opposite foot with 1/4 turn L to face in original direction - - - - - - - - - - - - - - - - - - - - - | 1  2  3 | 1 |
| Repeat all 3 X - - - - - - - - - - - - - - - - - - - - - - - - - - - - - - - - - - - - - - - - - - - | | 6 |
| | total - - | 8 |

D. 4/4 meter

| | cts. | meas. |
|---|---|---|
| Repeat heavy leap R as in "A" - - - - - - - - - - - - - - - - | 1 | |
| Step Bk., L R L - - - - - - - - - - - - - - - - - - - - - - - - - | 2  3  4 | 1 |
| Repeat all - - - - - - - - - - - - - - - - - - - - - - - - - - - - - - - - - - - - - - - - - | | 1 |
| Heavy Leap R - - - - - - - - - - - - - - - - - - - - - - - - - - - | 1 | |
| Step Bk. L - - - - - - - - - - - - - - - - - - - - - - - - - - - | 2 | |
| Repeat 2 X - - - - - - - - - - - - - - - - - - - - - - - - - - - | 3  4, 1  2 | |
| Whole turn R in place stepping R L R - - - - - - - - - - - | 3 & 4 | 2 |
| | total - - | 4 |

E. 4/4 meter

Repeat "A", "B" and "D" with partner No. 2 starting two beats after partner No. 1. Thus, No. 1 begins on count one of measure one; No. 2 begins the identical sequence on count three of measure one.

## 3. Percussive Hip Whip

Partners kneeling to sit back on heels, face each other with opposite hands joined across. No. 1 acts as a resisting force against No. 2 who rises to high kneeling level with an impulsive pull that whips sequentially from hips through torso and head, counts one, two. No. 2 returns to starting position as No. 1 repeats the same sharp lifting movement, counts three, four. Continue as desired.

## 4. Percussive Arm Whipping

A. 4/4 meter

| | cts. | meas. |
|---|---|---|
| Fists clenched leading upward arms bent Fd. with elbows turned outward. Whip R elbow inward crossing front of chest as R arm rotates inward - - - - - - - - - - - - - - - - - - - - - - - - - - - | 1 | 1 |
| Reverse movement to original position - - - - - - - - - - - | 2 | |
| Repeat all with L arm - - - - - - - - - - - - - - - - - - - - | 3  4 | 1 |
| Repeat all 3 X bringing arms higher with each whipping motion  - - - - - - - - - - - - - - - - - - - - - - - - - - - - - - - - - - - | | 3 |
| | total - - | 4 |

B. 4/4 meter                                                   <u>cts.</u>        <u>meas.</u>

   1) St. Wt. L. L arm curved low Sd. L, R
      arm in starting position of "A" above.
      Whip R forearm inward crossing front of
      chest while stepping R across in front of
      L - - - - - - - - - - - - - - - - - - - - - - - - - - - - - - - - - - -    1

      Step L elevated Sd. L while reversing the
      R arm movement to the original position - - - - - -    2

      Repeat traveling Sd. L 3 X - - - - - - - - - - - - - - - -    3  4
                                             1  2  3  4          2

      Quick catch-step R - - - - - - - - - - - - - - - - - - - - -    ah

      Repeat all traveling Sd. R and reversing
      arm and leg movements - - - - - - - - - - - - - - - - - - - - - - - - - - - - - -          2

   2) Repeat "1" cross and Sd. stepping 2 X;
      first Sd. L and again Sd. R - - - - - - - - - - - - - - - - - - - - - - - - -          2

   3) Repeat "1" cross and Sd. stepping 1 X;
      first Sd. L and again Sd. R - - - - - - - - - - - - - - - - - - - - - - - -          1

      Repeat again - - - - - - - - - - - - - - - - - - - - - - - - - - - - - - - - - - - - - -          1

                                                    total - -    8

5. **Percussive Contrasted with Sustained Movement**

4/4 meter

Wide stride stand. Bending body laterally L, L
arm out Sd. L, R arm reaching up over head to
Sd. L, push both arms sharply toward Sd. L 4 X - - - - - -    1  2  3  4          1

In sustained movement raise R leg Sd. R bring-
ing R arm Dn. to Sd. R - - - - - - - - - - - - - - - - - - - - - - - -    1  2  3  4          1

Leap-lunge Fd. R pushing heel of R hand Fd., L
leg extended Bk., body inclined Fd. - - - - - - - - - - - - - -    1

Hold - - - - - - - - - - - - - - - - - - - - - - - - - - - - - - - - - - - - - - - -    2

Elevate entire body sharply and two-step L
with 1/2 turn L to face in opposite direction - - - - - - - - -    3 & 4          1

Repeat leap-lunge Fd. R as above - - - - - - - - - - - - - - - -    1

Hold - - - - - - - - - - - - - - - - - - - - - - - - - - - - - - - - - - - - - - - -    2

Repeat elevated two-step L with 1/2 turn L to
end facing in original direction - - - - - - - - - - - - - - - - - - -    3 & 4          1

Repeat all bending and pushing laterally R - - - - - - - - - - - - - - - - - - - - - - - -          4

                                                    total - -    8

6. **Creative Clues**
   A. Walk percussively across the floor. The movement should be short, dynamic jerks which propel the body through space. Add a directional change on every fourth beat.
   B. Using one measure of 4/4, 3/4, 2/4 and two measures of 1/4 meter, and moving only on the first beat of each measure, all make up a movement pattern. No sustained movement allowed, no locomotor movement on the off-beats — only percussive movement on accented beats!

## VIBRATORY MOVEMENT

Vibratory movement is very exciting to do and see when used economically. The repetitive nature of vibratory movement tends to become wearing on the dancer and viewer alike if it is done too long or too often. The violent tensions involved coupled with the jerky movements that result from small, quick, repeated contractions and releases of muscle groups offer interesting contrasts in dance. This type of movement is very useful in expressing extreme emotions of fear and nervousness, and the tensions of modern life. A certain shock value may be obtained by the injection of this unusual kind of movement.

1. **Vibrating While Sitting**

| 4/4 meter | cts. | meas. |
|---|---|---|
| Sit on R hip, both legs bent Bk. L, head low over knees, hands Dn. by hips. Tense the neck muscles and vibrate or shake the head quickly as lift focus and straighten Bk. - - - - - - - - - - - - - - - - - - - | 1 2 3 4 | 1 |
| Bring arms straight out Sd. and up from body to diagonal reach above head, vibrate wrists as lift - - - - - - - - - - - - - - - - - - - - - - - - - - - - - - - - - - - - - - | 1 2 3 4 | 1 |
| Lower R arm circling L across body and up with focus following vibrating R hand - - - - - - - - - - - - - - | 1 2 3 4 | 1 |
| Suddenly drop both arms as body Wt. is lifted on both knees - - - - - - - - - - - - - - - - - - - - - - - - - - - - | 1 | |
| Circle both arms Dn. and around L vibrating both hands, focus following hands - - - - - - - - - - - - - - - - | 2 3 | |
| Settle onto L hip with focus Dn., hands low by hips - - - - - - - - - - - - - - - - - - - - - - - - - - - - - - - - - - - - - | 4 | 1 |
| Repeat all on opposite Sd. - - - - - - - - - - - - - - - - - - - - - - - - - - - - - - - - - - - - - - - - - - | | 4 |
| | total - - | 8 |

2. **Vibrating While Standing**

| 4/4 meter | | |
|---|---|---|
| St. face Fd. in bent knee position focus low, hands on knees. Tense feet and stamp in place with vibrating movement, head lifting in vibration at the same time - - - - - - - - - - - - - - - - - - - - - - - - - | 1 2 3 4 | 1 |

Figure Thirteen

|  | cts. | meas. |
|---|---|---|

Remain in bent knee position, vibrate feet as lift arms up Sd. until reach high diagonal, arms vibrating as lift - - - - - - - - - - - - - - - - - - - - - - - - - - - - - - - 1 2 3 4      1

Suddenly lunge L and circle R arm across body L and up with focus following vibrating R hand - - - - - - 1 2 3 4      1

Bring R foot over to L in bent knee position - - - - - - - - -    1

Circle both arms Dn. L, high overhead to R and return to center.   Focus following vibrating hands - - - - - - - - - - - - - - - - - - - - - - - - - - - - - - - - - - - - - 2 3

Hold focus low, hands on knees - - - - - - - - - - - - - - - - - - - 4      1

Repeat all with lunge going R and L arm circling across - - - - - - - - - - - - - - - - - - - - - - - - - - - - - - - - - - - -      4

                                                           total - -   8

### 3.  **Propelling Body Across Space with Vibrating Movement**

4/4 meter

St. vibrating feet in place, knees bent, hands on knees, focus Dn. - - - - - - - - - - - - - - - - - - - - - - - - - - - - - 1 2 3 4      1

Gradually straighten body, knees, lift focus, arms coming up as strong initial pulse propels body Fd. as feet and arms vibrate - - - - - - - - - - - - - - - 1 2 3 4      1

Move diagonally R as continue to vibrate - - - - - - - - - - 1 2 3 4      1

Change sharply to vibrate diagonally L, focus changes to follow body direction - - - - - - - - - - - - - - - - - - 1 2 3 4      1

Change sharply to vibrate circling R in place, arms down, body low - - - - - - - - - - - - - - - - - - - - - - - - - 1

Lift body and arms continuing to vibrate as complete circle - - - - - - - - - - - - - - - - - - - - - - - - - - - - - - 2 3

Lower into original position bent knees, focus Dn., hands on knees - - - - - - - - - - - - - - - - - - - - - - - - - - - 4      1

                                                           total - -   5

### 4.  **Combine Vibratory Movement with Percussive Steps**

4/4 meter

To the above vibratory pattern, continue the vibratory circling holding high on the 4th ct. of the 5th meas. Then suddenly return to original position with fists striking knees in percussive movement ct. 1 of 6th meas. - - - - - - - - - - - - - - - - - - - - - 1

Hold - - - - - - - - - - - - - - - - - - - - - - - - - - - - - - - - - - - - - - - - - - - - - - 2 3 4      1

                                                           total - -   6

5. **Vibratory Movement with Percussive Stops and Runs**

| 4/4 meter | cts. | meas. |
|---|---|---|
| Add to the previous pattern. St. R. run diagonally R 4 X - - - - - - - - - - - - - - - - - - - - - - - - - - - - - - - - - - - | 1 & 2 & | |
| Lunge R reaching R arm percussively R - - - - - - - - - - - - - | 3 | |
| Hold - - - - - - - - - - - - - - - - - - - - - - - - - - - - - - - - - - - - - - - - - - | 4 | 1 |
| St. L. Run diagonally L 4 X - - - - - - - - - - - - - - - - - - - - - - | 1 & 2 & | |
| Lunge L reaching L arm percussively L - - - - - - - - - - - - - | 3 | |
| Hold - - - - - - - - - - - - - - - - - - - - - - - - - - - - - - - - - - - - - - - - - - | 4 | 1 |
| Turn 1/2 R and run 8 X St. R arms swinging in opposition to legs - - - - - - - - - - - - - - - - - - - - - - - - - - - - | 1 & 2 & 3 & 4 & | 1 |
| Percussive stop, strike both knees with fists, focus low - - - - - - - - - - - - - - - - - - - - - - - - - - - - - - - - - - - - | 1 | |
| Hold - - - - - - - - - - - - - - - - - - - - - - - - - - - - - - - - - - - - - - - - - - | 2 3 4 | 1 |
| | total - - | 10 |

The entire sequence may be repeated in the opposite direction. Or by making one-half turn on the first measure, the pattern may be repeated with the original directional pattern.

6. **Creative Clues**
   A. Have the entire class start a vibratory stamping with feet. On cue from the teacher, start moving forward, diagonally left or right, backward, circling.
   B. As class vibrates, the teacher calls out various parts of the body to carry out the vibratory action — head, one arm, both arms.
   C. Work on increasing the dynamics. Have the class start with very tiny vibrations and gradually increase the size and intensity of the movement. As the teacher calls out a new direction or a different part of the body to emphasize the vibration, start all over in the building up of tension to increase the dynamics.
   D. With partners, number one vibrates for one measure as number two remains silent. Confine the dancers to a sit, then a stand. Now let them move across the floor.

## SUSPENDED MOVEMENT

Suspended movement appears to be an arrestment of action. Actually, it gives to dance a sense of growth and continuity of movement. The pulse of an action started and then held at its highest point until the movement grows in importance and excitement as the control becomes more difficult to maintain, often gives a lyric quality to dance. A sense of phrasing, so essential in music and dance, may be achieved by the judicial use of suspended movement.

It should be stressed that suspended movement is never static and so balanced as to cease growing. It is the off balance continuing pull of opposing muscle groups that makes for the suspense in the suspension!

1. **Suspended Movement from an Initial Swing Impulse**

| 3/4 meter | cts. | meas. |
|---|---|---|
| A. Swing R leg Fd.- - - - - - - - - - - - - - - - - - - - - - - - - - - - - - - | 1 2 3 | 1 |
| Hold high and balance on L toe, palms up, arms by Sds. Keep the movement growing (don't pop up and perch on toe) - - - - - - - - - - - - - - - | 1 2 3 | 1 |
| Drop body Fd. as step R, Bk. straight - - - - - - - - - - - | 1 2 3 | 1 |
| B. St. Sd. L. Swing body laterally L - - - - - - - - - - - - - - | 1 2 3 | 1 |
| Suspend stretching R leg R and reaching arms L overhead - - - - - - - - - - - - - - - - - - - - - - - - - | 1 2 3 | 1 |
| Swing body Dn. and laterally R shifting Wt. R - - - - - - - - - - - - - - - - - - - - - - - - - - - - - - - - | 1 2 3 | 1 |
| Suspend R - - - - - - - - - - - - - - - - - - - - - - - - - - - - - - | 1 2 3 | 1 |
| C. Swing body Dn. and up L as step L, turn complete L with R leg trailing - - - - - - - - - - - - - - - | 1 2 3 | 1 |
| Hold body high in suspension while completing turn - - - - - - - - - - - - - - - - - - - - - - - - - - | 1 2 3 | 1 |
| Repeat turn R - - - - - - - - - - - - - - - - - - - - - - - - - | 1 2 3<br>1 2 3 | 2 |
| Come up on both toes, cross hands low and circle arms in and up to suspend - - - - - - - - - - - - - - - - | 1 2 3 | 1 |
| Combine A, B and C - - - - - - - - - - - - - - - - - - - - - - - - - - | total - - | 12 |

2. **Suspension Starting from Circling Impulse**

| Slow 3/4 meter | cts. | meas. |
|---|---|---|
| Circle head and body Dn. L and up R suspending on toes and holding at highest point - - - - - - - - - - - | 1 2 3 | 1 |
| Repeat - - - - - - - - - - - - - - - - - - - - - - - - - - - - - - - - - - | 1 2 3 | 1 |
| Add arms circling and suspending with body - - - - - - - - - | 1 2 3 | 1 |
| Repeat - - - - - - - - - - - - - - - - - - - - - - - - - - - - - - - - - - | 1 2 3 | 1 |
| Add R leg circling with arms opening on suspension - - - - - - - - - - - - - - - - - - - - - - - - - - - - - - - - - - | 1 2 3 | 1 |
| Reverse circling as L leg opens on suspension - - - - - - - - - | 1 2 3 | 1 |
| Drop to L hand and L knee support circling R bent knee into tucked body - - - - - - - - - - - - - - - - - - - - | 1 2 3 | 1 |
| Open body circling R leg Dn. and out, up to extend and suspend while R arm opens wide - - - - - - - - - | 1 2 3 | 1 |
| | total - - | 8 |

3. **Creative Clues**
    A. Have the group walk across the floor to 5/4 meter catching and suspending the fourth step to hold the fifth count. Try walking across to 4/4 meter, stepping three times and holding in suspension the fourth count. Try 3/4 meter, stepping twice and holding the third count to give a lop-sided effect. Now try 2/4 meter across the floor stepping once on each foot. Remember to suspend the movement — don't just swing the free leg forward and wait for the next step!

    Try two measures of each meter respectively across the floor. Try decumulative and accumulative sequences. For example, two measures each of 5/4, 4/4, 3/4, 2/4 followed by two measures each of accumulative meter 2/4, 3/4, 4/4, 5/4.

    B. Experiment with any percussive movement that lifts the body up or out. Instead of stopping the movement, elongate it to take it into suspension. For example: upward or sideward slashes or strikes and sudden turns. Use various parts of the body to initiate the movement: knees, elbows, arms, head.

    Some of the results may tend to be comical because the serious initial dynamic movement loses its original purpose and becomes almost sentimental in contrast!

Never miss the opportunity to let half of the group observe the accomplishments of the other half. Encourage the group to choose several of the movements that seem to show the suspension quality best, and then all watch these. Have volunteers evaluate their observations. Through the process of appraisal the students begin to discover the significance of dance.

## VARIATIONS BUILT FROM SPATIAL ASPECTS

### FLOOR PATTERN

Any movement that involves a weight transference will necessarily show a floor pattern. The design on the floor which results from locomotor movement is called the floor pattern.

Dance studies stressing floor pattern are particularly valuable for beginners. They become involved in the design they are trying to form on the floor and can become quite objective about movement. The fear of "emoting" or "performing" in front of a group is lessened, and the beginner is able to project a very simple, yet well-defined statement which viewers will be able to understand.

Often very interesting dance movement develops out of studies of this type as the dancer moves through a complicated floor pattern. The beginner sometimes is so involved with the star shape or spiral pattern he is working on that he is completely unaware of the totally different and unusual uses he is making of his body in other spatial aspects — arms, concentrated focus, strong directional line and so on. The group will notice and should be encouraged to point out these aspects as they become aware of them.

There is always a great deal of overlapping in spatial studies because any movement of the human body involves using many if not all the spatial aspects. Just to stand still means that the body has direction, is focusing some place, has a certain level to maintain and is creating a contour in space. However, if the problem projected by the teacher is one of floor pattern, then that should be the first concern of the dancer. It should be obvious to all observers that the design developing on the floor is more important at the moment than such aspects as the rhythmic pattern or dimension of various movements.

Figure Fourteen

Simplicity and singleness of purpose is called for in specific studies. Even in the simplest study or pattern there should be a beginning — sometimes nothing more than a moment of stillness and concentration before movement of dance begins; middle — the main problem or work of the dance; and the end — a definite stop, fall, climactic movement or simply a gradually easing of tensions and hold. No doubt should be left in the mind of the viewer that the dance is over. It is worthwhile to stress and comment on these aspects of dance and thus arouse an awareness of them on the part of the participant-viewer from the moment the dancer starts to communicate through movement to an audience.

1. Teach the whole group to walk in a square. Refer to pages 62 and 63. Try walking first in the line of direction, and then walk on a square facing forward.
2. Teach all to walk in a circle taking six steps to complete a full circle.
3. Try a quick step on the last count of the six step circle to change sides and complete a six step circle on the opposite side making a figure eight.
4. Combine Zigzag with Circular Floor Pattern

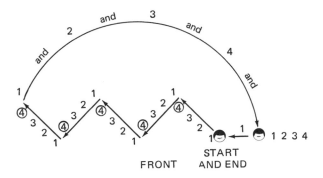

FRONT   START AND END

| 4/4 meter | cts. | meas. |
|---|---|---|
| St. facing Fd. Face diagonally L as step diagonally Bk. L, R, L - - - - - - - - - - - - - - - - - - - - - - - - - - - - - - - - - - | 1 2 3 | |
| Hold - - - - - - - - - - - - - - - - - - - - - - - - - - - - - - - - - - - - - - | 4 | 1 |
| Face diagonally R, step Fd. R, L, R - - - - - - - - - - - - | 1 2 3 | |
| Hold - - - - - - - - - - - - - - - - - - - - - - - - - - - - - - - - - - - | 4 | 1 |
| Repeat diagonally Bk. L, R, L; hold - - - - - - - - - - - - - - - - | 1 2 3 4 | 1 |
| Repeat diagonally Fd. R, L, R; hold - - - - - - - - - - - - - - - | 1 2 3 4 | 1 |
| Repeat diagonally Bk. L, R, L; hold - - - - - - - - - - - - - - - | 1 2 3 4 | 1 |
| Sharply turn R and run in large semi-circle around to starting position on floor R, L, R, L, R, L, R, L - - - - - - - - - - - - - - - - - - - - - - - - - - - - - - | 1 & 2 & 3 & 4 & | 1 |
| Wt. L, circle R toe Fd., Sd., Bk. - - - - - - - - - - - - - - - - - | 1 2 3 4 | 1 |
| Wide step Sd. R - - - - - - - - - - - - - - - - - - - - - - - - - - - | 1 | |
| Draw L foot to R and hold, focus Fd. - - - - - - - - - - - - | 2 3 4 | 1 |
| | total - - | 8 |

Repeat floor pattern.

Try dividing the group into two or three sections. Start them at two measure intervals.

Try starting them at one measure intervals.

Place the three groups facing different directions. All do the floor pattern together once, then the different groups start the sequence at two measure intervals. Hold at the end.

Let half of each group sit and watch the other half perform.

5. **"Easter Eggs" or "Pattern Within a Pattern"**

| 4/4 meter | cts. | meas. |
|---|---|---|
| Make an oblong on the floor walking in strong strides. St. L  - - - - - - - - - - - - - - - - - - - - - - - - - - - - - - | 16 | 4 |
| Grapevine Dn. the length of the egg. St. stepping Sd. L, Bk. R, Sd. L, Fd. R and so on  - - - - - - - - - - - - - - - | 8 | 2 |
| Turn 1/4 L, slide St. L all the way up the egg - - - - - - - - - | 1 ah 2 ah 3 ah 4 ah | 1 |
| Slide Bk. Dn. the egg St. L  - - - - - - - - - - - - - - - - - - - - | 1 ah 2 ah 3 ah 4 ah | 1 |
| Dot the egg all over with 8 jumps, turning on the jumps - - - - - - - - - - - - - - - - - - - - - - - - - - - - - - - - - - - - - - - - - - - - - - - |  | 2 |
|  | total - - | 10 |

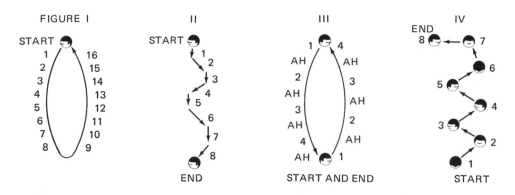

6. **Creative Clues**
   A. Draw patterns on the chalkboard and call for suggestions of others from the group.
   B. Have each one make up his own floor pattern and be able to draw it on paper as well as show it in movement.

## DIRECTION

Direction becomes evident either as the body moves or as the dancer travels to form a floor pattern. The focus of the eyes, the turning of the head, the pointing of a finger, the extension of a leg, or the leaning forward and backward of the torso illustrate the use of direction. The path traversed exemplifies another aspect of direction. In dance composition this course of motion is associated closely with the theme of the dance. For instance, a forward direction may denote an authoritative and unswerving course of action; a backward direction may convey a retiring and submissive feeling; and a sideward direction may suggest indecision and uncertainty. The direction to be followed is affected by the idea to be communicated.

1. **Emphasizing Direction in Locomotor Movement**
   A. Entire group start skipping around in a large circle in the line of direction. Have the music freeze. At every silence the group walks slowly toward the front of the room, four counts. As the music starts again the group skips in a circle.
   B. The same as above, except on the silence the teacher calls out the direction in which the group should move; sideward left, diagonally right, turning.
   C. Now try all skipping in any direction. At the freeze in the music, the teacher calls out the direction toward which all must move. Everyone is now facing a different direction so the teacher must call out "Front of room," "Toward exit," "Toward piano," and so forth.
   D. Move using any locomotor movement: runs, prances, or slides. On the silences move toward the direction called in a non-locomotor way: bend, twist, reach, or lunge to point up the directional line.

2. **Emphasizing Direction in Non-locomotor Movement**

| Slow 4/4 meter | cts. | meas. |
|---|---|---|
| St. facing Fd. L knee lifts to diagonal L - - - - - - - - - - - - - | 1 2 | |
| Lunge diagonally L - - - - - - - - - - - - - - - - - - - - - - - - - - | 3 4 | 1 |
| Point L elbow sharply diagonally L - - - - - - - - - - - - - - - | 1 | |
| Hold - - - - - - - - - - - - - - - - - - - - - - - - - - - - - - - - - - - - | 2 | |
| Open L arm up to extend diagonally L, focus follows line - - - - - - - - - - - - - - - - - - - - - - - - - - - - - - | 3 4 | 1 |
| R arm circles Dn. close to body and up to point toward the L diagonal - - - - - - - - - - - - - - - - - - - - - - | 1 2 3 4 | 1 |
| Pivot 1/2 turn R leaning Bk. diagonally L - - - - - - - - - - | 1 2 | |
| Hold reaching with both hands Bk. diagonally L - - - - - - | 3 4 | 1 |
| Continue turning R with L foot crossing over R to lunge again diagonally L - - - - - - - - - - - - - - - - - - - - | 1 2 3 4 | 1 |
| Clasp hands diagonally L as hop L - - - - - - - - - - - - - - - - | 1 2 | |
| Hop 2 X L moving as though pulled diagonally L - - - - - - - - - - - - - - - - - - - - - - - - - - - - - - - - - - - - | 3 4 | 1 |
| Bring R foot in to L quickly to push leap diagonally L - - - - - - - - - - - - - - - - - - - - - - - - - - - - - - | ah 1 2 | |
| Repeat diagonal L leap - - - - - - - - - - - - - - - - - - - - - | ah 3 4 | 1 |

Slowly reach R foot Fd. far across diagonally L,
extend L leg Bk., hands clasped, arms extended
Fd. diagonally L, focus Dn. - - - - - - - - - - - - - - - - - - - - - - - -      1 2 3 4                    $\underline{1}$

                                                                    total - -        8

3. **Creative Clues**
   A. Give everyone in the class a specific direction to emphasize. Every movement
      should be used toward stressing the chosen direction. Four measures of movement
      should be enough to see whether or not the problem is understood. If the group is
      ready, have individuals show their study; otherwise, have smaller groups of four or
      five move at the same time while the rest of the class watches.
   B. Divide the group into couples. Make an eight measure Advance and Retreat Study
      showing strong forward directional line as opposed to strong backward directional
      movement.
      1) One moves forward one measure as the other holds. Then the other moves
         backward while the first holds.
      2) Both move together — one advancing as the other retreats.
      3) Change after four measures to reverse the direction. A see-saw movement
         pattern results.
      4) See-saw advance and retreat four measures each way, then two measures, then
         one measure. Let the individual couples devise their own ending to the pattern
         — one end victorious, both advance at the same time, or turn and retreat
         together.
   C. Divide the group into partners. Have them stand facing each other about twenty
      feet apart.
      1) Advance toward each other and continue on with no recognition.

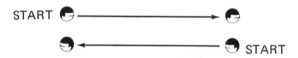

      2) Advance and both make one-half turn and walk backward the rest of the way.

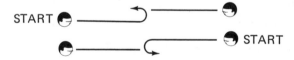

      3) As they meet in the center, only one does a one-half turn and walks backward.

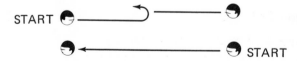

      4) As they meet in the center, one does a one-half turn and walks forward joining
         the other.

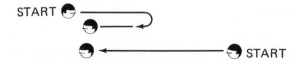

Note the feeling that is projected merely by a directional pattern of two people. Have the group comment on the expectant quality that grows as the two people move toward each other. The excitement can be built upon by emphasizing the moment of meeting. The interesting point to be observed is that so much can be said by simply moving toward an object or away from it.

FOCUS

The use of focus is extremely important to dance. Focus simply means the point to which the eyes are directed. By lifting the eyes or lowering the gaze a movement may be positively killed, or it may take on vitality and meaning. The most beautifully executed, joyful leap can be pulled right down into the ground by a downward focusing of the eyes and head.

The eyes are perhaps the most compelling single movement aspect in dance. Most everyone has experienced the irresistible desire to look up when seeing a group of people intently gazing into the sky. Or have you ever been talking to a friend when his eyes suddenly stop and focus with rapt attention on some object in back of you? Practically no power on earth can keep you from quickly turning to follow his gaze.

By concentrating the focus on a particular part of the body, this part becomes important. If the stare goes on for too long, the concentration becomes abnormal and a strange almost demented effect is created.

In floor pattern studies the focus is too frequently downward toward the floor. In directional studies the focus can be used to emphasize the line of the movement.

Beginners nearly always must be urged to keep their eyes off the floor. It is wise to stress the focus and lift of the eyes from the very beginning of dance work.

### 1. Simple Eye Movements

| 4/4 meter | cts. | meas. |
|---|---|---|
| Kneel-sit, hands on thighs. Keep the head completely still while only the eyes move. Focus straight ahead. Suddenly lift eyes and focus on a point diagonally up - - - - - - - - - - - - - - - - - - - - - - | >1  2 | |
| Center eyes - - - - - - - - - - - - - - - - - - - - - - - - - - | 3  4 | 1 |
| Eyes up diagonally L sharp - - - - - - - - - - - - - - - - | >1  2 | |
| Center- - - - - - - - - - - - - - - - - - - - - - - - - - - - - | 3  4 | 1 |
| Eyes Dn. diagonally L sharp - - - - - - - - - - - - - - - | >1  2 | |
| Center - - - - - - - - - - - - - - - - - - - - - - - - - - - - | 3  4 | 1 |
| Eyes Dn. diagonally R sharp - - - - - - - - - - - - - - - | >1  2 | |
| Center - - - - - - - - - - - - - - - - - - - - - - - - - - - - | 3  4 | 1 |
| Eyes up diagonally R sharp - - - - - - - - - - - - - - - - | >1  2 | |
| Center - - - - - - - - - - - - - - - - - - - - - - - - - - - - | 3  4 | 1 |
| Eyes up sharp - - - - - - - - - - - - - - - - - - - - - - - - | >1  2 | |

|  | cts. | meas. |
|---|---|---|
| Eyes up diagonally L sharp -------------------- | >3 4 | 1 |
| Eyes Dn. diagonally L sharp -------------------- | >1 2 |  |
| Eyes Dn. diagonally R sharp -------------------- | >3 4 | 1 |
| Eyes up diagonally R sharp -------------------- | >1 2 |  |
| Eyes up sharp and hold --------------------- | >3 4 | 1 |
|  | total -- | 8 |

## 2. Eyes Combined with Head Movement

| | cts. | meas. |
|---|---|---|
| Sitting on knees, hands on thighs, focus straight ahead. Eyes only move slowly Sd. L. --------------- | 1 2 | |
| Head turns sharply L ------------------------ | >3 | |
| Center ----------------------------------- | 4 | 1 |
| Eyes only move slowly diagonally Dn. L ------------ | 1 2 | |
| Head turns sharply diagonally Dn. L over L shoulder -------------------------------- | >3 4 | 1 |
| Repeat R Sd. ------------------------------- | 1 2 >3 4 | 1 |
| Repeat diagonally Dn. R ----------------------- | 1 2 >3 4 | 1 |
| Eyes and head focus sharply Sd. L --------------- | >1 | |
| Center ----------------------------------- | 2 | |
| Eyes and focus Dn. diagonally L sharply ----------- | >3 | |
| Center ----------------------------------- | 4 | 1 |
| Eyes and head focus sharply Sd. R --------------- | >1 | |
| Center ----------------------------------- | 2 | |
| Eyes and focus Dn. diagonally R sharply ----------- | >3 | |
| Center ----------------------------------- | 4 | 1 |
| Focus eyes and head up sharply ------------------ | >1 | |
| Gradually come up onto knee, stand, hands coming up to either Sd. of throat --------------- | 2 3 4 | 1 |
| Bend body suddenly Dn. over knees, focus Dn., hands over eyes --------------------------- | >1 | |
| Hold ------------------------------------- | 2 3 4 | 1 |
| | total -- | 8 |

3. **Creative Clues**
   A. Everyone sit on floor. With only the eyes and the head moving, trace a clear design that is projected toward the floor.
   B. All stand and draw a pattern in space with only the eyes and head moving.
   C. Now add an arm or sudden twist, a leg movement, to emphasize the pattern which the eyes have indicated.
   D. Take partners. Sit facing each other. Gaze into each other's eyes. One initiate a slow sustained hand movement; the other mirror image the movement. Continue the movements in any way; however, never change the focus from the eyes.
   E. Partners shadow movement. Sit or stand very close to each other with the focus in the same direction. The front person initiate a slow, sustained movement with the focus following the movement. The person in back follows the focus and movement exactly, and at the same time.

## LEVEL

The dancer can move from the lowest point on the floor through all the strata up to the highest jump he can reach. Usually if one wishes to express a feeling of dejection, he utilizes a low level and focus to clarify his emotion. Whereas, if he is elated and joyous, he lifts and reaches and bounds upward to help express this feeling.

A sudden change of level can be most dramatic and effective when used as a tool to emphasize a point or to reach a climax. A gradual change of level is less dramatic, but can be fully as satisfying by showing growth and development of movement themes, or by an augmenting or decreasing of body tensions.

Dancers should get acquainted and become fast friends with the floor. It has been said that some Asian dancers greet the floor before beginning to dance. The dancer uses the floor surface as an instrument from which to rebound, to strike, and even to receive succor. There should be a real understanding between the dancer and the earth or floor surface. The relationship may be tender or fierce. The floor should be thought of as a tool for the dancer's use as much as a rhythmic pattern or musical instrument is used as a tool for accompaniment.

1. **Non-locomotor Change of Level**

| 4/4 meter | cts. | meas. |
|---|---|---|
| St. standing tall, feet together hands reaching high, focus high. Reach from the shoulders up R, L, R, L - - - - - - - - - - - - - - - - - - - - - - - - - - - - - - - | 1 2 3 4 | 1 |
| Let R foot slide out Sd. to wide stride - - - - - - - - - - - - - | 1 2 3 4 | 1 |
| Arms open wide to Sd. shoulder level - - - - - - - - - - - - - | 1 2 3 4 | 1 |
| Gradually lower focus, bend upper torso Dn. between legs, fold hands in to touch elbows - - - - - - - - - | 1 2 3 4 | 1 |
| Swing hands out Fd. and walk on hands to fall Fd. with hands braced under shoulders - - - - - - - - - - - - | 1 2 3 4 | 1 |
| Suddenly roll onto L hip circling R leg and arm up and out, focus up, chest lifted - - - - - - - - - - - - - - - - | 1 2 | |
| Tuck body and roll up onto R knee - - - - - - - - - - - - - - - - | 3 4 | 1 |

|                                                                          | cts.      | meas. |
|--------------------------------------------------------------------------|-----------|-------|
| Stand on L foot, then R, lifting body and focus ------                   | 1  2      |       |
| Jump high and clap hands overhead ----------------                       | 3  4      | 1     |
|                                                                          | total --  | 7     |

2. **Combine Locomotor or Level Change**

   2/4 meter

| St. L, 4 runs ----------------------------------------          | 1  2  1  2 | 2 |
| L step, hop, step R -----------------------------              | 1  ah  2   | 1 |
| L step, hop, step R -----------------------------              | 1  ah  2   | 1 |
| L step, hop -----------------------------------               | 1  2       | 1 |
| Bend R knee in Bk. of L and fall R Sd. -------------           | 1  2       | 1 |
| Lift up to R knee and L foot, shift Wt. to R ---------         | 1  2       | 1 |
|                                                               | total --   | 7 |

3. **Creative Clues**
   A. Find the lowest position possible. In sixteen counts come to the highest point possible. Go down from high to low in sixteen counts. Now up in eight counts; down in eight counts. Up in four counts; down in four counts. Up in two counts; down in two counts. Up in one gigantic movement and down in one count.
   B. Explore the levels different parts of the body can reach — head, elbow, knee, big toe, shoulder.

## DIMENSION

Dimension or range relates both to the size of the movement employed and to the amount of space utilized on the floor. Dance studies comprising large, amplified movements tend to suggest the feeling of freedom, openness and release. In contrast, dance projects employing small contractive movements are likely to inspire the feeling of restraint, limitation and constriction. Certain compositional ideas by their very nature may limit the space areas through which the dancer moves. For example, a theme of "introversion" would automatically confine the movement to a limited floor pattern. By the same token, a dance idea on "wandering" would allow a greater latitude in spatial travel.

1. **Individual Experiences in Dimensional Movement**
   A. Skip in place, then gradually increase the space covered on each skip.
   B. Move across the floor with as many small, concentrated leaps as possible. Return with as few long, wide leaps as possible.

2. **Group Experiences in Dimensional Movement**
   A. Gradually increase and decrease the dimension of a circle. All stand close together in a circle facing counter-clockwise with left hand reaching toward the center of the circle. Run, widening the circle, to a phrase of sixteen counts. Make one-half turn left to face clockwise with right hand reaching toward the center of the circle. Run to another phrase of sixteen counts bringing the circle in very small.

Figure Fifteen

| | cts. | meas. |
|---|---|---|
| B. 4/4 meter | | |

Group forms a circle facing inward. Stand in
normal stance with feet slightly apart, hands
crossed low behind Bk. Sway body L and R
4 X - - - - - - - - - - - - - - - - - - - - - - - - - - - - - - - - - - - - -        1 2 3 4                1

Gradually increase dimension and force of
movement until it becomes step-hop L, R, L - - - - - -        1 & 2 & 3 &

Step-hop R turning 1/4 turn R - - - - - - - - - - - - - - - -        4 &                    1

All moving counter-clockwise in circle, long
forceful step-hops L and R with arms swing-
ing Fd. high in opposition to legs - - - - - - - - - - - - - - -        1 & 2 & 3 & 4 &
                                                                                                      1 & 2 & 3 & 4 &      2

Make sharp 1/4 turn R to face outward and
travel Fd. away from circle, 8 skips L and R  - - - - - -        1 ah 2 ah
                                                                                                      3 ah 4 ah
                                                                                                      1 ah 2 ah
                                                                                                      3 ah 4 ah            2

Make sharp 1/2 turn R to face inward and
walk slowly L and R 8 X toward center of
circle and finish in original position - - - - - - - - - - - -        1 2 3 4
                                                                                                      1 2 3 4             2
                                                                                                                       ____
                                                                              total - -    8

3. **Creative Clues**
   A. A theme of "Gossip" or "Rumor" may well lend itself to movement of changing
   dimension. To depict such an idea, movement of very small size may be increased
   gradually to movement of exaggerated dimension. Stylizing the movement
   suggests a means of making it incredibly humorous.

| 4/4 meter | cts. | meas. |
|---|---|---|

Standing in a long line, Sd. by Sd., first
dancer stamps R foot with the least force
possible - - - - - - - - - - - - - - - - - - - - - - - - - - - - - - - - - - - - - - - - -        1

Hold - - - - - - - - - - - - - - - - - - - - - - - - - - - - - - - - - - - - - - - - -        2

Clap hands softly - - - - - - - - - - - - - - - - - - - - - - - - -        3

Hold - - - - - - - - - - - - - - - - - - - - - - - - - - - - - - - - - - - - - - - - -        4                    1

Second dancer having watched first dancer
with strong focus, faces Fd. and repeats the
movement in wider dimension - - - - - - - - - - - - - - - - -        1 2 3 4                1

Third dancer focuses Fd. and repeats move-
ment in wider dimension - - - - - - - - - - - - - - - - - - - -        1 2 3 4                1

Fourth dancer stamps 2 X harder and claps
once wider - - - - - - - - - - - - - - - - - - - - - - - - - - - - - - - - - - -        1 2 3 4                1

| | | |
|---|---|---|
| Fifth dancer stamps 2X, claps 2 X, harder and bigger - - - - - - - - - - - - - - - - - - - - - - - - - - - - - - - - | 1 2 3 4 | 1 |
| Sixth dancer stamps 4 X turning completely R in place - - - - - - - - - - - - - - - - - - - - - - - - - - - - - | 1 & 2 & | |
| Claps 2 X as large as possible - - - - - - - - - - - - - - - - - - - | 3 4 | 1 |
| Last dancer runs to head of line - - - - - - - - - - - - - - - | 1 & 2 & 3 & 4 & | 1 |
| Repeat 4 stamps turning R and 2 claps - - - - - - - - - - - | 1 & 2 & 3  4 | 1 |
| Entire group throw hands in air and lean Bk. in silent laughter  - - - - - - - - - - - - - - - - - - - - - - - | 1 2 | |
| All rock Fd. and shake - - - - - - - - - - - - - - - - - - - - - | 3 & ah | |
| | 4 & ah | 1 |

total - -   9

Have the first dancer find his own movement for the first four counts. The others exaggerate the movement each time. The last dancer becomes the new leader after all have joined in the laughter movement at the end of the phrase.

B. Using the title, "The Power of a Fad," have the group form a small circle facing in. All bend knees and side-step to the right. The steps begin very small and gradually become wider and faster until one person whirls out from the group to "set the new fad." The group comes back close together and starts slow small side steps again gradually building up until two or three go out to copy the movement being done by the first dancer on the outside. Finally all are following the fad. At this point the magnetic power of the fad seizes the group and the size of the movement grows larger and larger, the floor pattern expands, the tempo accelerates to end in a frenzied climax.

C. Each dancer sit in a small ball as though inside a balloon. Explore the restricted area with diminutive movements. As the balloon or area expands, the exploratory movements grow in dimension. To end the study, the balloon could burst and all collapse.

## CONTOUR

Contour is the shape or outline of an individual or group in relation to space. As a dancer moves any part of the body — whether in place or while traveling through space — the contour changes. When individuals move in relation to other dancers in a group, the outline is constantly shifting. Whenever movement occurs, change in contour is inevitable. This constant variation in the outline or shadowing accentuates the fleeting and intangible quality of dancers in motion. At the same time, this momentary quality of movement underlines the excitement of ever-changing patterns.

1. **Experiments in Changing Contour**
    A. Sustain a movement that changes the bodily position through a series of turns that end in a slow fall.
    B. Experiment with a massed group before a mirror. Have a leader improvise with the group following in sustained movement involving changes of focus, direction and level. In this way individuals may see how they actually look in changing contour.

C. The first group forms a line in the background. The second group moves into view in file formation toward and across in front of the first group. Both groups focus directly forward. As the second group passes the first group, the first group moves directly forward. The continued floor pattern may be developed experimentally.

2. **Creative Clues**

A. 4/4 meter cts.        meas.

A group of 6 to 8 stand very close together facing Fd. Maintaining this massed relationship, walk slowly Fd. L and R 8 X, bringing arms to high vertical reach with focus upward - - - - - - - - - - - - - - - - - - - - - - - - - - - - - - - - - - - - - - -     1 2 3 4

                                                                         1 2 3 4          2

Slowly lower to kneel with focus continued upward - - - - - - - - - - - - - - - - - - - - - - - - - - - - - - - - - -     1 2 3 4

                                                                         1 2 3 4          2

Slowly flex torso Fd. with forehead coming to rest on folded hands in front of knees - - - - - - - - -     1 2 3 4

                                                                          1 2 3 4          2

total - -    6

B. Form groups numbered 1, 2 and 3 respectively.

Group 1, downstage left, moves through space with focal attention toward group 3, then away from group 3 as group 3 recoils. Group 2, center stage back, placed between groups 1 and 3, devise fast, continuing, whirling movements, left and then right, representing the link between groups 1 and 3.

Group 3, downstage right, in kneeling or sitting position, develops movements emphasizing extension toward group 1, as group 1 moves toward group 3, and then recoils from group 1, as group 1 moves away from group 3.

Repeat movement phrase several times gradually enlarging the dimension.

Suddenly group 2 rushes forward downstage between groups 1 and 3 and triumphantly. Groups 1 and 3 focus sharply away.

To emphasize further the varying contour of moving individuals and groups, divide the class into two parts allowing one to watch the other half.

## VARIATIONS BUILT FROM CHANGING DYNAMICS

Dynamics in movement cannot be dissected as easily as can the elements of space or rhythm. Simply, it is the energy released as a movement is performed. It is possible to vary this energy or intensity by releasing the energy quickly or slowly. The way in which the dynamic power in the body is used makes for the individualism and style in dance. Everyone moves differently in dance, but all dancers have a core of energy, a dynamism, that makes their every movement breathe life.

A good fashion model is graceful, but not necessarily a good dancer. The model plays down any dynamic power in her body; her purpose is to call attention to her garment and to display it to advantage. Energy and vitality exhibited on her part immediately detract from the dress, and the viewer's attention is diverted. The whole being of the model is subjugated to the personality of the costume.

One may have beautiful posture but not be a good dancer. A dance posture is charged with an expectant quality — it goes beyond positioning.

One famous dance teacher flew into a rage during a dance technique class when one of her pupils unwarily answered in the affirmative the question when asked, "Are you comfortable?" The answer, of course, should have been, "No, I'm drying," or "Ouch! It hurts!" Seriously, the point to be made is that one should always be trying to do more than his body is capable of doing. It is this extra stretch, pull and striving that makes for the tension necessary for dynamic dance movement.

Dynamism captures empathy in an audience. Modern dance is an audience-dancer participation art. It is not so much a spectator art. When a dancer soars into a leap, he should be able by sheer force of his dynamic power to lift his audience along with him. If he writhes and suffers on the floor, the audience should be physically affected with him.

After viewing a fine dance concert by such artists as José Limón or Martha Graham and her Company, one finds that one is physically as well as mentally exhausted. Incongruously perhaps, the whole experience is tremendously exhilarating. The dynamic power of the dancers has lifted and carried the viewer through exotic, terrifying, enchanting, unexplored territory.

1. **Examples of Dynamics in Dimensional Movement**
   The whole section on Dimension found on pages 152-156 can be done with special emphasis placed on the force of the movements involved. Dynamics plays an important role in dimensional movement. The two are closely related as the energy release of large movements usually requires more force than smaller ones. However, dynamics implies a great deal more than dimension, and one sees that sometimes the most interesting and unique patterns result from exerting unexpected vibrancy even in minute movements.

2. **Changing Dynamics Using Swinging Movement**
   Drain all the energy from a two-beat, forward and backward swing. Sustain the movement to make it smooth, relaxed and practically dead! Now gradually increase the dynamics until the big, vigorous two-beat swing literally takes the dancer off the floor into a full extension jump.
   Decrease the dynamics until the dancer sinks, devoid of energy, into the floor.

3. **Examples of Changing Dynamics with Vibratory Movement**
   See page 140 under Creative Clues, section 6C.

4. **Dynamic Execution of the Axial Movement Series**
   See page 102, section A, Unit IV.
   See page 103, section B, Unit I.
   See pages 106-109, section C, Units I, II, III.

5. **Examples of Dynamics in Percussive Movement**
   See page 136 under Creative Clues.

6. **Example of Dynamics in Suspended Movement**
   See page 142 under Creative Clues B.

7. **Examples of Dynamics in Contractions and Releases**
   See page 113 under 4C and Creative Clues.

Figure Sixteen

8. **Creative Clues**
   A. Sit on the floor inside an imaginary collapsible rubber ball. Push against resistance to find a way out. Use the head, arms, feet, back.
   B. Take a partner and join right hands. Pull and tug to get the feel of moving against a resisting force. Now do the same movements alone trying to exert the same amount of energy required as when working with a partner.
   C. Move across the floor as though pulled against your will.
   D. Move across the floor as though pushed by a strong wind.
   E. Walk across the floor as though moving through a vacuum; mud, mercury or jelly; flapping gauze and confetti.
   F. Divide the room into density areas. Have groups move from one section to another to show contrasts in movement dynamics.

## VARIATIONS BUILT FROM RHYTHM

There is joy in feeling and responding to the rhythmic quality of movement. The exhilarating effect springs from the recurring flow of measured motion. Rhythm sustains the dance and gives it breadth and depth.

1. **Samples Emphasizing Elementary Development of Rhythm**
   A. Note Values
      Divide the class into three groups, each with a leader. Group I represents eighth notes; Group II represents half notes; and Group III whole notes. All three groups signify quarter notes. The accompanist plays an unordered sequence of all the above notes. Each group moves according to the leader's improvisation in response to the designated note values. All groups walk to quarter notes. When a specified note or quarter note is not sounded, those respective groups kneel and gaze at the moving group.
      Leaders should be changed frequently.
   B. Primary Rhythm
      1) Beat on a drum a variety of simple and/or compound meters repeating each measure four times. Have the class respond by first clapping, then by stepping in place, and finally by moving through space.
      2) Have the group sit in a circle. The designated leader starts clapping a specific underlying rhythm of one measure. In sequence around the circle each person answers by clapping the same rhythmic measure without losing a beat. Repeat from a standing position stepping out the same rhythm in sequence. Try improvising a non-locomotor movement to coincide with the identical rhythm. Finally repeat the same procedure using locomotor movement to travel away from the circle.
   C. Secondary Rhythm

      Write out the following rhythmic pattern on the board.

Have the class clap and then step in place to the rhythmic pattern. Divide the class into groups of three or four members. Have them develop a movement pattern to coincide with the given rhythmic pattern. Encourage each group to indicate an initial starting position, to bring the movement to some kind of climax in either the third or fourth measure, and to complete the pattern with a specific ending.

D. Accent

| 4/4 meter | cts. | meas. |
|---|---|---|
| Step sharply L Fd. suspended on half toe while making 1/4 turn R - - - - - - - - - - - - - - - - - - - - | $\overset{>}{1}$ | |
| Walk Fd. R L R - - - - - - - - - - - - - - - - - - - - - - - - - - - - | 2 3 4 | 1 |
| Stamp L Sd. as body leans L - - - - - - - - - - - - - - - - - - - | $\overset{>}{1}$ 2 | |
| Stamp R Sd. as body leans R  - - - - - - - - - - - - - - - - - | $\overset{>}{3}$ 4 | 1 |
| Make complete turn L in place walking L, R, L, R while clapping eighth notes - - - - - - - - - - - - - | $\overset{>}{1} \& \overset{>}{2} \& \overset{>}{3} \& \overset{>}{4} \&$ | 1 |
| Walk Fd. L, R - - - - - - - - - - - - - - - - - - - - - - - - - - - - | 1 2 | |
| Jump strongly to stride stand, arms stretched high diagonally upward with focus directed up - - - - - - - - - - - - - - - - - - - - - - - - - - - - | $\overset{>}{3}$ | |
| Hold - - - - - - - - - - - - - - - - - - - - - - - - - - - - - - - - - | 4 | 1 |
| | total - - | 4 |

E. Tempo
  1) Have class respond with locomotor and non-locomotor movement to moderate tempo, fast tempo, very fast tempo, slow tempo, and very slow tempo.
  2) Have groups of twos, threes or larger groups develop short movement studies using the same tempo while moving in the same direction; using different tempos while traveling in opposing directions; and using changing tempos while moving toward and away from a fixed focal point.

F. Phrasing
  1) Divide the class in groups of six or eight each with a leader. The leaders create locomotor movement to a series of 8-beat phrases with respective groups following. At the beginning of each new phrase the leaders change direction, level or focus. The leaders themselves should be changed frequently.
  2) Have partners respond to a series of four 16-beat phrases. Partners dance together for one phrase; alone for the next phrase. Developing new locomotor movement for each succeeding phrase, complete the 64 total beats alternating duo and solo dancing.

2. **Samples Emphasizing Advanced Development of Rhythm**
  A. Variable Accents
  Have different groups devise movement studies emphasizing the shifting accents indicated in the following pattern:

B. Syncopation

4/4
```
1  2  3  4   | 1 & 2 & 3 4 ah | 1-2 & 3 &-4 & | 1 2 3 4 &
```

| 4/4 meter | cts. | meas. |
|---|---|---|
| Step Fd. R placing Wt. on R heel - - - - - - - - - - - - - - - | 1 | |
| Forcibly slap R foot to floor taking Wt. on whole foot and pushing far Fd. with heel of R hand - - - - - - - - - - - - - - - - - - - - - - - - - - - - - - - - - - | >2 | |
| Repeat L - - - - - - - - - - - - - - - - - - - - - - - - - - - - - - | 3 >4 | 1 |
| Cross R foot in front of L - - - - - - - - - - - - - - - - - | 1 | |
| Slip on ball of R foot Bk. toward L - - - - - - - - - - - - | >& | |
| Step Bk. L - - - - - - - - - - - - - - - - - - - - - - - - - - - - - | 2 | |
| Step Sd. R - - - - - - - - - - - - - - - - - - - - - - - - - - - - - | & | |
| Slip on ball of R foot diagonally Bk. toward L - - - - - - - - - - - - - - - - - - - - - - - - - - - - - - - - - - | >3 | |
| Step Bk. L - - - - - - - - - - - - - - - - - - - - - - - - - - - - | 4 | |
| 1/4 turn L as hop L - - - - - - - - - - - - - - - - - - - - - - | ah | 1 |
| Traveling Fd. on L diagonal, step R - - - - - - - - - - - - | 1 | |
| Hold - - - - - - - - - - - - - - - - - - - - - - - - - - - - - - - - - | 2 | |
| Stamp L - - - - - - - - - - - - - - - - - - - - - - - - - - - - - - | >& | |
| Step R - - - - - - - - - - - - - - - - - - - - - - - - - - - - - - - | 3 | |
| Stamp L - - - - - - - - - - - - - - - - - - - - - - - - - - - - - - | >& 4 | |
| Step R - - - - - - - - - - - - - - - - - - - - - - - - - - - - - - - | & | 1 |
| 1/2 turn L lunging L - - - - - - - - - - - - - - - - - - - - - - | 1 | |
| Pivot 1/2 turn R lunging R - - - - - - - - - - - - - - - - - - | 2 | |
| Pivoting on ball of L foot, make 1/2 turn L in place, dragging R toe in wider circle - - - - - - - - - - - | >3 | |
| Step Fd. R and L - - - - - - - - - - - - - - - - - - - - - - - - | 4 & | 1 |
| | total - - | 4 |

C. Mixed Meters

2/4
```
1  2  | 1  2
```
3/4
```
1-2 & 3 | 1-2 & 3
```

6/8
```
1-2 ah 3 4 5 6  | 1-2 ah 3 4 5 6
```

|  | cts. | meas. |
|---|---|---|
| To the above phrase step Fd. L raising R leg Fd. with L arm swing Fd. and R arm Bk. -------- | 1 2 | 1 |
| Repeat R ------------------------------------ | 1 2 | 1 |
| Step Fd. L --------------------------------- | 1 | |
| Raise R leg Fd. swinging L arm Fd. and R arm Bk. ----------------------------------- | 2 | |
| Hop L --------------------------------------- | & | |
| Step Fd. R --------------------------------- | 3 | 1 |
| Repeat on same foot ------------------------ | 1 2 & 3 | 1 |
| Step Fd. L---------------------------------- | 1 | |
| Hold -------------------------------------- | 2 | |
| Hop L -------------------------------------- | ah | |
| Run R L R --------------------------------- | 3 4 5 | |
| Leap lunge L-------------------------------- | 6 | 1 |
| Repeat on opposite foot --------------------- | 1 2 ah 3 4 5 6 | 1 |
| | total -- | 6 |

D. Accumulative and Decumulative Meter

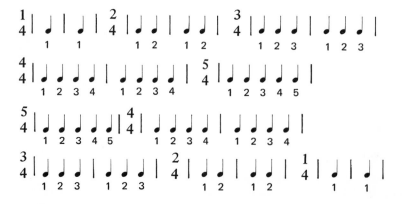

|  | cts. | meas. |
|---|---|---|
| St. in slight stride facing Fd. Shift Wt. R, body pivoting 1/4 turn L, L heel on floor, toe up ---------------------------------------- | 1 | 1 |
| Twist body to R, Wt. L, R heel on floor, toe up ------------------------------------------ | 1 | 1 |
| Step Sd. R --------------------------------- | 1 | |
| Twist body L, Wt. R, L heel on floor, toe up ------ | 2 | 1 |

| | cts. | meas. |
|---|---|---|
| Repeat stepping Sd. L, twisting body R - - - - - - - - - - | 1  2 | 1 |
| Step Sd. R - - - - - - - - - - - - - - - - - - - - - - - - - - - | 1 | |
| Cross L over R - - - - - - - - - - - - - - - - - - - - - - - - | 2 | |
| Step Sd. R while twisting body L, L heel on floor, toe up - - - - - - - - - - - - - - - - - - - - - - - - - - | 3 | 1 |
| Repeat L - - - - - - - - - - - - - - - - - - - - - - - - - - - - | 1  2  3 | 1 |
| Step Sd. R - - - - - - - - - - - - - - - - - - - - - - - - - - - | 1 | |
| Cross L over R - - - - - - - - - - - - - - - - - - - - - - - - | 2 | |
| Step Sd. R - - - - - - - - - - - - - - - - - - - - - - - - - - - | 3 | |
| Twist body L, lift L leg Sd. L, arms parallel and following line of L leg - - - - - - - - - - - - - - - - - - - | 4 | 1 |
| Repeat to L - - - - - - - - - - - - - - - - - - - - - - - - - - | 1  2  3  4 | 1 |
| Step Sd. R - - - - - - - - - - - - - - - - - - - - - - - - - - - | 1 | |
| Cross L over R - - - - - - - - - - - - - - - - - - - - - - - - | 2 | |
| 3-step turn R, L, R - - - - - - - - - - - - - - - - - - - - - - | 3  4  5 | |
| Hop R lifting L leg Sd. L - - - - - - - - - - - - - - - - - - | ah | 1 |
| Repeat to L - - - - - - - - - - - - - - - - - - - - - - - - - - | 1  2  3<br>4  5  ah | 1 |
| Repeat 4-beat movement 2 X - - - - - - - - - - - - - - - - - - - - - - - - - - - - - - - - - - - | | 2 |
| Repeat 3-beat movement 2 X - - - - - - - - - - - - - - - - - - - - - - - - - - - - - - - - - - - | | 2 |
| Repeat 2-beat movement 2 X - - - - - - - - - - - - - - - - - - - - - - - - - - - - - - - - - - - | | 2 |
| Repeat 1-beat twist 2 X - - - - - - - - - - - - - - - - - - - - - - - - - - - - - - - - - - - - - | | 2 |
| | total - - | 18 |

E. Rondo

## A B A C A D A

Divide into groups and have each construct a simple composition based on a rondo (see Chapter 3, page 44). One person moves alone on the A theme; joins a partner for B; repeats the A theme alone; joins a group and moves in unison for C; repeats the A theme alone; joins a new group that introduces a different movement for D; completes the study by repeating the same A theme alone.

F. Round

For an example of a Round Form, use the rhythmic and movement pattern of the Syncopation Study found in "B" under Sample Variations Emphasizing Advanced Development of Rhythm. (See page 163.)

Divide the class into three groups. Start Group I moving from upstage left toward center stage. After two measures, Group II starts to repeat the same movement pattern from upstage right progressing diagonally toward center. After four measures, Group III starts to repeat the same movement pattern from downstage right and progresses diagonally across and upstage facing toward Group I. Once each group has started, they continue their pattern three times and then hold in a final position placing right heel forward and the heel of the right hand pushing diagonally forward.

Now try the Round with groups entering after a one measure interval. Continue three times and hold at the end until all movement ceases.

## FLOOR PATTERN FOR SYNCOPATED ROUND

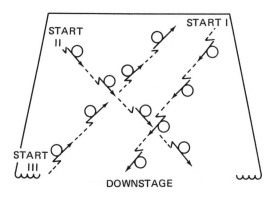

G. Polymeter — Resultant Rhythm Study

Charting 3/4 against 4/4, see Chapter 3, page 43.

The rhythm which results is:

1 ② ③ 4 5 ⑥ 7 ⑧ 9 10 ⑪ ⑫

Two groups work as contrasting units. Group I develops a movement pattern for four measures of 3/4 meter. Group II creates a movement pattern for three measures of 4/4 meter. Group I does their 3/4 pattern two times and holds final position while Group II does their 4/4 pattern two times. Introduce an eight beat transition during which the two groups combine into a massed unit. In unison, both groups move to the accents, 1, 4, 5, 7, 9, 10, of the resultant rhythm twice. Devise a climactic ending.

## THEME AND VARIATIONS DANCE STUDY

| Theme: 4/4 meter, slow, stately | cts. | meas. |
|---|---|---|
| All face Fd. start L walk 4 steps Fd. ------------- | 1 2 3 4 | 1 |
| Lunge L Sd., reach slowly out with L hand from L hip, palm up, focus L ------------------ | 1 2 3 4 | 1 |
| Circle R almost in place: St. R walk 4 ---------- | 1 2 3 4 | 1 |
| Step wide Sd. R --------------------------- | 1 | |

|                                                                 | cts.        | meas. |
|-----------------------------------------------------------------|-------------|-------|
| Open arms up diagonally overhead, focus high - - - - - - - - - - - - - - - - - - - - - - - - - - - - - - - - - - - - - - - - | 2  3  4     | 1     |
|                                                                 | total - -   | 4     |

**Variation No. 1**  4/4 meter, same pulse, but twice as fast in feeling — use 1/8 notes and runs

|                                                                 | cts.        | meas. |
|-----------------------------------------------------------------|-------------|-------|
| All run Fd. 8 St. L - - - - - - - - - - - - - - - - - - - - - - - | 1 & 2 & 3 & 4 & | 1 |
| Lunge L and reach L - - - - - - - - - - - - - - - - - - - - - - - | 1  2        |       |
| Change Wt. R quickly, bring L hand into hip again - - - - - - - - - - - - - - - - - - - - - - - - - - - - - - - - - - - - | ah |       |
| Lunge L again and reach L out from hip, focus L - - - - - - - - - - - - - - - - - - - - - - - - - - - - | 3  4 | 1 |
| 8 runs circling to R, St. R - - - - - - - - - - - - - - - - - - - | 1 & 2 & 3 & 4 & | 1 |
| Step Sd. R - - - - - - - - - - - - - - - - - - - - - - - - - - - | 1 |       |
| Jump with legs apart, hands reaching up from shoulders - - - - - - - - - - - - - - - - - - - - - - - - - | 2 |       |
| Pull hands to shoulders - - - - - - - - - - - - - - - - - - - - - | 3 |       |
| Jump, reach up from shoulders again - - - - - - - - - - - | 4 | 1 |
|                                                                 | total - -   | 4     |

**Variation No. 2**  4/4 meter, slow sustained

|                                                                 | cts.        | meas. |
|-----------------------------------------------------------------|-------------|-------|
| Lunge Fd. R bringing both hands slowly up from hips, palms Fd. reaching Fd. - - - - - - - - - - - - - | 1  2  3  4 | 1 |
| Twist body slowly R, reach L leg far to R in Bk. of supporting R foot - - - - - - - - - - - - - - - - - - - | 1  2 |       |
| Fall sustaining movement to L hip, letting L hand reach out L along the floor as stretch full length L - - - - - - - - - - - - - - - - - - - - - - - - | 3  4 | 1 |
| Contract pull up to knees - - - - - - - - - - - - - - - - - - - - | 1  2 |       |
| Cross L over R spiralling upward and on around to face Fd., keep low - - - - - - - - - - - - - - - | 3  4 | 1 |
| Straighten back slowly, arms lift to diagonal overhead reach, lift focus - - - - - - - - - - - - - - - - - - | 1  2  3  4 | 1 |
|                                                                 | total - -   | 4     |

**Variation No. 3**  4/4 meter, medium tempo, strong quality

|                                                                 | cts.        | meas. |
|-----------------------------------------------------------------|-------------|-------|
| 4 wide, vigorous lunge walks Fd. St. L, arms swing shoulder high in opposition - - - - - - - - - - - - - | 1  2  3  4 | 1 |

|  | cts. | meas. |
|---|---|---|
| Strong Sd. lunge L, flinging L arm out Sd. shoulder level, hand in fist, focus L - - - - - - - - - - - - | 1 | |
| Hold - - - - - - - - - - - - - - - - - - - - - - - - - - - - - - - - - - - | 2 | |
| Percussively bend R elbow in front of body shoulder high, fist near L shoulder, focus L - - - - - - | 3 | |
| Thrust both arms straight to L - - - - - - - - - - - - - - - - - | 4 | 1 |
| Circling R one complete turn, take wide low walks circling R with R heel lead, L foot closing to R on the "and" beat, arms reaching out shoulder level, hands in fists - - - - - - - - - - - - - | 1 & 2 &<br>3 & 4 & | 1 |
| Big circular swing of R leg to step R, heel lead to R, focus to R - - - - - - - - - - - - - - - - - - - - - - - | 1 | |
| Big circular swing of L leg to step L, heel lead to L, focus L - - - - - - - - - - - - - - - - - - - - - - - - - | 2 | |
| Both fists flung diagonally overhead, body lifted, strong, wide stride - - - - - - - - - - - - - - - - - - - | 3 | |
| Hold - - - - - - - - - - - - - - - - - - - - - - - - - - - - - - - - - - - | 4 | 1 |
| | total - - | 4 |
| Theme and three variations | total - - | 16 |

Figure Seventeen

# Chapter 7

# DANCE COMPOSITION

Dance composition is the achievement of creative endeavor. Although improvisation and experimentation are involved in the procedure, dance composition is more than this. It represents a logical planning, the organizing of materials, and the developing of a specific concept with respect to the overall form which may range from stark reality to pure abstraction. Interestingly enough, creativity is not something that may be turned on and off at will. Rather, it presupposes the need for some kind of motivation to inspire originality. From the simplest beginnings creative experiences should be stimulated by solving specific and tangible problems. The actual process of making fundamental techniques creative forms a base for the development of short movement patterns or studies; in turn, these become the threshold of simple, and then, more advanced dance compositions. In other words, if basic movement and rhythmic experiences are approached creatively, they tend to span the gap between techniques and composition. This is a vital step in helping dancers begin to explore the joy of discovery and expression. In the meantime the teacher should learn to know the students as individuals and to be able to understand the goals they have set for themselves. Only in this way can dance become meaningful for them. Initially the dancer needs to know how to use his body — his instrument of expression — efficiently and effectively. Then, through varied movement exploration and experimentation he begins to approach a more mature form of expression. Gradually, as the dancer is allowed freedom from limitation, his movement becomes more direct and purposeful. As he achieves greater confidence, his concepts of dance are enlarged, his suppositions show noticeable clarification, his ability to organize materials is apparent, and his skill in communicating his dance ideas is reinforced.

The whole process of learning to dance creatively should be one of self-exploration under competent direction rather than that of teacher dictation. Breadth and depth in development do not accrue from experiences that are teacher imposed. Conversely, the teacher, through guidance and suggestion, should help the student open just the right doors to creative endeavor.

The ways of seeking and finding are innumerable. For beginners the choice of dance ideas may be either too overwhelming, or may be lacking entirely. The problem is, where and how to begin. Certainly, the concept to be developed must be appropriate for the maturity and interest of the dance composer. For the less experienced, compositional materials should be simple and somewhat limited. Otherwise, discouragement and disinterest may follow. Even though the first efforts may seem meager, the results should be respected and evaluated in a helpful, positive manner. Frequently, the beginner's first approach will be one of pantomime. At this point he should be encouraged to use the movement in a more objective and less literal fashion. Similarly, the more advanced student should be challenged to reach as far as his means and understanding will permit.

Having equipped himself with an understanding of the various elements of movement, analyzed and classified basic movements, and experienced many examples of dance movement built from these various aspects, it seems reasonable for the dancer to proceed to the real purpose of all this intensive dissection — to dance! This calls to mind the wise man's counsel to his son. "Go to college, my boy, and then forget that you have ever been there." After dancers struggle for years training their bodies in order to achieve some kind of technical competence, they should then forget all the mechanics that went into the movement and just dance! The knowledge and technique should become a part of the dancer so that movement literally flows out and the body is able to express that which the mind dictates. The body then becomes truly a fine instrument in the hands of a skillful dance artist.

This does not mean that at last one can relax and move freely and emotionally without regard to form, subject matter, and technique. It means that the dancer must apply all the intelligence he possesses in tackling the larger problem set before him, or which he sets for himself — that of communicating an idea through movement. This is the real challenge of dance!

When working with an idea the same dedicated, honest attack is required as in studying floor pattern, swinging movement, or even in analyzing a skip. Look at the heart of the problem, cut away all embellishments and extraneous material and find the essence of the thought. Determine if the idea is danceable. A stone seems very dead. It would be difficult to dance about one. However, a certain contour or texture might excite some dancers to build a quite interesting movement study around an idea of a stone.

Does the problem seem worthwhile? Does it merit time and thought or does it seem trite? A wheel may seem at first glance quite uninteresting — it just goes around and around. But to a dancer it may kindle a whole dance theme — a perpetual motion study, showing the rut in which many human lives get caught. One approach might indicate the progress of civilization in which the wheel made such a tremendous impact. Other themes might emphasize the work quality, or stress various characteristics of wheels, such as: delicate, spindle-like, hard, soft, rigid or flexible.

Does the subject hold sufficient interest for the dancer and his audience? After all, the dancer has to work with the idea, be inspired by it, and have enough insight and interest in the problem to sustain him to complete the dance once he has started it. If he has not this much inspiration he cannot hope to interest an audience who perhaps has not given the idea any thought at all. The reason the dancer creates the dance is to be able to communicate his contribution to an audience. True, he gains great personal satisfaction in attacking the problem and being able to arrive at some possible conclusion. But the urge, need and, indeed, obligation of the artist is to show his results to others.

Is the idea timely and meaningful? Not long ago a dancer was captivated by the story of Poe's, "The Mask of the Red Death." But she fell into the trap of being so literal and enthralled with medieval costumes and court dances, masks and pageantry, that she missed the great opportunity of seizing the theme itself and relating this old story to life today.

The story concerned a Prince who because of the tragedy of violent death around him withdrew into a walled refuge of frantic pleasure seeking. How much more timely and apropos this dance would have been had it adapted the idea to the twentieth century danger of total destruction from the bomb and our efforts to escape into private shelters. This would have emphasized much more clearly the true dance theme, which was selfish withdrawal — refusing to face the challenge of life.

One might say that it is the dancer's business to see movement possibilities in practically everything. He must carefully select his idea and then proceed to develop it choreographically. Assuredly, this process is not reduced to the mere synthesis of combining parts into a whole.

After a general dance concept has been selected, it may help to narrow the idea to at least an initial working title. This point of departure tends to hold together the developing materials and sets a tangible goal toward which to work. After the composition has been completed, the process of reanalyzing and refining the materials of the dance may result in the discovery of a new title.

## SUGGESTED SOURCES FOR DANCE IDEAS

From Key Words to Suggest Moods, Feelings and Reactions

| | | |
|---|---|---|
| adversity | deceitful | foolish |
| affectation | dedication | frail |
| agitation | defenseless | frank |
| anger | defiant | frenzy |
| anticipation | deflated | frighten |
| anxiety | dejection | frustration |
| aspiration | denial | furious |
| awe | depressed | futility |
| bashfulness | derisive | generous |
| belligerent | desperation | gentle |
| bereavement | despondency | glad |
| bewildered | determination | gossip |
| bitter | disappointment | gratitude |
| boasting | discontent | greedy |
| boisterous | discouragement | grief |
| bored | disillusionment | gullible |
| brave | dissatisfaction | habit |
| calmness | distraction | harmony |
| carefree | distress | haste |
| careless | docile | hate |
| casual | dominating | haughty |
| cheerful | downhearted | heaviness |
| cheerless | dynamic | helpless |
| comfort | eager | holiness |
| composed | embarrassment | hope |
| compassionate | enthusiastic | hopelessness |
| complaining | envious | horror |
| composure | erratic | humility |
| conceit | exaggerated | humor |
| confident | excitable | hysterical |
| confused | expectant | idler |
| contentment | exuberant | impatient |
| courteous | failure | impetuous |
| convulsive | falter | impulsive |
| cowardice | farewell | indifference |
| crying | fatigued | infectious |
| curiosity | fear | inferiortiy |
| daring | flattery | innocence |
| daydreaming | flighty | insecurity |

insolent
intimidate
intolerance
irritation
jealousy
jeer
joy
jubilant
just
kind
lament
languid
laughter
lethargy
liberal
listless
liveliness
magnify
majestic
meddlesome
meditation
melancholy
merciful
merciless
migration
misery
modesty
morose
mourning
mystify
nervous
nobility
nonchalance
nonconformist
nonsense
nostalgic
obedience
obstinacy
old
opposition
optimism
ostentatious
overpower
pain
peace
peculiar

penitence
perish
persistent
persuasion
pessimism
piety
pity
plea
pleasure
plight
power
pride
prim
proud
quarrel
quick
quiet
rage
ramble
rebellious
reckless
refusal
regret
rejoice
reluctant
remorse
repress
reproach
repulsion
resentment
resistance
restraint
restrict
revelry
revenge
reverence
revolt
ridicule
roving
sad
sarcastic
satirical
secure
sedate
sentimental
serenity

serious
severity
shame
silence
sinister
small
smooth
solemn
sorrow
spontaneous
stately
steadfast
stern
strife
struggle
submission
subtle
sullen
superficial
superiority
suppress
surprise
surrender
temerity
temptation
tender
terror
timidity
tragic
tranquil
tribulation
turbulent
uncertainty
unchangeable
uniformity
useless
vacillation
veneration
vigilance
vivacity
wander
weary
worry
wrath
yearning
youth

From Combined Locomotor Movements (see Chapter 5, pages 81-95)
From Patterns Emphasizing Spatial Aspects (see Chapter 6, pages 142-157)
From Patterns Emphasizing Changing Dynamics (see Chapter 6, pages 157-161)
From Patterns Emphasizing Rhythm (see Chapter 6, pages 161-168)
From Literary Sources:

1. Drama from early ritual down to the present time.
2. Poems by such poets as Walt Whitman, Carl Sandburg, Vachel Lindsay, Robert Frost, Archibald MacLeish, Edgar Lee Masters, Rupert Brooke, and Frederico Garcia Lorca.
3. Books such as biographies and novels.
4. Short stories.
5. Bible.
   Books of Ruth, Esther, Joshua, Job, Psalms, Proverbs, and Ecclesiastes.
   Characters of Ruth, Esther, Job, Jonah, John the Baptist, David, Joseph, Judas Iscariat, Sampson and Delilah, Mary the Mother, and Mary Magdalene.
6. Historical Characters such as Catherine the Great, Nero, Mary, Queen of Scots. Henry VIII, Marie Antoinette, Kublai Khan, Cleopatra, Lady Hamilton, Madame Pompadour, Catherine de Medici, Elizabeth I, Joan of Arc, Florence Nightingale and Clara Barton (nurses), Susan B. Anthony (women's suffrage), Jane Addams (social settlement, Hull House), and Brigham Young.

From Legendary Sources
From Current Events:

1. Famous murder trials.
2. Floods, famines, earthquakes and other disasters.
3. Space flights.

From Dance Suites:

A dance suite usually comprises three to five short though related dances. The following samples are intended to be merely suggestive listings to allow a range of choice and to permit ample leeway in personalizing the development of the suite. In some instances only general ideas are included; in others, specific titles are proposed.

1. Folk Suite
   Cowboy themes such as Round-up, Saturday Night Whoopie, Along the Trail, Around the Campfire, Westward Ho!, Sea Chanteys and folk ballads.

2. Pioneer Suite
   Barn Warmin'
   Corn Huskers' Frolic
   Hoe-Down
   Dance Time

3. Historical Suite
   The Overland Trail
   The Trail of Tears
   Northwest Passage
   The Pony Express
   The Erie Canal

Paul Bunyan
Johnny Appleseed

4. Regional Suite
   New England Suite
      Salem Lore
      Prayer Ritual
      Witchcraft Magic
      Thomas Morton versus the Puritans
   Mississippi Suite
      Indian Influences
      Spanish, French and English Authority
      Steamboat Days
   Virginia Suite
      The English Settlers
      The Struggle for Independence — poverty, humiliation, and strife.
      Colonial Virginia — social life.

5. Spiritual Suite
   Work Songs
   Religious Songs
   Blues Songs

6. Pre-Classic Suite
   Allemande
      Noble Entrance
      Tender Moment for Trio
      The Letter
   Bourrée
      Lusty Dance
      The Bacchanalia
      The Reveler
   Chaconne
      The Duennas
      Majestic Ceremony
      The Grand Duchess
   Courante
      Hasty Exit
      Gay Incident
      Holiday Dance
   Galliard
      The Lighthearted
      Poppy-cock
      The Gay Young Blade
   Gavotte
      Flexible Stateliness
      Flirtation
      Greetings
   Gigue
      Rural Sketch
      Traffic Problem
      Dimension of Gossip

Minuet
    Afternoon Tea
    Flirtation
    Her Ladyship Shops for a Chapeau
Passacaglia
    Royal Gaiety
    The Processional
    Where the Elite Meet
Pavane
    Evil Intent
    Pioneer Woman
    The Illustrious Patrician
Passepied
    Woman's Prerogative — to Change Her Mind
    Chicanery
    Adventures in Deception
Rigaudon
    A Satire on a Lesson from the Ballet Master
    The Singing Tambourine
    Indecision of a Young Girl
Sarabande
    Farewell
    The Sophisticate
    The Intrigues of Catherine de Medici

## SELECTED LIST OF DANCE TITLES WITH PROGRAM NOTES

Titles are used on a printed program to aid the audience in clarifying the general intent of the dance composition. At times the titles are self-explanatory. At other times additional choice remarks help in explaining the significance of the dance to the audience.

1. Alone in a Crowd
2. Directions to a Stranger
3. The Introvert
4. Exuberance
5. Indecision
6. Vesperale
Depicting the serene and meditative mood inspired by eventide.
7. A Cry in the Wilderness
A study in loneliness.
8. Movement Studies
Changing Levels.
Changing Dynamics.
9. Better Late Than Never
Meet me under the clock.

10. Chauvinism
    Exaggerated patriotism — blind devotion to a lost cause.

11. Social Strata
    Depicts the three levels of society — upper, middle and lower. The drape signifies convention, tradition, comfort, and luxury of life.

12. Behind These Walls
    A psychological study of the morbid effect of routine, the rebellion against it, and the final resignation to the inescapable monotony.

13. The Lens
    A psychological study of three types of individuals developed from three forms of optical deviation and the ultimate conformity to the normal.
    The Nearsighted — seeing only the immediate and the superficial.
    The Farsighted — moving in intangible dreams; oblivious to the immediate.
    The Astigmatic — living in a state of confusion with conceptions constantly changing.
    The Conformation — realization of true values resolves into a totally integrated personality.

14. A Saga of East Tennessee
    A group of dances dedicated to all those people who destined that there should be an East Tennessee.

    Spirit of the Land
    A dance, based on abstract movement, conveying the grandeur, ruggedness, and scenic majesty of the terrain of East Tennessee.

    Native Dispossession
    Dance of Avowal
        The sturdy pioneers force their way into the land of the Redmen, bravely meeting their furtive opposition, and finally triumphing over them.

    Lamentable Departure
    The banished Indians lament their lost land and turn their eyes westward.

    Pioneer Episode
    Dance of the Settlers
        These pioneers - rugged and courageous individualists — accepting their heritage, bend their efforts to meet the hardships imposed by the environs, to overcome marauding invaders, and to insure an existence that is their lot.
    Mountain Ballad
        A dance parody to one of the mountaineer's favorite play party tunes that he saved for his happiest moods of singing and dancing.
    Mechanical Power
        Man harnesses and utilizes the natural power of his immediate surroundings.

## DANCES DERIVED FROM SPECIFIC CONTENT

The following suggestions for dance choreography derive from varied sources to demonstrate the manner in which a particular form may be utilized to augment the chosen theme.

Figure Eighteen

## DANCES BASED ON RHYTHMIC DEVICES

The rhythmic devices which are related to dance movement (See Chapter 3) may serve as a source for choreographic material. The explicit factors inherent in any one of these rhythmic devices may become a firm point of departure for developing a dance composition. The more advanced rhythmic devices, such as shifting accents, accumulative and decumulative meter, mixed meter, counterpoint, polymeter, and the several rhythmic forms are peculiarly adapted to dance and are suitable as choreographic content.

Samples:

1. **Dance of Greeting**

   A B A Sequential Form
   A is done in a Three-Part Canon
   B is done in Decumulative Meter
   A is done in a Two-Part canon

   Synopsis of Dance
   An entrance of three groups is completed in a three-part canon. The middle section of the dance makes use of decumulative meter to help produce a feeling of expectancy, and to build the intensity through the use of the entire group moving in unison to a pronounced rhythmic base. The two-part canon is a variation of the three-part entrance canon, thus making an overall sequential form.

2. **Primal Power**

   Program Note
   Based upon a resultant rhythm — a two counter to a three. Initially, the two and three beat patterns are introduced simultaneously. Eventually, only the resultant accents of the combined meters are evident in the movement.

   Synopsis of Dance
   Three dancers produce an exacting and powerful dance by utilizing movement which exploits the resultant rhythm of a two counter to a three. A primitive quality is maintained throughout. The climax is achieved by a gradual increase in tempo and by a sudden shift to movement in unison which responds only to the accents of the resultant rhythm.

3. **Passacaglia**

   Program Note
   A theme and variations based upon a traditional dance form of the court and stage; characterized by imposing majesty coupled with the gaiety of its social form.

   Suggested Music: Passacaglia by Cyril Scott.
   This dance suggests a specific piece of music as accompaniment. Many choreographers prefer to work from a previously composed musical selection. The form is already established. The tempo, mood, and quality are set. The composer has been sufficiently inspired to communicate an idea in musical terms. It is the responsibility of the choreographer not only to be able to understand the composer's intentions but also to be able to

enrich this original concept with the indelible stamp of his own personality, and to express these ideas in vital movement terms.

Starting Formation on Stage:

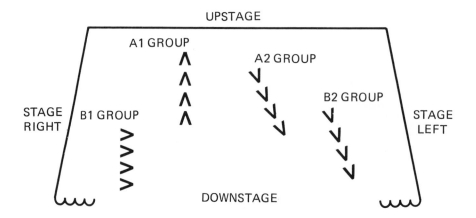

Synopsis of Dance

The Passacaglia is a theme and variations form which is often favored by dancers. In this dance an initial theme is introduced and is followed by eight variations. Large groups are woven together to enhance a majesty of design. The ever-shifting contour of the dancers adds interest to the unfolding drama of line.

## DANCES EVOLVING FROM IDEAS

Particular care should be taken in the selection of a suitable title for the original dance work. The written title is the first contact between the choreographer and his audience. The tone is established by these few highly selective words for the expectation of a light, amusing episode, a brutal comment, or a dramatic and emotional dance experience. The choreographer is concerned with communicating his concept, not confusing his audience. In some instances a subtitle or a brief explanation could be useful in clarifying the content. For example, following the title "Song in Counterpoint" it might be suggested that the word counterpoint is used not so much as a musical term but to illustrate the pulls and counter forces of the dance.

Dances based on ideas and developed to completion should have music composed especially for the dance. Ideally, the choreographer and the composer work very closely together from the first conception of the dance idea in order to achieve the most harmonious and artistically satisfying result.

Samples:

1. **Song in Counterpoint**

   Program Note

   This dance attempts to show the effort of a modern woman toward an inner acceptance of and joyful commitment to her role.

Dancers:
  Wife
  Husband
  Five stairstep size children
  Friends — three women and two men

Synopsis of Dance
  Part I
    A. Wife's Theme
       A solo establishes the willing, careful, very earnest character of the woman. A square floor pattern helps to establish the narrow, confined rut into which modern woman often finds herself.
    B. Introduction of Groups
       1. Husband
          This dance section sets the relationships of the couple which is open, mutual regard and respect. The movement varies between the vigorous and gay to the more tender.
       2. Children
          The woman's relationship with her children is established with tender moments interspersed with regimentation collapsing into confusion.
       3. Social Group
          The artificial and forced hilarity of being with a group of associates is explored.
    C. Build-up
       A gradual increasing carousel type of movement whereby the entire group circles the stage is utilized to create a hypnotically oscillating setting in which the woman finally collapses.

  Part II  "Growing Pains"
    After an introspective time of despair, the woman finds the inner strength to face her problems.

  Part III  Song
    Led by the wife, the group dances lyrically and harmoniously to re-affirm their love, joy and strength in each other.

2. **Child of the Earth**

   A study of the conflicting pagan and religious forces in Mexico.

   Dancers:
     Earth Figure
     Children of the Earth
     Monk
     Four Religious Fanatics

   Synopsis of Dance
     Part I
       The dance opens with a solo by the Earth Figure. There is a quiet, but powerful primitive quality in her movement theme. Later she is joined by two children of the earth. The dance expands to include five children

of the earth and the dance turns into a wild, gay, uninhibited fiesta theme.

Transition

A Monk, carrying a large cross, followed by four religious fanatics, breaks into the merry-making, and progresses across diagonally from upstage right to downstage left and exits. The Earth Figure exits downstage right. As the cross passes, the children genuflect and become influenced by the restrained, off-center movement of the religious procession.

Part II

The four religious fanatics establish a dance theme. Gradually more and more of the earth children are caught up in the movement. At the height of the strained, sustained pulls the Earth Figure re-enters.

Part III

A struggle of the wills results. The children of the earth are influenced by both the religious and the pagan themes.

Transition

The Monk with the cross re-enters and progresses across stage on the same long diagonal. All genuflect as the cross passes, and the religious fanatics fall in behind to form a processional as in their first appearance. The Earth Figure waits downstage right, facing the audience, pulsing in place.

Part IV

As the processional exits, the Earth Figure dominates the stage, gathering up her children in a strong, building accumulative rhythmic pattern. The group exits diagonally downstage right.

Part V

There is a restatement of the Earth Figure's solo theme as the curtain closes.

## DANCES BASED ON PLAYS

When attacking the problem of making a dance based on a play, the first step is to come to understand what the playwright is trying to communicate through his medium and then translate this perception into the dance medium. The dramatic line must be determined. The characters that are needed to push the action forward and the incidents which throw the essence of the plot into the sharpest possible focus must be carefully selected. Many times two or three dancers can represent a large group of characters. If words are to be injected to emphasize the dance action, they should be used sparingly. The voice or voices are introduced to set the mood or to act as a rhythmic base rather than as a crutch to clarify ideas that are best said through movement. A moment in dance can often say volumes. It is important to be clear in dance statements. Never play down to an audience, but stay true to the art of dance and compliment the viewer's imagination and intelligence. The purpose is not to transplant the literal format of the play into dance expression, but rather to extract the substance of the plot and interpret it into a meaningful dance impression.

Sample:

### The House of Bernarda Alba

Program Note
A dance based on the play by the Spanish poet-dramatist, Frederico Garcia Lorca. The action takes place in Bernarda's house during the days following her husband's funeral.

Dancers:
Bernarda
Five Daughters; Adele, the youngest.
Women in Mourning.

Properties:
The cane carried by Bernarda. A large white filigree Moorish arch – on the right side of which hangs a man's heavy dark cloak; on the left side is a filmy white wedding veil.

Synopsis of Dance
Part I   Opening
A funeral procession begins the dance. Words may be used to give the background of the tragedy to follow. The solemn measured beat sets the atmosphere of foreboding.

Part II   The Character of Bernarda
Bernarda enters holding a long black cane which she actively uses throughout the dance as a symbol of authority. Through movement she establishes her relationship with her daughters.

Part III   The Relationship of the Sisters
In the development of a sewing theme the sisters establish their relationship to each other.

Part IV   Adele's Effort to Break Conventional Ties
Adele's rebellion against the stifling boundaries of tradition, and her wilful, passionate nature are developed.

Part V   Climax
The conflict of wills develops. There is one brief time of hope when the establishment is shaken, but then youth and passion are destroyed.

Coda
The women in mourning return with their original theme. Authority is re-established. All is as before, except now the knowledge of hopelessness is more real.

## DANCES EVOLVING FROM POETIC CONTENT

Many choreographers compose dances based on poems, poetic phrases or simply ideas which a poet has inspired. In some cases, no words are needed to help the dancer communicate his own interpretation. Sometimes he may introduce the poem in its entirety to add power, clarity, or rhythmic intensity to his dance. He may use one speaker or a choral choir to accompany the dancers as they move. He may even have his dancers speak at significant moments.

In the dance, "Song of Life," a choral choir is used offstage and conducted much as a symphony orchestra. The speaking voices introduce themes, set tempos, establish moods, and are used as accompaniment to dance movement. A percussion ensemble accompanies parts of the work to add even greater variety and support.

If the speakers are to be used on stage and in view of the audience, care must be taken to arrange all entrances and exits, and to choreograph the speaker's movements so that they will not destroy the quality of the dance being performed. If one speaker is to be used at several points in the dance, it may be effective to freeze the action of the dancers as the speaker recites his line or lines. Lights, if available, are very useful in directing attention to and from the necessary points of emphasis.

Whenever another art medium is used with the dance, a delicate balance must be observed. When an art work has inspired the choreographer to compose his piece, the intricacies are especially challenging. It is important that the dance will not lack the efficacy of its original art form. In other words the power of the dance should be significant and should not be sublimated to the other art form. The choreographer must offer new insights, expand and enrich the ideas of the initial concept, or make additional and unique contributions in order for the dance to be equally successful.

José Limón's dance, "Lament for Ignacio Sanchez Mejias," based on the poem by Frederico Garcia Lorca, represents a masterful fusion of the arts of poetry, drama, music, and dance.

Samples:

1. **Eastport to Block Island**

   Program Note
   Depicting some of the typical events that occur in a seaboard area.

   Cast Off!
   Splice your patience, lads, we'll soon be off!

   Seaman's Sermon
   Steady at the helm!
   Weather eye peeled!
   Through changing wind and tide
   Hold true your course
   Look to harbors aloft!

   Storm Warning
   A seaman's blood is salty stuff
   And we must live on land,
   They back and fill and tack and luff
   And we must live on land,
   So wait and watch and wonder why
   And pray this time they will not die.

   Synopsis of Dance
   Part I   Cast Off!
   Depicting the light, carefree antics of sailors on shore leave.

   Part II   Seaman's Sermon
   The seamen, representing scoundrels, ruffians and bullies from all walks of life tend to be non-conformists. As emergencies such as severe storm

warnings arise, they demonstrate uncontrolled feelings of fear and superstition. In the foreboding situation the steadiness of the captain quiets the group and helps them accept their plight by teaching them to rely on a power much greater than themselves.

> Choral Speech Choir: during the unfolding of the dance, periodically the voices present the following poem, "The Seaman's Sermon."

> Who are these fellows?
> Where are they going?
> Where do they come from? Do they know?
> Do they see the hatches of sin battened
> Down above them by the evil one?

> No, my breathren, the helm spins wildly but
> You are too far below to realize it.

> Watch the weather, brethren, the helm
> Needs a steady hand before the wind and
> Tide take you far off your course.

> And what is your course?
> Aloft! Aloft! That's where you're going.

> With a steady helm and a fair wind
> That's the place. That's the port.

> Peace . . . peace . . . only peace in that harbor aloft!

Part III  Storm Warning

This is a dance of the mother and her three daughters who wait for their captain to return from sea. They watch from the "widow's walk" (a small, open porch-like area surrounded by a railing and located on top of the house), the vantage point from which all women of seafaring men may catch a first glimpse of returning ships. Although the mother is deeply concerned for the safety of her husband, she walks proudly to assure her daughters that all is well despite her inner misgivings concerning the outcome of the watch. The strength and significance of the entire dance is augmented by the resolute though serene appearance of the mother who leads her three daughters in a square floor pattern.

## Song of Life

Program Note

A dance depicting the vital forces of human existence.

Synopsis of Dance

<u>Opening Statement</u>
   Choral Choir:
      We are the spirit of a people.
   Dancers
<u>Work Theme</u>
   Choral Choir:
      We are the plowshares, stevedores, millhands, road crews,

Sullen
Struggling
Sweating.
Dancers
Choral Choir:
The puppets of a universal stage, coming and going
To the melody of sun and moon,
Yesterday, now and forever!
Dancers
Choral Choir:
We are the power that dams rivers, fells forest giants,
Forces energy from black diamonds.
Dancers

Laughter Theme
Choral Choir:
We are the surly, stormy laughter of a people
Its blood
Its pulse
The throbbing blend of a hundred nations.
Dancers

Struggle Theme
Choral Choir:
We are the dynamo that creates life
Lives for it
Dies for it
Fights, cries, kills!
Dancers

Hope Theme
Choral Choir:
In blood shot eyes is always the obscure horizon,
Horizon of hope
The golden tomorrow.
Dancers
Choral Choir:
We are the universal law, the
Master's most genial creations.
Created to last a span of time,
Transient or constant,
Plodding or coasting,
Drowned in tears,
Interrupted with laughter.
We are the universal law,
The family of man.
Dancers

# DANCE MOBILE

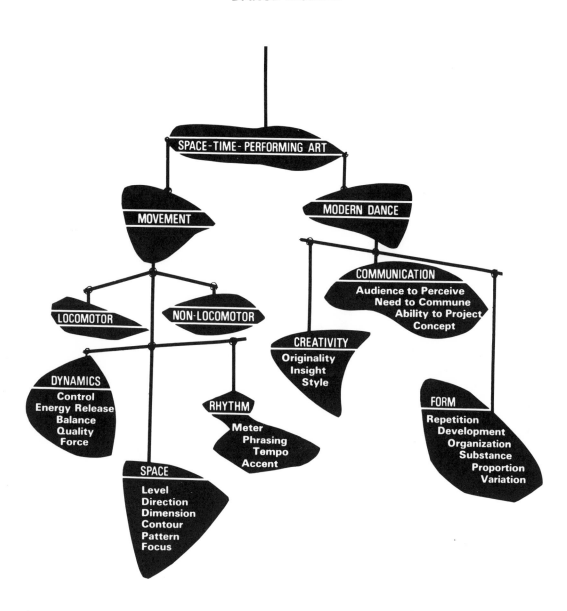

Figure Nineteen

Design by Dan Estes

## THE PROCESS OF CHOREOGRAPHY

Once the basic idea has been decided upon, the process of choreographic development follows. The central concept and the core substance of the dance is defined and established — indelibly imprinted on the composer's mind. This vision and insight will guide him and color every decision in the selecting, organizing, arranging and developing of his movement material. In constructing his dance to make a whole and a completely finished work, he must first have something to say — a personal view or deep emotional conviction — and then systematically and logically move toward revealing this concept. A dance results from clarifying and illuminating a mental image. It is a symbolic rendering of a truth.

The Dance Mobile was conceived to try to help clarify some of the similarities and differences between all movement, and in particular, dance movement. The term mobile was thought to be especially applicable because of its connotation of the inter-dependence and inter-relationships of all of its parts, and its delicate balance of ever-changing planes and points of emphasis. By actually naming and grouping many of the various aspects in a concrete way, it was thought that a visual presentation might establish a point of contact whereby an overall view of the extremely vast and complex dance area could be achieved. The danger of over-simplification is immediately apparent. Whole books have been written on the various segments of dance. In previous chapters of this book many of the categories have been dealt with in considerable detail. Although pointed out previously, once again it should be stressed that all the elements — every item of the Dance Mobile — are inter-related and interwoven, irrevocably latched together in greater or lesser degree when dance happens.

The composer of a dance seeks to bring under his control all of these elements, to build them by adherence to form, and to communicate them effectively through his own personal insight. Form grows out of the unfolding of the dance. Form may be planned for but does not exist before the dance. The parts of form can not be listed, numbered, and produced at the choreographer's call to be placed here and there and pronounced good. Form is the thing that results and is recognized when a work of art is complete. Still, in the study of composition and in the persistent effort to break down and to see and know what takes place, one can recognize the elements of form that have been apparent in works of art in the past. It can be noted that time and again those works which have been most satisfying contained certain commonalities.

Perhaps the single most important aspect of form is the recognition of substance — a central theme, a motivating idea — which propels the movement forward toward the goal of revelation. This unifying purpose ties the moving forces together to strive for totality.

One apparent aspect of form involves the organization of selective materials so that they may be arranged into a harmonious whole. Of equal importance is the development of materials into an orderly sequence. Development refers to the growth of one movement into the next, one phrase into another, one section into the next as power and dramatic line build toward final enlightenment.

Proportion is inherent in form. Proportion emanates from the fusion of sound judgment, good taste, sensitive balance, and a delicate relationship between each move-ment and the various parts of a work.

The most readily recognizable aspect of form is repetition. To repeat a movement is to give it more importance, to stress the significance of the statement, and to allow the audience time to absorb the idea which is being expressed. Clarity of the image is further impressed on the mind of the viewer through repetition of single movements, themes, or whole sections of the dance. Through careful use of repetition the central motivating force may be strengthened and intensified.

Finally, variation becomes clearly apparent in considering the aspects of form. A variety of ways to present materials is indispensable to dance composition. The need to change, to contrast, to alter, or to utilize the ingredients of form in a different and new way is essential to the developing process. Such a variety of stimuli may challenge the viewer to a deeper insight into the message that is being conveyed. Diversity of movement is exciting to watch. Variety is the enemy of monotony and boredom.

As a dance is being composed, all the elements of form must be considered. The possibility for a successful dance achievement is greatly increased if the choreographer has an understanding of form. The dance movement and the form develop simultaneously. Each one excites the other until a whole symphony of elements fuse to become a complete entity. Movement is selected which has as its sole purpose to objectify the central idea, mood, feeling, or image. To clarify the theme, movement is expanded, repeated, contrasted, and varied. The rhythm employed augments and supports the movement and is characteristic of the idea to be expressed. The development of the movement from the myriad multiple stimuli grows in a logical, ordered sequence. This builds an overall dynamic line from the first moment of movement until the dance is complete. The way in which the materials are structured identifies the form. Unity of the whole is effected by the balancing of all the constituent elements making up the dance composition.

At last when a dance has been nurtured through its various stages until what has had to be said has been said, and the dance is choreographically sound, all that remains is for the work to be performed. The dancer must dance, the musicians play, the audience view and the message be passed. Dance must take place.

Still you ask, "But what makes it dance?" After all is prepared, memorized, arranged for — all is in readiness, what is the illusive quality that makes the magic of movement; that makes alive the thing we call dance?

Dance is total involvement, complete absorption, all consuming. Dance happens when a being, forgetful of self, is functioning to his fullest capacity burning with a need to communicate. Dance is performance and is all engulfing. When contact is made, when communication occurs between dancer and audience, a spark of recognition is ignited. Response is immediate and both the giver and receiver are enriched.

If one moves with this total commitment, dance will be present. One may not always produce a dance masterpiece. Many elements go into the production of a complete work of art. However, the spirit of dance must touch the performance or there is nothing. Dance is serious business; it is profound and complicated; but one need not be unusually gifted to have that devine spirit touch him. Agonizing, soul searching macerations are unnecessary. As baby ducks take instinctively to water, children commit their whole beings boldly and joyously to dance. How daring does one wish to be in giving of one's self to the art of dance? The individual must make his personal decision.

The individual who is serious about dance will subject himself to the discipline of technical training, will drive himself relentlessly toward the discovery of his own limits in mind and body, and will whole-heartedly involve himself in life experiences knowing that the result will lead to mature artistry. A way of life will be established and one day he will not only dance, but he will be a dancer.

Dance is a selfish deity and is not humble or modest in its demands. Dance is not sympathetic or understanding. One either serves dance or does not. There is no half-hearted or easy way. Dance is dance.

Figure Twenty

APPENDICES

## Selected Musical Composers for Dance

Antheil, George
Babbitt, Milton
Bach, Johann Sebastian
Barber, Samuel
Bartok, Bela
Bennett, Robert Russell
Berners, Lord
Bernstein, Leonard
Bliss, Arthur
Bloch, Ernst
Bowles, Paul
Brant, Henry
Britten, Benjamin
Cage, John
Clarke, Henry Leland
Colman, John
Copland, Aaron
Cowell, Henry
Creston, Paul
DeBoeck, Evelyn Lohoefer
Debussy, Claude
Dello Joio, Norman
Dohnanyi, Ernst von
Falla, Manuel de
Feldman, Morton
Foss, Lukas
Gershwin, George
Gilbert, Pia
Gillis, Don
Ginastera, Alberto
Goosens, Eugene
Gould, Morton
Griffes, Elliot
Grofe, Frede
Guion, David
Handel, George Frederick
Hanson, Howard
Harris, Roy
Heiden, Cola
Hindemith, Paul
Honnegger, Arthur
Horst, Louis
Hovhaness, Alan
Ives, Charles
Jahn, Daniel

Jenkins, Gordon
Kagel, Mauricio
Khachaturian, Aram
Krenek, Ernst
Lloyd, Norman
Lowe, Frederick
Luening, Otto
Malament, Sarah
Mancini, Henry
Mann, Herbie
McCosh, Cameron
Milhaud, Darius
Miller, Freda
Mompou, Feredico
Mussorgsky, Modest
Nordoff, Paul
North, Alex
Nowak, Lionel
Orff, Carl
Persichetti, Vincent
Poulenc, Francis
Previn, Andre
Prokofiev, Serge
Ravel, Maurice
Riegger, Wallingford
Rogers, Bernard
Roto, Nino
Ruggles, Carl
Satie, Erik
Schoenberg, Arnold
Schuman, William
Scriabin, Alexander
Sessions, Roger
Shostakovich, Dmitri
Siegmeister, Elie
Stravinsky, Igor
Tansman, Alexander
Taylor, Deems
Thomson, Virgil
Toch, Ernst
Verese, Edgar
Walton, William
Williams, Ralph Vaughn
White, Ruth

# Appendix B

## Selected Recordings for Teaching Modern Dance

COLMAN, JOHN. *Music for Contemporary Dance.* Directed by Oliver Kostock, Hanya Holm School of Dance. Dance Records, Inc., Waldick, New Jersey.
1 – 12″    33 1/3 R.P.M.                                                                    No. HLP 3046

A series of inspiring musical selections for floor technique and locomotor movement.

COLMAN, JOHN. *The Dancer Creates.* Directed by Joan McCaffrey. Dance Records, Inc., Waldick, New Jersey.
1 – 12″    33 1/3 R.P.M.                                                                    No. HLP 3086

Designed as accompaniment for moods and character studies.

DE BOECK, EVELYN LOHOEFER. *Music for Movement Expression.* Educational Activities, Inc., Freeport, L.I., New York.
1 – 12″    33 1/3 R.P.M.                                                                    No. LP 615

Usable for techniques and improvisations. Includes a blending of piano with percussion and bass. The bands are untitled.

GILBERT, PIA. *Music for the Modern Dance.* Coordinated by Aileene Lockhart. Hoctor Dance Records, Inc., Waldick, New Jersey.
1 – 12″    33 1/3 R.P.M.                                                                    No. HLP 4015

Accompaniment for locomotor and non-locomotor movement, and for varied rhythmic devices.

HEIDEN, COLA. *Music by Cola Heiden for Keynotes to Modern Dance* by Dorothy E. Koch Norris and Reva P. Shiner. Educational Activities, Inc., Freeport, L.I., New York.
1 – 12″    33 1/3 R.P.M.                                                                    No. 610
1 – 12″    33 1/3 R.P.M.                                                                    No. 611
1 – 12″    33 1/3 R.P.M.                                                                    No. 612

The music, composed in modern idiom, is vibrant and rich in varied qualities and tempos. The breadth of selections allows for continuous action in technique, and offers exciting accompaniment for locomotor movement, dance studies, and composition.

No. 610 includes Fundamental and Intermediate Locomotor Movements; Technique Units and Qualities of Movement.

No. 611 includes Traditional Forms (traditional dance steps) and certain of the Musical Forms; and Pre-Classic Suite.

No. 612 includes Advanced Development of Rhythm (seven challenging rhythmic devices); and Suggested Compositions (six varied pieces designed especially for dance studies and/or composition).

KEIG, BETTY and MADELINE NIXON. *Modern Dance Music for Techniques.* Educational Activities, Inc., Freeport, L.I., New York.
1 – 12″    33 1/3 R.P.M.                                                                    No. LP 502

Includes music for a variety of axial and locomotor movements. Sections are adaptable to improvisations.

**KEIG, BETTY and MADELINE NIXON.** *Modern Dance Music for Composition.* Educational Activities, Inc., Freeport, L.I., New York.

1 — 12″    33 1/3 R.P.M.                                                  No. LP 503

The musical selections are varied in length, mood, and historical scope.

**MALAMENT, SARAH.** *Improvisations for Modern Dance.* Sarah Malament, 3215 Netherland Ave., New York 63, New York.

1 — 12″    33 1/3 R.P.M.                                                  No. Series 1

Interesting and varied qualities of music in modern idiom suitable for locomotor and non-locomotor movement and selected dance studies.

**MALAMENT, SARAH.** *Improvisations for Modern Dance.* Sarah Malament, 3215 Netherland Ave., New York 63, New York.

1 — 12″    33 1/3 R.P.M.                                                  No. Series 2

Includes 18 improvisations for floor work, locomotor movement, rhythmic emphasis, and for dance studies and/or composition.

**McCOSH, CAMERON.** *Music for Modern Dance.* Supervised by Mary Anthony. Dance Records, Inc., Waldick, New Jersey.

1 — 12″    33 1/3 R.P.M.                                                  No. HLP 3053

Designed as accompaniment for floor work, locomotor movement, and aerial work.

**MERRIL, KATHLEEN.** *Studies and Sketches for Modern Dance.* Arranged in collaboration with Gertrude X. Mooney. Kathleen Merril, 6484 S.W. 25th St., Miami 55, Florida.

2 — 10″    33 1/3 R.P.M.

A collection of short pieces composed for axial and locomotor techniques, rhythmic studies, and composition.

**MILLER, FREDA.** *Records for Dance.* Freda Miller Records for Dance, 131 Bayview Ave., Northport, New York 11768.

1 — 12″    33 1/3 R.P.M.                                                  Album No. 1
1 — 12″    33 1/3 R.P.M.                                                  Album No. 2
1 — 12″    33 1/3 R.P.M.                                                  Album No. 3
1 — 12″    33 1/3 R.P.M.                                                  Album No. 4
1 — 12″    33 1/3 R.P.M.                                                  Album No. 5

The music is of fine quality. Each selection is moving and exhilarating.

Album No. 1 includes Accompaniment for Technique and Daily Paper.

Album No. 2 includes Music for Technique and Fable of the Donkey; and Dance Project.

Album No. 3 includes Compositions and Improvisations; and Time Out for a Dream.

Album No. 4 includes Music for Rhythms and Dance (primarily for children); and The Pied Piper.

Album No. 5 includes Technique/Improvisation; and Pre-Classic Suite.

**WHITE, RUTH.** *The Compact Library of Music for Dance.* Cheviot Corp., Dept. M 672, Box 34485, Los Angeles, California 90034.

This basic activities library of 5 albums (15 records) may be obtained as a complete set or in single albums as listed below.

*The Fundamentals of Music for Dancers.*
3 — 7"     33 1/3 R.P.M.                                                          No. CC 609

Short lectures precede suggested examples. Emphasizes concepts relating melody, harmony, time, accent, form and counterpoint to dance studies.

*Motivations for Modern Dance.*
3 — 7"     33 1/3 R.P.M.                                                          No. CC 610

Includes music for technique, percussion patterns, dance studies, and a pre-classic suite.

*Motifs for Dance Composition.*
3 — 7"     33 1/3 R.P.M.                                                          No. CC 611

Includes Studies for Creative Composition, Texures, Space Motifs, and studies. Electronic music and influences from eastern cultures are offered.

*Music for Contemporary Dance.* Vol. 1.
3 — 7"     33 1/3 R.P.M.                                                          No. CC 612

Style and quality of music vary from ethnic and classical to electronic.

*Music for Contemporary Dance.* Vol. 2.
3 — 7"     33 1/3 R.P.M.                                                          No. CC 613

Accompaniment for contemporary choreography comprises both the modern and the electronic styles and qualities — a challenge for individual or group experimentation. The reading of a poem is a part of one selection.

## Selected Recordings for Dance Composition*

### SOLEMN, MEDITATIVE, RELIGIOUS

BACH, JOHANN SEBASTIAN. *Jesu, Joy of Man's Desiring.* Religious hymn. Piano.
Columbia GB 10.                                                        Time: 3 minutes.

BLOCH, ERNST. *Three Jewish Poems:* Danse — mystical and somber (time: 8
minutes); Rite — emotional, then solemn (time: 6 minutes); Cortege Funebre —
sorrowful (time: 6 minutes).
Vanguard VRS 1067.

HOVHANESS, ALAN. *Mysterious Mountain*: Andante — meditative (time: 8 minutes); Double Fugue and Presto (time: 6 minutes); Andante — chanting style
(time: 3 minutes).
Victor LM 2251.

RAVEL, MAURICE. *Pavane for a Dead Princess.* ABACA form. Strong, dignified
and stately. Piano and orchestra.
Columbia ML 5878.                                                     Time: 3 minutes.

ROGERS, BERNARD. *Dance of Mourning.* Three Japanese Dances. ABA form.
Somber with focal mid-section.
Mercury MG 50713.                                                     Time: 3 minutes.

### SLOW, SMOOTH, TENDER, SENTIMENTAL

GILLIS, DON. *Prairie Sunset: Portrait of a Frontier Town.* Legato, quiet.
London LL 176.                                                        Time: 4 minutes.

LOWE, FREDERICK. *Come to Me, Bend to Me*: *Brigadoon.* Lyric and tender, a love
setting. Instrumental.
Victor LOC 1001.                                                      Time: 3 minutes.

ROTO, NINO. *Andre and Natasha*: *War and Peace.* Slow, sentimental song. Strings
and woodwinds.
Columbia CL 930.                                                      Time: 3 minutes.

ROTO, NINO. *Musical Moment*: *War and Peace.* ABA form, 4/4 moderate tempo.
Light melody.
Columbia CL 930.                                                      Time: 2 minutes.

### EMOTIONAL, DRAMATIC

BARBER, SAMUEL. *Essay for Orchestra, No. 1, Op 12.* Slow, lyric quality; then
powerful, light, powerful climax and resolution.
Mercury MG 50148.                                                     Time: 6 minutes.

---

* Whenever the length of a musical selection is not listed in exact minutes, the approximate length will be indicated as
follows: <u>short</u>, 3 to 4 minutes; <u>medium</u>, 5 to 8 minutes; and <u>long</u>, 9 minutes or more.

KHACHATURIAN, ARAM. *Sabre Dance.* Wild, on-rushing with a more subdued middle part. Incessant rhythmic pattern.
Victor ML 2744.                                          Time:  2:21

PROKOFIEV, SERGE. *Scythian Suite.* Barbaric, savage, frenzied, pagan, ritualistic. Interwoven with quieter moments and ending with a procession.
Columbia ML 4142.                                        Time:  short.

ROGERS, BERNARD. *Dance With Swords.* Three Spanish Dances. Fierce, clashing, thrusting rhythms. Quiet sections with overlay of attack.
Mercury M6 – 50713.                                      Time:  short.

ROTO, NINO. *Leaving For War: War and Peace.* Slow, foreboding legato. Brass. Entry and march, fanfare interspersed with battle effects.
Columbia CL 930.                                         Time:  5 minutes.

SMETANA, BEDRICH. *Moldau.* ABCA form. A section – quiet beginning building to surges and strong flow with running figure underneath, then fading; B section – dancey, gay, in strict meter; C section – quiet, peaceful; A section – building to strong pomp, then fading away.
Columbia ML 6279.                                        Time:  10 minutes.

## ETHNIC, FOLK

CHAMBRIER, EMMANUEL. *España Rapsodie.* Energetic Spanish styled rhythms with varied themes.
RCA Victor, VIC 1057.                                    Time:  5 minutes.

CHORALE, ROGER WAGNER. *Sea Chanties.* Interesting vocal arrangements of familiar songs: Sailing; Erie Canal; Blow the Man Down; A Roving; Wide Missouri (Shenandoah); and others.
Capitol P 8462.                                          Time:  short.

COPLAND, AARON. *Hoedown.* Lively, in modern idiom. Saturday night atmosphere in country style.
Victor LM 2744.                                          Time:  3:10.

COPLAND, AARON. *Outdoor Overture: Music for Young America.* Clear and exhilarating. Brasses, woodwinds and strings. Some syncopated percussion.
Epic LC 3819.                                            Time:  8:53.

GILLIS, DON. *Ranch House Party: Portrait of a Frontier Town.* Typical hoe-down in lively tempo including the polka and gallop. Fiddles and orchestra.
London LL 176.                                           Time:  3 minutes.

GINASTERA, ALBERTO. *Malambo from Estancia.* Fast rhythm with a Latin flavor. Xylophone and tambourine.
Everest 6013.                                            Time:  short.

SIEGMEISTER, ELIE. *American Indians of the Southwest.* Chanted songs and dances of Hopi, Zuni, Navajo, and Apache Indians.
Ethnic Folkways Library P 420.

_____ . *Fiesta Italiana.* Includes Tarantella, Polkas, Mazurkas and Waltz.
Fiesta FLP 1382.

_____ . *I Remember Austria.* Includes: Schulplatter, Yodels, March, Polkas and Landler.
Fiesta FLP 1291.

_____ . *Music of Vietnam.* Short selections including: Highland Tribal Music; Ancient Imperial Music; Chamber Music; and Ancient Folk Songs.
Folkways FE 4352.

_____ . *Songs of Israel Today.* Includes: Horas; Harvest Prayer; and Celebration Songs. Chorus and orchestra.
Fiesta FLP 1351.

_____ . *Tahitian Percussion.* Primitive sounds of drums, voice, and screaming birds.
Al — Fi — C 4075, 5810 South Normandie Ave., Los Angeles, California.

_____ . *Tribal Music of Australia.* Includes ten selections. Unusual sounds with percussion, chants, and songs.
Folkways P 439.

_____ . *Voodoo Suite, Part I.* Jungle drums predominate; voices introduced.
Victor SPL 12-13 (Voodoo Suite complete), EPB/LPM 1101.

## DANCE FORMS, MUSIC FORMS

BACH, JOHANN SEBASTIAN. *French Suite No. 6, E Major.* Includes eight short dances: Allemande (fast); Courante (fast); Sarabande; Gavotte; Polonaise (very light); Bourrée; Minuet (fast); Gigue. Piano.
Columbia ML 2196.                                         Time: short.

BACH, JOHANN SEBASTIAN. *Suites For Lute, Nos. 1 and 2.* Dance forms in the Pre-Classic style. Very formal. Includes: Prelude; Sarabande; Gigue. Solo instrument.
Victor LM 2896.                                          Time: short.

BOWLES, PAUL. *Concerto for Two Pianos, Winds and Percussion.* Includes: Allegro; Scherzo; Andante; Gallop.
Columbia ML 2128.                                         Time: long.

DEBUSSY, CLAUDE. *Snow Is Dancing: Children's Corner Suite.* Very light, delicate music, dancey. Piano.
Columbia ML 4539.                                         Time: short.

HANDEL, GEORGE FREDERICK. *Bourrée and Hornpipe: Water Music Suite.* A rapid Bourrée with string accompaniment. The Hornpipe in moderate tempo.
Fidelio ATL 4008.                                      Time: 2 minutes.

LOWE, FREDERICK. *Ascot Gavotte.* Moderate 4/4. Instrumental.
Columbia KOL 8000; OS 2015.                               Time: short.

MILHAUD, DARIUS. *Les Songs.* Includes a lilting Scherzo, a short Valse, and a Polka. Two pianos.
Columbia ML 2128.                                         Time: short.

RIEGGER, WALLINGFORD. *Dance Rhythms: Music for Young America.* Varied rhythms with syncopation.
Epic 3819.                                                      Time: medium.

RODGERS, RICHARD. *March of the Siamese Children: The King and I.* Delightfully danceable.
Capitol W 740.                                                   Time: short.

ROGERS, BERNARD. *Dance With Pennons.* Three Japanese Dances. Oriental tone that is jolly and bright.
Mercury MG 50713.                                               Time: short.

## JAZZ AND JAZZ VERSIONS OF CLASSICAL STYLES

BRUBECK, DAVE. *Jazz Impressions of New York.* Easy-going jazz. Includes a bossa nova and a rumba.
Columbia CL 2275.                                              Time: short.

ELLINGTON, DUKE. *Mood Ellington* (1948 Ellington). Includes: H'ya Sue (slow); Lady of the Lavender Mist (evasive); The Clothed Woman (with variations); Progressive Gavotte (swing time); On A Turquoise Cloud (slow band and voice sounds); New York City Blues (sophisticated style); Golden Cress (slow trombone); Three Cent Stamp.
Columbia NL 6024.                                          Time: 3 minutes each.

FINEGAN, SAUTER. *Solo For Joe* (from Concert for Jazz). Slow, quiet jazz. Vibraharps and voice sounds.
Victor SPL 12-13 (also Concert for Jazz, EPC/LPM 1051).        Time: 4 minutes.

GOULD, MORTON. *Interplay.* Includes: Gavotte (3 minutes); Blues (3 minutes). Piano and orchestra.
Victor LM 2532.                                               Time: 6 minutes.

MANN, HERBIE. *Mann Alone.* Includes: Happy Happy (3:30); Looking Through the Window (4:00); Like You Know Baby (5:50); Loce (5:15); All Day Monday (6:20); From Midnight On (3:25); For the Love of Kali (4:20); Ruth, Ruth (3:40). Solo flute.
Savoy MG 12107.

## MODERN, ELECTRONIC, PERCUSSION, NOVELTY SOUNDS

HONEGGER, ARTHUR. *Three Symphonic Movements.* Includes two pieces: Rugby (7:25); and Pacific 231, giving the impression of the sounds of machinery at work (6 minutes).
Columbia ML 6059.

KAGEL, MAURICIO. *Transicion II for Piano, Percussion and Two Magnetic Tapes.* Electronic sound. Utilizes the piano as a percussive instrument.
Time – Series 2000, # 58001.                                  Time: 17:35.

SOUNDS OF THE HOME. *Experimental Resources for Improvisation.*
Offbeat Records –95706, Bill Gaver Productions,
235 West 46th St., New York 36, N.Y.

STOCKHAUSEN, KARLHEINZ. *Refrain for Three Performers.* Light, varied percussion.
Time — Series 2000, # 58001.                                              Time: 8:10.

STOCKHAUSEN, KARLHEINZ. *Zyklus for One Percussionist.* Utilizes a variety of percussive sounds with marimbaphone, wood drums, Indian bells, tom-toms, cymbals, triangle, vibraphone, gong, and sticks.
Time — Series 2000, # 58001.                                              Time: 11:48.

VARÈSE, EDGAR. *Music of Edgar Varèse.* Déserts in four sections with electronic and instrumental sounds (25 minutes); Arcana with constant sounds (non electronic) but without moments of silence (16 minutes).
Columbia ML 5762.

## COLLECTIONS OR SUITES OF VARYING MOODS

ELWELL, HERBERT. *Suite from The Happy Hypocrite in Music for Young America.* Includes five parts: Opening Scene (4:06); Dance of the Saint, lyric (1:39); Dance of Merry Dwarf, gay and playful (2:42); Dance of Jenny Mere (3:18); Finale (3:03).
Epic — 3819.

JOIO, DELLO. *Symphonic Suite* (Air Power). Suite of pieces in varying moods.
Columbia ML 5214. .                                                       Time: 30 minutes.

JOIO, DELLO. *Variations.* The six variations include lyric, dramatic, presto, light, wild, and gay.
Columbia ML 5263.                                                         Time: 8 minutes.

PROKOFIEV, SERGE. *Concerto No. 3 in C Major for Piano and Orchestra.* Includes Andante Allegro, lively tempo (7 minutes); Theme and Variations, polyrhythms (7 minutes); Allegro, persistent but calm (7 minutes). 20th century sounds.
Angel 2 XLA 311.

VINCENT, JOHN. *Symphony in D.* An Andante Moderato continuing into an Allegro. Interesting melodic and rhythmic treatment of varied moods from the lyric, to the exhuberant, and finally, to the triumphant climax.
Columbia ML 5263.                                                         Time: 18 minutes.

## COMIC, PLAYFUL

BERNERS, LORD. *The Triumph of Neptune.* Includes nine humorous pieces: Harlequinade, Dance of the Fairy Princess, Schottische, Cloudland, Sunday Morning, The Sailor's Return, Hornpipe, The Frozen Forest, and Apotheosis of Neptune.
Columbia ML 4593.                                                         Time: short.

BOWLES, PAUL. *Music for a Farce.* Short pieces in comic style.
Columbia ML 4845.                                                         Time: short.

BRITTEN, BENJAMIN. *Sonfonietta Op. I.* Unexpected rhythms.
London CM 9465.                                                           Time: 4 minutes.

SHOSTAKOVICH, DMITRI. *Age of Gold — Polka.* Gay, humorous, polka rhythm.
Capitol P 8576.                                                           Time: 2:14.

## BACKGROUND PIECES

**FELDMAN, MORTON.** *New Directions in Music/2.* Limited tones, plinks, brushing across the keys. Possibilities for improvisation. Piano and strings.
Columbia ML 5403                                        Time: medium.

**HOVHANESS, ALAN.** *Orbit No. I.* Gives a floating impression. Flute, celeste, harp, and tympani.
MGM – E 3164.                                           Time: 3 minutes.

**LA MONTAINE, JOHN.** *Birds of Paradise.* Non-melodic with single notes, thin and fragmented.
Mercury 50430.                                          Time: long.

**SATIE, ERIK.** *Trois Gymnopedies.* Slow and quite unemotional. In Greek religious style.
Capitol P – 8244.                                       Time: medium.

## Films for Dance*

### APPRECIATION OF DANCE ART THROUGH FILMS

Fine films can serve in many ways to enrich the dance experience. They can introduce material, supplement and support the existing dance program, extend the knowledge of great dance personalities, and act as a document for our dance heritage in preserving dance masterpieces.

Films cannot be a substitute for the live performance, but they can offer an exciting second choice. Films can make possible, at relatively minor expense, an opportunity to view the finest dancers performing all forms of dance in many diversified styles. The expenditure of time and effort in arranging a viewing is minimal compared to the details involved in scheduling an actual concert. Films and live dance performances compliment each other. Through the use of both, an intelligent appreciation of the dance art can be fostered.

In listing and evaluating the following films, this two-fold purpose was kept in mind: to appraise them according to their informative and educative values; and, to be aware of their merit in furthering an appreciation of the dance art.

All the films listed have the potential for rendering some useful purpose educationally. To attain the utmost value from the viewing of a film, the teacher should assume the responsibility of preparing the audience with a knowledge of what to look for before presenting the film. In some films such as, *Thai Traditional Music and Classical Dance,* more teacher guidance and explanation would be needed than in other films such as, *Sadler's Wells Ballerina.*

### A DANCER'S WORLD

Distributors or Producers:     WQED Pittsburgh, Rembrandt Films.
                               NET, Indiana University, A-V Center

Time:  31 minutes
B & W, Sound
Rental:  $6.40
Grade level:  Senior High School; College
Comment:  An artistically conceived and beautifully performed film which allows a glimpse into the world of the creative dance artist.

### APPALACHIAN SPRING

Distributors or Producers:     WQED for NET; Rembrandt Films Library.
                               NET, Indiana University, A-V Center

Time:  31 minutes
B & W, Sound
Rental:  $6.90
Grade level:  Senior High School; College
Comment:  Martha Graham and members of her fine dance company perform this outstanding modern dance "classic" with music by Aaron Copland.

---

* It should be noted that rental and sales prices of films as listed may flucuate. The grade level as listed may vary according to the background of the respective group.

*A STUDY OF CHOREOGRAPHY FOR CAMERA*

    Distributors or Producers:    Maya Deren and Talley Beatty.
                                     NET, Indiana University, A-V Center
    Time:  4 minutes
    B & W, Silent
    Rental:  $3.15
    Grade level:  Senior High School; College
    Comment:  A fine experimental film in which the camera becomes a part of the dance
        action.

A TIME TO DANCE SERIES

This appears to be one of the most ambitious and comprehensive attempts at educational dance filming to date. There are nine films in the entire series. Each film is complete in and of itself with no need to view the whole series in order to understand each segment. The three major dance forms — ethnic, ballet, and modern — are explored in the series. Martha Meyers introduces each film, then proceeds to interview prominent dancers, choreographers and critics in the field of dance. Professional dancers illustrate material, and usually a staged presentation of a partial or complete work is viewed.

*A TIME TO DANCE:  A CHOREOGRAPHER AT WORK*

    Distributors or Producers:  NET, Indiana University, A-V Center
    Time:  29 minutes
    B & W, Sound
    Rental:  $5.40
    Sale:  $125.00
    Grade level:  Senior High School; College
    Comment:  John Butler is the dancer-choreographer interviewed. He discusses and
        illustrates how he develops his dances. He presents "Three Promenades with
        the Lord."

*A TIME TO DANCE:  ETHNIC DANCE — ROUNDTRIP TO TRINIDAD*

    Distributors or Producers:  NET, Indiana University, A-V Center
    Time:  29 minutes
    B & W, Sound
    Rental:  $5.40
    Sale:  $125.00
    Grade level:  Senior High School; College
    Comment:  Geoffrey Holder, a dancer-choreographer who is a native of Trinidad,
        is interviewed. Some movements used in contemporary dance can be traced to
        ethnic sources. "Banda" a Haitian dance about death is performed by Geoffrey
        Holder and Carmen de Lavallade.

*A TIME TO DANCE:  GREAT PERFORMANCE IN DANCE*

    Distributors or Producers:  NET, Indiana University, A-V Center
    Time:  29 minutes
    B & W, Sound

Rental: $5.40
Sale: $125.00
Grade level: Senior High School; College
Comment: Walter Terry, dance critic, is interviewed. Some rare film clips are shown of Anna Pavlova, Irene and Vernon Castle, and Argentinita. Alexandra Danilova and Frederick Franklin are interviewed and then perform "Le Beau Danube."

## A TIME TO DANCE: INVENTION IN DANCE

Distributors or Producers: NET, Indiana University, A-V Center
Time: 29 minutes
B & W, Sound
Rental: $5.40
Sale: $125.00
Grade level: Senior High School; College
Comment: Alwin Nikolais, controversial and innovative choreographer, is interviewed. A variety of shapes and sounds are presented with movements coordinated in time and space. "Web," "Fixation," danced by Murray Louis, and "Disc" are performed.

## A TIME TO DANCE: THE LANGUAGE OF DANCE

Distributors or Producers: NET, Indiana University, A-V Center
Time: 29 minutes
B & W, Sound
Rental: $5.40
Sale: $125.00
Grade level: Senior High School; College
Comment: José Limón, dancer-choreographer, is interviewed. He shows how a dancer extends and sustains feeling through movement. Excerpts from "There Is A Time" are performed with music by Norman Dello Joio.

## A TIME TO DANCE: MODERN BALLET

Distributors or Producers: NET, Indiana University, A-V Center
Time: 29 minutes
B & W, Sound
Rental: $5.40
Sale: $125.00
Grade level: Senior High School; College
Comment: Anthony Tudor, well-known choreographer, is interviewed. Nora Kaye and Hugh Laing demonstrate new trends in the modern ballet by using excerpts from two famous ballets, "Pillar of Fire" and "Romeo and Juliet."

## A TIME TO DANCE: A REFLECTION OF OUR TIME

Distributors or Producers: NET, Indiana University, A-V Center
Time: 29 minutes
B & W, Sound
Rental: $5.40

Sale: $125.00

Grade level: Senior High School; College

Comment: Herbert Ross is the dancer-choreographer interviewed. The use of dance as one means of expressing social concerns is examined. "Caprichos," a dance based on Goya's etchings, is presented. It is a harsh but effective social comment.

## A TIME TO DANCE: A TIME TO DANCE

Distributors or Producers: NET, Indiana University, A-V Center

Time: 29 minutes

B & W, Sound

Rental: $5.40

Sale: $125.00

Grade level: Senior High School; College

Comment: This is the first film of the complete series. An attempt is made to explain and illustrate each of the three major dance forms — ethnic, ballet and modern.

## BUILDING CHILDREN'S PERSONALITIES WITH CREATIVE DANCING

Distributors or Producers:    Frank Goldsmith Prod.
                              NET, Indiana University, A-V Center

Time: 29 minutes

B & W, Color, Sound

Rental: $5.65 (B & W)

Sale: $175.00 (B & W); $275.00 (Color)

Grade level: College

Comment: The film shows a growth of security within a group of children and a development of more freedom in movement expression. The film could provoke a stimulating discussion among teacher trainees.

## FABLE OF THE PEACOCK

Distributors or Producers:    Jo Schaeffer; Regency Prod.
                              NET, Indiana University, A-V Center

Time: 15 minutes

Color

Rental: $5.40

Grade level: All levels

Comment: An authentic Indian dance is performed by Lakshimi Waba Singh as narration accompanies symbolic gesture.

## FOCUS ON CONTROL

Distributors or Producers:    Educational Activities, Inc.,
                              Freeport, New York, Producers

Time: 11 minutes

B & W, Sound

Sale: $65.00

Grade level: Senior High School; College

Comment: This film illustrates the intense physical and intellectual discipline essential to accomplishment in contemporary dance. The movement selected for the film is the non-locomotor technique series presented in this book, pages 100-109. The film attempts to present sound educational material in an artistic and imaginative way.

## FOLK DANCES IN THE U.S.S.R.

Distributors or Producers:     Lenfilm Studios; Artkino.
                               NET, Indiana University, A-V Center

Time: 9 minutes
B & W, Sound
Rental: $1.90
Grade level: All levels
Comment: Three Russian folk dances are presented by the Soviet State Ensemble of the Folk Dance.

## HELEN TAMIRIS IN HER NEGRO SPIRITUALS

Distributors or Producers:     Nagtam Prod.:  Contemporary Films.
                               NET, Indiana University, A-V Center

Time: 16 minutes
B & W, Sound
Rental: $4.65
Grade level: Senior High School; College
Comment: John Martin introduces the Negro spirituals performed by Helen Tamiris. These dances show how contemporary dance may be exemplified through folk themes.

## INTRODUCTION TO DANCE

Distributors or Producers:     Associated Film Services,
                               Burbank, California

Time: 15 minutes
Color, Sound
Sale: $165.00
Grade level: Upper Elementary; Senior High School; College
Comment: The film presents the basic locomotor steps and their combinations to form traditional dance steps. It compares the use of these steps in some of the social dances of today and then relates them to some of the dances performed in certain foreign lands.

## LAMENT FOR IGNACIO SANCHEZ MEJIAS

Distributors or Producers:     Walter Strate.
                               NET, Indiana University, A-V Center

Time: 16 minutes
B & W, Sound
Rental: $3.90
Grade level: Senior High School; College
Comment: José Limón performs in a dance based on Lorca's poem. Dance, music, poetry and cinematographic art combine to present an exciting production.

## MEDITATION ON VIOLENCE

Distributors or Producers:     Maya Deren, producer.  Cinema 16.
                               NET, Indiana University, A-V Center
Time:  13 minutes
B & W, Sound
Rental:  $2.65
Grade level:  College
Comment:  An interesting attempt is made in this film to capture the intensity of
dance with imaginative cinematography.

## MODERN DANCE: SEQUENTIAL FORM

Distributors or Producers:     Bailey Films.
                               NET, Indiana University, A-V Center
Time:  12 minutes
Color, Sound
Rental:  $4.15
Grade level:  Junior and Senior High School; College
Comment:  Primarily this is an educational dance film. The information is sound and
clearly narrated, but it has little aesthetic appeal.

## SADLER'S WELLS BALLERINA

Distributors or Producers:     NET, Indiana University, A-V Center
Time:  12 minutes
Color, Sound
Rental:  $3.90
Grade level:  All levels
Comment:  A young ballerina prepares for her debut in "Beauty and the Beast."

## STEPS TO THE BALLET

Distributors or Producers:     Contemporary Films, Inc.
Time:  26 minutes
B & W, Sound
Rental:  $4.65
Grade level:  Upper Elementary; Junior and Senior High School; College
Comment:  An informative, understandable film presentation which shows how
various arts combine to produce a finished theater piece.

## TCHAIKOWSKY'S SWAN LAKE

Distributors or Producers:     Mosfilm Studio; Artkino.
                               NET, Indiana University, A-V Center
Time:  9 minutes
B & W, Sound
Rental:  $1.90
Grade level:  Upper Elementary; Junior and Senior High School; College
Comment:  This fine classical ballet is beautifully performed by The Corp de Ballet of
the Moscow Bolshoi Theatre.

*THAI TRADITIONAL MUSIC AND CLASSICAL DANCE*

   Distributors or Producers:     Gov. of Thailand; Thailand Embassy.
                                   NET, Indiana University, A-V Center
   Time:  28 minutes
   Color, Sound
   Rental:  $6.40
   Grade level:  Upper Elementary; Junior and Senior High School; College
   Comment:  An explanatory introduction would be helpful in preparing the audience
      for an understanding of this Eastern art form. The authentic costumes filmed in
      color are splendid. The film seems long and strange to Western eyes and ears.

U S A SERIES

   U S A is a series of forty-five films designed to portray the state of the arts in the
   United States today. There are a total of six dance films in the series. These have been
   video taped and reproduced on 16 mm film. While the content of the six dance films
   is excellent, the aesthetic appeal is diminished by this process. The exception is the
   film *In Search of Lovers.* The viewer almost takes part in the action as it happens. In
   this highly personalized approach, one can forgive technical inadequacies since they
   are used many times to further the sense of immediacy and excitement. However, in
   the other films in the area of performance some of the magic is lost.

   *U S A DANCE: ANNA SOKOLOW'S ROOMS*

      Distributors:  NET, Indiana University, A-V Center
      Time:  30 minutes
      B & W, Sound
      Rental:  $5.40
      Sale:  $125.00
      Grade level:  College
      Comment:  This film shows a powerful, provocative dance about the isolation of
         man. Parts of the dance are named, "Escape," "Going," "Desire," and "Pain."

   *U S A DANCE: ECHOES OF JAZZ*

      Distributors:  NET, Indiana University, A-V Center
      Time:  30 minutes
      B & W, Sound
      Rental:  $5.40
      Sale:  $125.00
      Grade level:  College
      Comment:  This film traces the development of the jazz dance by presenting
         illustrations of tap dance, theatrical style jazz, couple dances with the "big
         band" sound, and today's jazz dance with choreography by John Butler.

   *U S A DANCE: FOUR PIONEERS*

      Distributors:  NET, Indiana University, A-V Center
      Time:  30 minutes
      B & W, Sound
      Rental:  $5.40

Sale: $125.00

Grade level: College

Comment: The four "greats" of modern dance, Graham, Weidman, Humphrey, and Holm are introduced. The film is full of dance heritage. A presentation of Doris Humphrey's "Passacaglia" is performed.

## U S A DANCE: IN SEARCH OF LOVERS

Distributors: NET, Indiana University, A-V Center

Time: 30 minutes

B & W, Sound

Rental: $5.40

Sale: $125.00

Grade level: College

Comment: This is an exciting contemporary film that shows how a dance is developed. Much information is presented, but in a striking, refreshing way. Glen Tetley is the choreographer with Mary Hinkson, Carmen de Lavallade and Scott Douglas his able dancers.

## U S A DANCE NEW YORK CITY BALLET

Distributors: NET, Indiana University, A-V Center

Time: 30 minutes

B & W, Sound

Rental: $5.40

Sale: $125.00

Grade level: College

Comment: Dances by George Balanchine are performed by the members of the very excellent New York City Ballet Company. "Tarantella," "Meditation," and excerpts from "Agon" and "Pas de Deux" are presented.

## U S A DANCE: ROBERT JOFFREY BALLET

Distributors: NET, Indiana University, A-V Center

Time: 30 minutes

B & W, Sound

Rental: $5.40

Sale: $125.00

Grade level: College

Comment: The film shows the wide range of styles and themes possible in ballet today.

Appendix E

## Distributors of Dance Films

Cinema 16
175 Lexington Avenue
New York, New York  10016

Contemporary Films, Inc.
267 West 25th Street
New York, New York  10001

Dance Films, Inc.
250 West 57th Street
New York, New York 10019

Media Center
University of California Extension
2223 Fulton Street
Berkeley, California  94720

NET Film Service
Indiana University
Audio-Visual Center
Bloomington, Indiana  47401

# GLOSSARY

ABSTRACTION — The process of transforming realistic movement into stylized or non-representational design while retaining recognizable elements of the original.

ACCUMULATIVE METER — A process of collecting one or more beats in each successive measure or a given sequence.

AXIAL MOVEMENT — Non-locomotor movement.

BINARY DIVISION — The process of dividing a note into two equal parts.

CANON FORM — A composition of two or more voice parts utilizing strict imitation by each successive voice.

CHOREOGRAPHIC PROCESS — The aspects related to the developing of dances.

CHOREOGRAPHY — The art of composing dances.

CLIMAX — The high point of compositional development, either structurally or dramatically.

CODA — A brief passage in music or dance that may be used to bring the composition to a close.

COMPOSITION — The welding of form and content into a whole and complete work.

COMPOUND METERS — Multiples or combinations of simple meters with a strong accent on the first beat and one or more weaker accents on the other beats in the measure.

CONSECUTIVE ACCENTS — The transferring of accents within a group of like measures from one beat to another in consecutive order.

CONTOUR — The profile or outline of a figure or mass projected upon a background.

CONTRACTION — The tightening of a muscle causing it to become shorter and thicker.

CONTRAST — Change for the purpose of providing new insights.

COUNTERPOINT — Plural melody.

DANCE SUITE — A number of related dances constituting a series or complement.

DECUMULATIVE METER — A process of casting off one or more beats from each successive measure in a given sequence.

DEVELOPMENT — The process of evolving a dance idea.

DIMENSION — Denotes size or range of movement.

DIRECTION — The path produced by moving, and the apparent line toward which someone is pointing or facing.

DISTORTION — To move in a manner away from the natural.

DOWNSTAGE — The area of the stage closest to the audience.

DUPLE METER — The alternation of one strong and one weak beat.

DYNAMICS — The force of movement with variations in the amounts of power, intensity and energy exerted.

EXTENSION — The straightening of a body part.

FALL — To descend in a downward plane.

FLEXION — The bending of a body part.

FLOOR PATTERN — The apparent floor design that develops as the dancer or dancers move through a pathway in space.

FOCUS — The conscious attention toward a converging point.

FORM — The essential nature of a thing resulting from a particular ordered arrangement of its parts.

FREE FORM — A composition that falls into no specific category but allows freedom in unlimited structural development.

FUNDAMENTAL LOCOMOTOR MOVEMENTS — The base from which all locomotor movements derive (walk, run, hop, jump).

HARMONY — The agreement of the forces involved in the whole.

IMPROVISATION — Impromptu movement — created extemporaneously.

INTERMEDIATE LOCOMOTOR MOVEMENTS — Outgrowths of fundamental locomotor movements (leap, slide, gallop, skip).

LEAP-LUNGE — A leap landing with a slightly bent knee.

LEVEL — Gradations of height from the floor to the highest possible elevation.

LOCOMOTOR MOVEMENT — Traveling from one place to another.

METER — The metric division of the measure as indicated by the time signature.

MIXED METER — No set order of meter. Metrical units may change from measure to measure.

MOVEMENT PATTERN — An uninterrupted succession of related movements grouped to form an entire design.

MOVEMENT THEME — The development of one or more movement phrases to project a specific idea, emotion, characterization, and the like. The theme is sufficiently important to be repeated more than once and gives emphasis to the total dance composition. It represents a small dance within a larger dance. Examples: hope theme, struggle theme, work theme, laughter theme, sister's sewing theme, wife's theme, mourning theme.

NON-LOCOMOTOR MOVEMENT — An "in place" movement performed on a fixed base.

ORGANIZATION — The systematizing of inter-related parts into a whole.

PERCUSSIVE MOVEMENT — A sharp, forceful and ballistic type of movement with a marked initial impetus which later is quickly checked on the follow-through.

PERFORMANCE — Skillful presentation in which communication occurs.

PHRASE — A rhythmic or movement unit — ordered, progressive, and proportioned in form.

PLANES — Gradations of level.

PLIÉ — Bend (the knees).

POLYMETER — Multimeter, a combining of two or more contrasting meters.

PRIMARY ACCENT — The strong accent in a measure preceded by a vertical line (bar line).

PRIMITIVE QUALITY OF MOVEMENT — Simple, unembellished, straightforward kind of movement. Not subtle, sophisticated, or complex.

PROBLEM SOLVING — The learning process of finding a satisfactory solution to a dance problem — a structured situation with clearly defined limits.

PROPORTION — A considered, harmonious arrangement.

RECOVER — Rising from a low level.

RELATIONSHIP — The affinity between two or more parts.

RELEASE — A relaxation of contracted muscles while maintaining decided control.

RELEVÉ — Lift (on the toes).

REPETITION — That which repeats in order to clarify and emphasize.

RESULTANT RHYTHM — A form of polymeter in which cross accents are produced.

RHYTHMIC PATTERN — A grouping of rhythmic units developed in consecutive order to form an entire design.

RONDO FORM — A form in which a principal theme occurs several times with contrasting themes interposed.

ROTATION — The turning or twisting of a body part on or around an axis.

ROUND FORM — A form of imitation in which three or four voices or dancers follow each other at specific time intervals.

SECONDARY RHYTHM — A variation of the fundamental beat in the measure while maintaining a value equal to that of the respective time signature.

SEQUENCE — The orderly, progressive placement of parts to effect coherence of a whole.

SEQUENTIAL FORM — The arrangement of one or more phrases that follow in succession. The phrase parts or "periods" are indicated by letter symbols as: A, A B, A B A.

SIMPLE METERS — Units of two or three with a strong accent on the first beat of the measure.

STAGE LEFT — The area of the stage to the left of center as the dancer faces the audience.

STAGE RIGHT — The area of the stage to the right of center as the dancer faces the audience.

SUBSTANCE — The unchanging essence or underlying reality of a thing.

SUSPENDED MOVEMENT — Movement initiated by a marked impulse and continuing until the peak of elevation is achieved with a momentary arrestment of movement. Thus, the movement is prolonged producing the effect of hanging in space without relationship to gravity.

SUSTAINED MOVEMENT — A steady and continuous type of movement marked by the equalization of force, and by the fusion of impulse and follow-through.

SWINGING MOVEMENT — A pendular and unrestricted type of movement characterized by a marked impulse and an unrestrained follow-through.

SYNCOPATION — Accenting a weak beat or an unaccented part of a beat.

TECHNIQUE — The skill essential to the components of performance.

TEMPO — The rate of speed (relative rather than absolute).

TERNARY DIVISION — The arbitrary division of a beat into three equal parts.

THEME AND VARIATIONS FORM — The introduction of an initial statement in music or dance that is followed by two or more variations of the original theme.

TRADITIONAL DANCE STEPS — Derived from combinations or expansions of both fundamental and intermediate locomotor movements.

TRANSITION — Separates one movement from another, or one dance phrase from another and at the same time acts as a connecting link between the two respective parts.

TRIPLE METER — One strong beat followed by two weak beats.

UNITY — The force which binds the parts of composition together.

UPSTAGE – The area to the rear of the stage.

VARIABLE ACCENTS – The shifting of accents within a group of like measures from one beat to another in variable order.

VARIATION – The diversification of thematic material.

VIBRATORY MOVEMENT – A shaking, tremulous type of movement resulting from the rapid tensing of certain muscle groups causing the contractions and relaxations to occur exceedingly close together.

# SELECTED BIBLIOGRAPHY

## BOOKS

Chujoy, Anatole, editor. *The Dance Encyclopedia.* New York: A. S. Barnes and Company, 1949.

Dixon, C. Madeleine. *The Power of Dance.* New York: The John Day Company, 1939.

Ellfeldt, Lois. *A Primer for Choreography.* Palo Alto, California: National Press Books, 1967.

Fisk, Margaret Palmer. *The Art of the Rhythmic Choir.* New York: Harper and Brothers, 1950.

Gilbert, Pia and Aileene Lockhart. *Music for the Modern Dance.* Dubuque, Iowa: Wm. C. Brown Company, 1961.

Hawkins, Alma M. *Creating Through Dance.* Englewood Cliffs, New Jersey: Prentice-Hall, Inc., 1964.

————. *Modern Dance in Higher Education.* New York: Teachers College, Columbia University, 1954.

Hayes, Elizabeth R. *An Introduction to the Teaching of Dance.* New York: The Ronald Press Company, 1964.

————. *Dance Composition and Production.* New York: The Ronald Press Company, 1954.

Hering, Doris, editor. *Twenty-five Years of American Dance.* New York: Dance Magazine, Rudolph Orthwine, Publisher, 1951.

Horst, Louis. *Modern Dance Forms.* San Francisco, California: Impulse Publications, 1961.

————. *Pre-Classic Dance Forms.* New York: Kamin Dance Publishers, 1953.

H'Doubler, Margaret N. *Dance: A Creative Art Experience.* Madison: The University of Wisconsin Press, 1962.

Humphrey, Doris. *The Art of Making Dances.* New York: Rinehart and Company, 1959.

Hutchinson, Ann. *Labanotation.* New York: New Directions, 1954.

Joiner, Betty. *Costumes for the Dance.* New York: A. S. Barnes and Company, 1937.

Jones, Ruth Whitney, and Margaret DeHaan. *Modern Dance in Education.* New York: Bureau of Publications, Teachers College, Columbia University, 1947.

Laban, Rudolf. *The Mastery of Movement.* London: MacDonald and Evans, 1950.

La Meri. *Dance as an Art Form.* New York: The Ronald Press Company, 1933.

————. *Dance Composition.* Lee, Massachusetts: Jacob's Pillow Dance Festival, Inc., 1965.

Lloyd, Margaret. *The Borzoi Book of Modern Dance.* New York: Alfred A. Knopf, Inc., 1949.

Lockhart, Aileene. *Modern Dance — Building and Teaching Lessons,* rev. ed. Dubuque, Iowa: Wm. C. Brown Company, 1957.

Magriel, Paul, editor. *Chronicles of the American Dance.* New York: Henry Holt and Company, 1948.

Mains, Margaret Small. *Modern Dance Manual.* Dubuque, Iowa: Wm. C. Brown Company, 1950.

Martin, John J. *America Dancing.* New York: Dodge Publishing Company, 1936.

Martin, John J. *Introduction to the Dance.* New York: W. W. Norton and Company, Inc., 1939. Brooklyn: Dance Horizons; 1965.

———. *The Dance.* New York: Tudor Publishing Company, 1946.

———. *The Modern Dance.* New York: A. S. Barnes and Company, 1933. Brooklyn: Dance Horizons, 1965.

Melcer, Fannie Helen. *Staging the Dance.* Dubuque, Iowa: Wm. C. Brown Company, 1955.

Murray, Ruth. *Dance in Elementary Education,* rev. ed. New York: Harper and Row, 1963.

Nettl, Paul. *The Story of Dance Music.* New York: Philosophical Library, Inc., 1947.

Palmer, Winthrop. *Theatrical Dancing in America.* New York: Bernard Ackerman, Inc., 1945.

Pease, Esther E. *Modern Dance.* Dubuque, Iowa: Wm. C. Brown Company, 1966.

Radir, Ruth Anderson. *Modern Dance for the Youth of America.* New York: The Ronald Press Company, 1944.

Rogers, Frederick R., editor. *Dance: A Basic Educational Technique.* New York: The Macmillan Company, 1941.

Sachs, Curt. *World History of Dance.* New York: W. W. Norton and Company, Inc., 1937.

Selden, Samuel. *The Stage in Action.* New York: Appleton-Century-Crofts, Inc., 1941.

Sheehy, Emma D. *Children Discover Music and Dance.* New York: Henry Holt and Company, Inc., 1949.

Sheets, Maxine. *The Phenomenology of Dance.* Madison and Milwaukee, Wisconsin: The University of Wisconsin Press, 1966.

Shurr, Gertrude, and Rachael D. Yocum. *Modern Dance — Techniques and Teaching.* New York: A. S. Barnes and Company, 1949.

Sorell, Walter, editor. *The Dance Has Many Faces.* Cleveland and New York: The World Publishing Company, 1951.

———. *The Dance Through the Ages.* New York: Grosset and Dunlap, 1967.

Tabouret, Jehan (Arbeau, Thoinot). *Orchesography.* Translated by Cyril W. Beaumont. London: C. W. Beaumont, 1925.

Terry, Walter. *Invitation to Dance.* New York: A. S. Barnes and Company, 1942.

———. *The Dance in America.* New York: Harper and Brothers, 1956.

Turner, Margery, J. *Modern Dance for High School and College.* Englewood Cliffs, New Jersey: Prentice-Hall, Inc., 1947.

———. *Dance Handbook.* Englewood Cliffs, New Jersey: Prentice-Hall, Inc., 1959.

Ulrich, Homer. *Music: A Design for Listening.* 2nd. ed. New York: Harcourt, Brace, and World, Inc., 1962.

Wessel, Janet. *Movement Fundamentals.* Englewood Cliffs, New Jersey: Prentice-Hall, Inc., 1961.

Wigman, Mary. *The Language of Dance.* Translated by Walter Sorell. Connecticut: Wesleyan University Press, 1966.

N.B. Several of the above books may be out of print but may be available at a library.

## PAMPHLETS

Bascom, Frances, and Charlotte Irey. *Costume Cues.* Washington, D.C.: National Section on Dance, American Association for Health, Physical Education and Recreation, 1952.

Committee on Visual Aids, National Section on Dance, Vol. III. *Selected Visual Aids for Dance.* Washington, D.C.: American Association for Health, Physical Education and Recreation, 1955.

Erlander, Margaret, Coordinator Committee on Supplementary Materials, National Section on Dance, Vol. I. *Modern Dance and Children's Dance.* Washington, D.C.: American Association for Health, Physical Education and Recreation, 1953.

Lippincott, Gertrude, editor. *Dance Production.* Washington, D.C.: National Section on Dance, American Association for Health, Physical Education and Recreation, 1956.

Rochlein, Harvey. *Notes on Contemporary Dance.* Baltimore, Maryland: University Extension Press, Box 1233, 1965.

## PERIODICALS

Dance Magazine, 268 W. 45th Street, New York, New York 10036.

Dance Perspectives, 29 E. 9th Street, New York, New York 10003.

Dance Scope, 124-16, 84th Road, Kew Gardens, New York 11415.

Impulse, Impulse Publications, Inc., 160 Palo Alto Avenue, San Francisco, California 94114.

Journal of Health, Physical Education and Recreation, The American Association for Health, Physical Education and Recreation, 1201 Sixteenth Street, N.W., Washington, D.C. 20036.

Theatre Arts, 104 E. 40th Street, New York 16, New York.

# INDEX